DEMOCRACY FROM THE HEART

By the same author -

Greg Calvert and Carol Neiman,

A Disrupted History (Random House, 1971)

DEMOCRACY FROM THE HEART

Spiritual Values, Decentralism, and

Democratic Idealism

in

the Movement of the 1960s

Gregory Nevala Calvert

COMMUNITAS PRESS

EUGENE, OREGON

Published in the United States of America by

COMMUNITAS PRESS
P.O. BOX 3784
EUGENE, OREGON 97403

ISBN 0-9628800-0-0 (Paperback)
ISBN 0-9628800-1-9 (Cloth)

For Ken Carpenter

Friend, Lover, Companion

CONTENTS

Contents

PREFACE

This book is not a history of the New Left, but a study of the political ideas of the New Left from a viewpoint that regards political philosophy as a branch of ethics to be studied in historical context. It also presents the viewpoint of philosophical idealism, which holds that "mind and spiritual values are fundamental in the world as a whole."[1] I hope to contribute to a philosophy of democratic idealism that places spiritual and ethical considerations at the heart of human life while insisting that the realization of democratic values is a necessary goal of all political and spiritual undertakings and a fundamental objective on the path towards human maturity.

The book is, in part, an attempt to restore political philosophy and theory to their rightful place as a branch of inquiry that draws upon the historical experience of humankind and its social, economic, and cultural heritage for insights but does not subordinate the role of political thought to sociological or economic categories. Nor does the book accept the reduction of political philosophy to language analysis. The lack of a proper appreciation of the role of political philosophy and theory was one of the deficits that the New Left inherited both from the academic world and from the Old Left.

Democratic radicalism is a central concern of this work and I am fully aware of the disputed status of the word radical. *Radix* in Latin means "root" and political radicalism implies "getting to the roots" of the problems of human political association. In my view, the roots cannot be reduced to issues of economic reorganization or political reform (the socialist and liberal viewpoints), but involve a complex tapestry of questions including political, economic, cultural, spiritual, sexual, and psychological growth and change. I wish to retain the use of the word radical and its concern with "getting to the roots" while rescuing its usage from those who would equate it with "tearing up by the roots."

The book falls into two parts although it follows a line of thought that runs throughout. Part I explores the Foundings of the major segments of the Movement of the 1960s and the spiritual-philosophical convictions that underlay their beginning documents. Part II examines the mature years of the New Left particularly in the context of the anti-war and draft resistance movements. I also probe here my own political experience.

Portions of this work are highly autobiographical--a development nurtured by three days of intense interviews conducted by Ron Grele of the Columbia University Oral History Project in the summer of 1987. I make no pretense of scientistic objectivity. My argument is for self-investigation and self-revelation as an integral part of political acting and thinking. One of the most important lessons of the 1960s Movement might be summarized in a revised version of the Delphic dictum: "Know thyself and articulate your self-understanding to others as part of any politics you uphold." The social scientistic worldview is contrary to this understanding and those who still believe in positivist social science (whether liberal or Marxist) may find this book offensive. It will certainly incur the standard Marxist charge of "subjectivism."

The very idea of political philosophy and theory so central in this undertaking will also run counter to the basic premises of many anarchists and social ecologists. By the mid-nineteenth century, "society" had replaced "polity" as the central category of much of supposedly "political" thinking and both Marxists and traditional anarchists accepted and promoted this reversal of categories for the understanding of human community. Democratic political theory as conceived in this work rejects that inversion and argues that political thought linked with ethical inquiry is the proper approach to understanding human affairs. The author believes that much of the political thought of the 1960s was based on just such an attempt to restore the political to its preeminent, Aristotelian position and, in particular, to make value-centered democratic political theory the framework for discussion of political change. In unexpected ways, my search for a deeper understanding of politics, morality, and spirituality brought me to a new appreciation of the Western tradition of political philosophy rooted in classical Greece and in the work of Plato and Aristotle, for whom "the political art, or the quality of acting rightly in the State [or polis] is the same as virtue, or the quality of right action in general."[2] For Plato, the quest for individual human goodness and the search for the good community were not only convergent and inseparable, but inevitably linked to spiritual goodness itself.

The emphasis that the book places on personal openness in the debate about the relationship between "the personal" and "the theoretical" is not meant to obscure important distinctions between "the private" and "the public." Since the late 1960s, the phrase "personal politics" has thrown this debate into confusion. Self-disclosure is used selectively in this book to elucidate the experiential viewpoint of the author, to expose the way in which a particular blindspot and prejudice (homophobia) obscured thinking in the Movement, and to provide a narrative framework for the discussion of the period (1965-1970) when the author was part of the leadership of the New Left. Personal references are designed to take what has remained hidden out of the shadows and to shed light on a long-tabooed subject area.

In reflecting on my experiences of the 1960s, it became clear that I had been unable to resolve satisfactorily two very important aspects of my experience and beliefs: the spiritual and the political. My involvements since the sixties in the worlds of psychotherapy and spirituality have never been divorced from political commitments but have been deeply concerned with the integration of those two realms of experience. My immersion in the American New Left had been preceded by a long journey of self-discovery during which I had struggled to resolve the difficult issues of gay-bisexual identity in a militantly homophobic world. Throughout this book, the term "gay" is used to describe a sexual orientation, not an "essence." I believe, as do many psychotherapists, that we all have a bisexual potential that is expressed in varied ways along a complex continuum of orientations and preferences. I also believe in the fundamental importance of homoerotic relationships in the process of human growth and that their denial or repression results in serious distortions of human personality including identity confusion, neurotic guilt, homophobia and violence. "Gay" is a word that emphasizes self-awareness and self-respect among persons of a particular orientation and is not used in this work as an exclusivist category to deny the bisexuality of all of us.

I came to the New Left with a view of human nature and consciousness informed by a long spiritual quest that had led me to a faith in a blend of Quaker, Buddhist, and Franciscan ideas of non-theistic, inner-light spirituality. These convictions were deeply felt but difficult to articulate in a political context. The primary spiritual involvement of my adult years has been in the non-theistic Buddhist tradition, but I have also learned and drawn inspiration from a variety of spiritual teachings.

The central insight of all great spiritual traditions, as best I can understand it, is the unity of life and of all beings. It is the realization that beyond all of the divisions of ego, social class, ethnicity, or genetic grouping we are basically an expression of the same fundamental consciousness and that we must transcend our petty differences in order to find peace in a truly just community of humankind which also recognizes its unity with nature and other species. This insight into oneness is not the property of any single tradition or sect. In fact, institutionalized religions functioning in collusion with the state have frequently been among the worst betrayers of a universalist spirituality.

The spiritual values that animated the Movement of the 1960s were not tied to any particular organized religion. The value placed on an ego-transcendent community of love, brotherhood, and sisterhood which moved activists of that period was frequently at odds with organized religion. A new attitude towards spirituality and spiritual values was developing that was perhaps best articulated by one of the leaders of the emerging humanistic psychology movement, Abraham Maslow. In a book that appeared on the eve of the 1960s and that was called *New Knowledge in Human Values*,[3] Maslow argued that spiritual values were no longer the exclusive property of organized religions; and, in *Religions, Values, and Peak-Experiences*, he flatly stated that "Organized Religion, the churches, finally may become the major enemies of the religious experience and the religious experiencer." However, his opposition to atheistic materialism was as great as his disenchantment with organized religion. "One could say," he wrote, "that the nineteenth-century atheist had burnt down the house instead of remodeling it. He had thrown out the religious questions with the religious answers" because "organized religion presented him with a set of answers which he could not accept."[4]

My background and experience when I became part of the New Left were not confined to spiritual and psychotherapeutic matters. I also came to the Movement of the 1960s in the United States with extensive academic training in history (including economic and social history) and a direct experience of the French left that gave me an unusual grounding in radical social and political thought. The insights of radical political economy and political sociology, most often grounded in a materialist world-view, were not easily reconcilable with my spiritual convictions, which seemed to imply a radical philosophical idealism. When I think of spiritual awareness, it involves at least four elements of perception: first, that the human mind is somehow commensurate with the universe; secondly, that human morality and ethical inquiry are intimately connected with our spiritual awareness; thirdly, that mind and nature are "a necessary unity";[5] and, fourthly, that the nature of the universe or of reality is consciousness in the Buddhist sense of awakened emptiness. At the same time I believe that such a view is compatible with the Christian assertion that "God is love" if God is understood in Paul Tillich's sense as the "Ground of All Being." There are other formulations of the human experience of ultimate reality in the mystical currents of the Hindu and Islamic traditions that have been important guideposts for me on the way.[6] The simple dignity of the Native American belief in the Great Spirit with its manifestations as Father Sky and Mother Earth has come to have even deeper significance for my quest than it first did when I was a youth roaming the hills and mountains of the Pacific Northwest.

The emergence in the last decade of ecologically- and spiritually-centered movements with a commitment to radical, decentralist, grassroots democracy has been for me one of the vehicles for the resolution of these conflicts. What was unsaid for me in the 1960s is much stronger than the insights of "sexual politics" or the statement that "the personal is political," although both of these questions were central to the struggle for a more integrated politics. What was struggling to be born in my experience of the New Left and which found no voice or audience was the realization that the spiritual is political. I need, however, to qualify that statement by adding that just as sexuality and the personal are political but are not "the political," each having points of unity as well as realms of distinction and separateness, so too is spirituality political in the sense of informing politics without being synonymous with it. Politics remains a branch of ethics concerned with the art of creating human community in harmony with nature.

The viewpoint is democratic-decentralist spiritual and ecological humanism and I have named the political philosophy "democratic idealism." It has taken me almost twenty years to understand and integrate my experiences of the New Left of the 1960s and to be able to articulate that. My ten years of involvement with psychotherapy as both therapist and client were followed by a renewed study of political theory in the History of Consciousness program at the University of California at Santa Cruz in the 1980s. Throughout these two decades the study and practice of Western psychotherapies in addition to Quakerism, Buddhism, Sufism, Native American, and other spiritual traditions have been central to my life and work.

It is difficult to find a framework for discussing the all-important question--What went wrong with the Movement of the 1960s?--which is the issue that haunts this work. Many studies have tried to deal with one or another aspect of that question, but most tend to draw narrow boundaries around the subject matter by limiting their focus to single organizations like SNCC or SDS or to the civil rights or anti-war movements. Since this book attempts to answer the question by investigating the political-moral-spiritual framework of sixties radicalism, its focus is broader. It is my conviction that in order to understand what happened in the 1960s it is necessary to draw on a broad spectrum of thought, organizations, and movements, none of which have been treated exhaustively here, but which form a configuration--a gestalt--of ideas and experience that can be analyzed if we recognize that it does not cohere neatly but is nonetheless comprehensible as a whole. I have used the term "New Left" to describe what is common to the whole without applying a rigid definition to that term. "New Left" is roughly equivalent in this writing to the politically and culturally radical portions of what is sometimes called "the Movement"--that is, to those parts of the Movement of the 1960s that consciously strove to build an alternative social, cultural, and political world. Different groups and individuals participated in different ways and at different times in this endeavor and many of those that are treated in the following pages consciously took on the label "New Left." I do not use the term to imply a narrowly-defined allegiance to strictly-held beliefs. At the same time, the term implies an exclusion of certain groups and thus provides some useful boundaries.

The power of the ideas and political activism that emerged in the New Left of the 1960s and to which I have given the name "democratic idealism" has reverberated throughout the spiritual and political life of the human community since the premature implosion of the Movement. Notions of grassroots democracy, decentralism, nonviolence, feminism, gay and lesbian liberation, cultural revolution, the rejection of consumerism and the critique of work, and concern for ecological values, were all either developed or nourished in the milieu of the New Left. Democratic idealism is not conceived here as a totalizing system or grand theory that I want to graft onto the experience of the 1960s. It is an idea that grew in my mind as I lived and studied the New Left and as I tried to understand what was missing in the notion of participatory democracy that made it so vulnerable to attack from the materialisms of the Marxist or liberalist traditions. What was lacking, in my perception, was an explicit invocation of the spiritual values and roots of participatory democracy, the frank statement of the idealist philosophical assumptions that underlay this new vision of radical, grassroots and decentralist democracy. This insight deepened as I read and pondered the experience of the democratic radicals of the 1960s, and I found more and more evidence to justify this assertion.

In the back of my mind was the taunting voice of an academic who had once argued to me that "the problem with [my brand of] political theorists is that they are always looking for what is missing." That is what I was looking for when I undertook this study seven years ago. I knew that most of the theories and interpretations which had been imposed on the New Left violated my deepest intuitions about the meaning of a set of spiritual, political, and cultural experiences that had radically altered and enriched my life and I needed to discover "what was missing" through a dialogue between my innermost being and the remnants of the Movement, be they documents or memories or unshed tears.

Courage to continue in this task came in part from the

realization that what I was calling democratic idealism was alive in grassroots movements for change in the First, Second, Third, and Fourth Worlds. The marriage of spiritual values and democratic convictions that had inspired the advocates of participatory democracy was animating movements as apparently diverse as liberation theology and Buddhist political activism in the Third World and Green Politics in the First. The common theme was evident: how to unite spirituality with radical democratic politics when inherited political ideologies are materialist.

The first major political document to sketch a timid outline of such a vision, the "Values" sections of the *Port Huron Statement* of the Students for a Democratic Society (SDS), was the creation of students in the advanced industrial world, but it has been re-articulated with new understandings and insights around the globe and may be the American New Left's most enduring contribution to political philosophy for the planet's most endangering species, the one in whose hands rest the decisions that affect the lives of all of us.

If the subject matter of this book is democracy, its subject pure and simple is the human heart--the source of caring and moral courage in this life. The heart and its caring gave the Movement of the 1960s its strength, hope, and creativity. That spirit of caring and moral courage was the New Left's most valuable legacy, and the truths of the heart were its most profound lessons. The echo of the Movement rang in the words of Vaclav Havel, the playwright-president of liberated Czechoslovakia, when he argued:

> the salvation of this human world lies nowhere else than in the human heart, in the human power to reflect, in human meekness and in human responsibility.[7]

ACKNOWLEDGMENTS

First to Ken Carpenter with whom I have shared life for many years and throughout the difficult enterprise of writing this book. As editor, critic, and literary guide, his help was indispensable. He never lost faith in the work even when I did.

My thanks to John Schaar, J. Peter Euben, and David Wellman who were my professors at the University of California at Santa Cruz and who served patiently on my doctoral committee. John Schaar provided me with much of the intellectual stimulation that fueled this work and was the most significant teacher of my adult years in the area of political philosophy. As mentor and friend he helped restore my faith in the pursuit of knowledge and truth. I would not have proceeded with my studies in political theory without his inspiring example.

Special gratitude is due Billie Harris, the guiding spirit of the History of Consciousness program at UCSC, without whose care, good humour, and concern no undertaking such as this would ever have reached fruition.

My debt to Lon Laughlin is exceedingly great. His warmth, generosity of spirit, patience, and wisdom made the final arduous year of work on this project both possible and a blessing.

The spiritual debt I owe to Maximo and the peoples of the Western Highlands of Guatemala as I completed this journey is immeasurable.

Several people have read this text in whole or in part and made important contributions to the final shaping of the work. Eleanor Foster was an early reader and valuable commentator. Others who offered constructive criticism include David Wellman, Alfred H. Jones, Larry Casalino, Herb Foster, David Albert, Ellen Herman, and Alice Lynd. Stewart Burns made a very valuable contribution towards the end of the project as reader, commentator, and copy editor. Staughton Lynd contributed innumerable gifts toward the shaping of the manuscript and made an heroic effort as final copy reader just as war was breaking out in the

Persian Gulf. The wit, warmth, and kindness of Dilshad Ahmed were integral to the successful completion of the project. The generous support of my father, Clyde Calvert, helped make production of the book possible. None of these persons is responsible for the final product.

Finally, to my faithful friend Jocko and his beloved, departed Mariah, and to Patch, without whom long hours in my study would have been lonely indeed.

May All Beings Be Happy.
May They Be Peaceful.
May They Be Free Of Suffering.

INTRODUCTION

THE INTERPRETATION OF BROKEN DREAMS

I think that one of the most potent things about SDS was its moral stance. We became morally informed and we used that in order to expose what was really going on. What we did was take political analysis and attach it to a moral driving force and use that to communicate about what was really going on. That was in some way our most effective tool--to discover that we do live in a moral universe and to take that knowledge and apply it to the world around us.[1]

Paul Potter (1940-1984)

An interpretation of the New Left as a whole is difficult to achieve both because the New Left was unable to interpret itself and because its business remains unfinished, leaving no whole to interpret. It is this "unfinished business" of the New Left which, however, still haunts political life and thought in our time--not only in the United States but throughout the advanced technological societies and the larger world that they shape increasingly in their image. It will soon be three decades since the *Port Huron Statement* of the Students for a Democratic Society (SDS) proclaimed its vision of "participatory democracy"[2] yet virtually none of the hopes articulated in that manifesto have been fulfilled. The call of conscience that moved the largest generation ever of young Americans to political action echoes only faintly from the ruins of radical hope--young hope crushed by war and greed and the party of political cynicism. Many former New Left activists remain politically and socially committed,[3] but generally speaking, accommodation has replaced freedom as the watchword of political life. While the rest of the planet is being revolutionized by a vision of nonviolent, grassroots, democratic change that the sixties Movement helped construct, the majority of the activist generation of yesteryear in the United States does not even vote.

In the absence of a whole to interpret there are, nonetheless, insights to be gained from the study of some of the parts--even the broken parts. These insights may help us piece together a new vision for the future and work more creatively with the materials of the present. Perhaps they can help fashion a bridge between the experience of the 1960s and the politics of tomorrow. This country (and the Western Civilization of which it is a part) is having a hard time relinquishing the drive to domination that created its present course in the world. The New Left was the product of the need to change that course and any "new politics" which seeks to guide us must respond to that imperative. It is the path of peace we need to find--with others, with nature, with ourselves. This book is about peacemakers who lost their way and the legacy they left.

One of the basic theses of this book is that the New Left, and the larger radical movement of the 1960s, had no political theory that could adequately express the nature of its intuitions and instincts and that it therefore succumbed to the methods and ideologies of the traditional left, Marxist and liberal.[4] In fact, the New Left was closest in spirit and practice to the decentralist political traditions: grassroots democracy of the type associated with the American Populist movement and the libertarian socialism of the syndicalist and anarchist-communalist varieties. These traditions differ from centralist political movements (whether Marxist or liberal) in that they do not aim at the conquest of state power but at the development of decentralized democratic alternatives to the centralized bureaucratic forms of the modern state. In short, they aim to replace the hierarchical, top-down power structures of the state with new democratic forms that maintain power at the grassroots. In addition, they maintain that political "democratic decentralism" cannot be attained without the democratization of economic power.

American New Leftists did not generally come to their belief in grassroots democracy or libertarian socialism through the study of political theories. Their politics were by and large the product of their experience and were often informed by spiritual and moral teachings rather than by "political science." In fact, one of the great weaknesses of the American New Left was the widespread ignorance of the history of the decentralist tradition as a source of alternatives to statist Marxist socialism or liberalism. This relative ignorance of history meant that the New Left was theoretically unprepared to defend its "intuitive decentralist politics" when it was faced with an organized takeover by Marxist-Leninists. It was, by comparison, less informed than its counterparts in the British New Left who had benefited from a revival of left libertarian thought in the late 1950s that had produced new directions in libertarian socialist theory, in particular through the group called London Solidarity.[5] Of course some American activists were aware of the indigenous anarcho-syndicalist tradition in the American labor movement represented by the Industrial Workers of the World (the IWW, also called "Wobblies"). By the mid-1960s there were SDSers who joined the IWW for reasons of sentimental identification.[6] But knowledge of the traditions and theories of democratic decentralism were spotty at best.

The Movement of the 1960s in the United States was not, however, just an unconscious revival of left libertarianism. It contained an important new element: the theory and practice of nonviolence. Although political nonviolence was not new to American social movements, its renewed importance for the New Left was due to the influence of the Indian Gandhian movement on spiritual and political thought around the world, and particularly on the radical pacifist and early civil rights movements in the United States.[7] Whatever its failures, Gandhi's movement had established the ability of a political movement based on a spiritually-grounded practice of nonviolence to challenge state power--in that case British imperial rule in India. In fact, the Indian Congress Party won independence but failed to establish the decentralist society based on village communes that Gandhi had envisioned.

The Movement of the 1960s in America was basically nonviolent and libertarian or decentralist until 1967-68, but because the tradition of radical social and political change that espoused libertarian and nonviolent approaches was not knowledgeably defended, the Movement and the New Left reverted to "orthodox" leftism, namely Marxism. Furthermore, the very bases on which it would have been possible to argue for a nonviolent libertarian radicalism were partly spiritual not materialist. And neither in the liberal tradition nor in Marxism were ideas of spirituality taken seriously. Unless one was willing to break with the philosophical tradition of secular materialist discourse--liberal or Marxist--there was no way to ground the intuitions of New Leftists about nonviolence. And, where in the early years of the Movement, religious or spiritual language and categories were commonplace, they were abandoned as the ideological struggle with Marxism was engaged. Secular materialism seemed to win out over the earlier spiritually-inspired language with little difficulty.

There is a long-standing taboo on spiritual and moral language within the left, both liberal and Marxist. It goes back to Machiavelli and Hobbes and the dawn of modern political theory, which separated spiritual, moral, and political concerns. The New Left and the Movement of the 1960s violated that taboo and for a time, in thought and action, political, moral and spiritual concerns were joined in the decentralist politics of nonviolent direct action. Not everyone who participated in that activism was comfortable with the spiritual language of the Movement and within the largest New Left organization, SDS, the taboo was reimposed as Marxist discourse came to dominate and then overwhelm political debates. It seems probable, however, that the adoption of Marxist language was a minority phenomenon operating only in special arenas like SDS, and to a certain extent the Student Nonviolent Coordinating Committee (SNCC), where there were large numbers of intellectuals and where there were actual organizations in which Marxists made a bid for power and control. For many if not most of the participants in the movements of the 1960s, spiritually- and morally-inspired political discourse remained their most natural mode of expression. Certainly the interest in the relationship between spirituality, morality, and politics survived the implosion of the New Left and became a major theme in the 1970s and 1980s.

The beliefs and practices involving democratic decentralism, nonviolent direct action, or libertarian radicalism were not the only force in the New Left. Rather, the somewhat disparate groups and individuals representing this viewpoint came to have an influence on the American New Left far out of proportion to their numbers or organizational strength because their politics made so much intuitive sense to so many people. Furthermore, it is their politics largely that survived and grew and informed new movements after the New Left of the 1960s had been torn apart by the sectarian battles of the authoritarian leftists--the Marxists and Marxist-Leninists. It was their spiritual values and sensibilities that made them the bearers of a non-sectarian point of view which was able to recreate unity and community.

This work will include an investigation of the traditions of nonviolent decentralist politics that fed the development of the Movement of the 1960s and have since given birth to a number of opposition political movements in the United States and abroad--especially in Europe. Anyone who has been involved in the nonviolence movement finds difficulty with the negative stance implied by the terms "nonviolent or nonviolence." In order to portray the positive face of nonviolent libertarianism, I have chosen to name it "a politics of compassion." This is, in part, a book about the origins, recent history, and possible futures of a politics of compassion.

It is also a book about democracy and rebirth, for the New Left's vision of participatory democracy entailed a faith that democratic political life could be reborn on new grounds with new values. From this vantage point, the New Left can be understood as a movement for the rebirth of democracy within the most advanced capitalist society on earth. It was not just another socialist movement in the tradition of the American Socialist or Communist parties because Stalinism had already made "socialism" problematic, and even "democratic socialists" had been compromised by their virulent anti-communism that had made them pawns in the Cold War. The need for democratic rebirth grew out of the increasing contradiction between the rhetoric and publicly proclaimed ideals of the American political tradition and the increasingly hierarchical, bureaucratic, imperialist, and technocratic character of American political and social life since the end of World War II.

The New Left was not naive: it did not assume there was a pristine democratic past that could simply be revived from slumber. The United States had never achieved even formal

political democracy for all its people because blacks had been
denied effective citizenship in the South. Furthermore, the United
States remained well behind other advanced industrial nations in
the achievement of social and economic democracy. Nonetheless,
the particular power that the language and vision of participatory
democracy had for American New Leftists was due to their faith in
the democratic ideals that were a part of American political
culture. Whatever else they may have disagreed about, they were
united in their commitment to extend the scope and practical
effectiveness of those ideals.

It was this democratic faith that created the spirit of the
community which called itself the New Left. Because their faith
was strong, New Leftists were often not rigorous in spelling out
the practical functional details of their political vision. This was a
positive source of strength as long as there was ample room for
political experimentation, but it proved to be a fatal weakness
when the New Left came under attack and found itself invaded by
undemocratic ideological leftists. Faith in a democratic rebirth
faltered in the face of organized cadres with a message of
"scientific socialism", and the New Left betrayed its own
uniqueness when it tried to respond in kind. Instead of a rebirth
there was a kind of tragic miscarriage in which values were
reversed and, for a moment, there was a terrible pastiche of the
worst aspects of the Old Left--Stalinization, ideological rigidification, factionalization, denunciation, dogmatism, sectarianism, and
pseudo-revolutionary violence.

Whatever had been embryonically most promising in the
experience of the New Left was shattered in the organizational
rending that accompanied its demise. And in its wake came
cynicism and despair fed by the dismal history of Watergate and
the brutal, useless prolongation of the Southeast Asian War.
Perhaps now--two decades after the destruction of SDS in 1969--it
may be possible to see beyond the ruins and determine more
clearly the legacy of the New Left. But it is not, in any case, an
easy task simply because the choice of categories and concepts for
understanding the New Left is itself problematic.

The New Left of the 1960s changed not only the character of
political radicalism in America and other advanced industrial
societies, it changed the character of politics in general in those
societies. The legacy of the New Left is revealed in a complex

redefinition of "the political" that incorporates a number of new politicized movements--feminism, gay liberation, ecology, decentralization. Additionally, it involves a complex set of cultural phenomena centering on personal, transpersonal, and spiritual growth that often share a common theme and metaphor: rebirth. The underlying movement of cultural transformation appears to give unity to the new politics of the post-1950s era, a politics that incorporates elements of personal growth and spiritual questing with demands for ecological sanity and democratic decentralization. Perhaps its most unexpected feature is the vigorous interest in spirituality that differentiates it from traditional secular leftism. It is not, however, a revival of religious fundamentalism, which has occurred simultaneously in the ideology of the New Right.

While the New Right is authoritarian, militaristic, fundamentalist, patriarchal, and homophobic, the movements that are the heirs of the New Left are for the most part libertarian, anti-militarist, sexually liberationist, feminist, and spiritually eclectic. Had it not been for the factionalism and adventurism that destroyed the political organizations of the 1960s (particularly SDS), the political spectrum of successor movements might have retained the name "New Left." In fact, there has been no unified political opposition on the left since the demise of the sixties Movement.

Only if we understand the New Left as the first wave of protest against advanced technological society--both capitalist and "state socialist"--can we appreciate its importance and uniqueness, a uniqueness that was lost in the ideological phrasemongering and the orthodox sectarianism that destroyed it. In fact, although the demise of the New Left is usually identified with the collapse of SDS in 1969, much of its spirit was quickly reborn in a variety of movements that were prefigured in its work and analysis. There is not one major issue that has been a focus of political activism in the period since 1970 (with the important exception of gay liberation) that had not been raised in SDS by 1968. Racism, sexism, militarism, decentralization, and ecological issues were all debated in the New Left and proposals to deal with all these issues were raised in debates within SDS.

I want then to argue that the New Left of the 1960s is alive though dispersed in the successor movements since 1970. In so doing, I am attributing a meaning to the phrase "New Left," a meaning I will later clarify in distinguishing it from the "Old Left." It would, however, be unfair to paint the New Left simply as the seedbed of a politics of libertarian nonviolence. It was more complex, for it also sparked a temporary renewal of liberalism and spawned the Weather Underground. However, it is fair to say that nonviolence and libertarianism were central themes in the New Left and that the libertarian and nonviolent eco-politics that has emerged since then is the most vital descendant of those very trends in the sixties. The true heirs of participatory democracy have been the ecology, anti-nuclear and disarmament movements: the Clamshell, Lonestar, and Abalone Alliances, the Livermore Action Group, the Green Party of West Germany, and the proliferation of decentralist, nonviolent groups and movements in the advanced industrial world that organize for peace against arms, for a survivable environment against pollution and waste and consumerism, for a politics of human scale against bureaucracy and bigness.

In addition, these movements have developed themes that were largely absent from the New Left until 1968-69: feminism and gay liberation. Had the New Left survived the invasion of Marxism-Leninism that disoriented and shattered it, women and gay people might have challenged and transformed from within a movement marred by male chauvinism and homophobia. But the largest organization of the New Left, the Students for a Democratic Society, was split by invading Maoists in 1968-69 before feminism had developed a major impact and before the banner of gay liberation was raised. In general, the impact of feminists and lesbians and gay men has been supportive of libertarian trends, but this has not always been the case. Because libertarian politics are by definition anti-hierarchical and anti-authoritarian, supportive of grassroots democracy and the decentralization of power, feminist and gay opposition to structures of power generally dominated by authoritarian straight men has a built-in libertarian bias. But it is also important to realize that where feminists and gay activists have become involved in narrowly defined "interest group politics," they have tended to adopt the political style of the liberal Democratic Party mainstream.

It is the libertarian socialist or anarchist tradition that has embodied, since the 19th century, a recurrent left-wing or anti-capitalist version of the politics of rebirth--although millenarian spiritual movements have a much longer history. In the 17th century, in particular, radical political movements of a millenarian persuasion, drawing on spiritual inspiration, were widespread in England. Modern libertarian, decentralist movements share a common rejection of the modern state--its authority, its centralization, its militarism, and its massification of life. Whether expressed in terms of Christian millenarianism as in the 17th century, or more frequently in secular anarchist language in the 19th and 20th centuries, left libertarianism has as its common thread a belief in the possibility of "holistic" human social or political organization: society should be reorganized on the basis of decentralized, self-governing communities, not from the top down by the centralized, authoritarian state.[8] Left libertarianism or democratic decentralism represents a radical rejection of some of the major tendencies and forms of modernity--centralization, bureaucratization, conformity, and the state. It has exercised its greatest appeal when and where the modern state was in the process of formation or where modern industrialization was least successful in its development: seventeenth-century England, nineteenth-century Russia, twentieth-century Spain, and the mines and logging camps of the American industrial frontier, wherever the new forms of state control or economic organization were still imperfectly achieved.

Until the 1960s, it was generally assumed on the left that libertarian socialist or anarchist movements were dead. An "atavistic ideology"[9] was the term used by Marxists confident of the truth of "scientific socialism" to describe that libertarianism. Quite unexpectedly, left libertarianism or decentralism in a variety of forms reappeared in the movements of the 1960s and has since exerted a powerful continuing influence on opposition political movements in the advanced technological societies, from the American ecology and anti-nuclear movements to the West German Green Party. Just what the decentralist revival means will be one of the questions this book attempts to clarify. Both the libertarian renaissance and the rapid spread of groups and movements concerned with spiritual growth are two key phenomena in the alternative cultural milieu that issued from the 1960s. Their interrelationship will also be a subject of further inquiry in this work.

From the standpoint of political theory, the New Left was much broader in its importance than a simple anarchist renaissance would imply. With the appearance of the *Port Huron Statement* of SDS in 1962, New Left discourse broke from the deadlock of 19th century scientism and rejoined the classical tradition of Western political philosophy, which had its roots in ancient Greece and particularly in the work of Aristotle.[10] In many ways the questions raised by the New Left were present in the political crises and thinking of Athenians in the 5th and 4th centuries.[11] The conviction that true knowledge could not be divorced from Goodness was central to the teachings of Socrates whose example of opposition to the state in questions of conscience stands as a beacon of political courage at the beginning of the Western tradition. And it was Aristotle who argued in opposition to Realpolitik that morality and politics could not be separated and that:

> The study of ethics may not improperly be termed a study of politics. (*Rhetoric,* Book I, c.II, #7.)

Without the gift of the *Port Huron Statement,* the contribution of the New Left to political thought might have remained a footnote to the 19th century debates between Marxists and anarchists. In fact, the notion of participatory democracy reopened the windows of political thought onto the broad landscape of the Western tradition of political philosophy and laid the groundwork for a reexamination of the concept of direct democracy that the world inherited from 5th century Athens and that had not been seriously reevaluated since Rousseau in the 18th century. The New Left opened up the possibility of recasting the discussion of modern radicalism in terms of democratic discourse thus establishing the framework in which serious political debate would proceed in our time.

The greatest problem posed by the development of decentralist democratic politics in the 1960s and today is this: how is it possible to pursue both short and long range decentralist goals and continue to participate meaningfully in "politics" as defined by the present system, that is by the system of liberal electoral democracy? The hip answer of the sixties--Tune In, Turn On, and Drop Out!--was a disaster for the Movement. It was in fact not a political strategy but an avoidance of politics.

The problem can be formulated in another way: how is it possible to pursue an alternative decentralist politics without abandoning meaningful participation in "politics"? How is it possible to create the "new politics" while recognizing that one must participate effectively in the existing political culture? The New Left of the 1960s was never able to answer those questions satisfactorily, and became trapped in an increasingly negative expression of its alienation from "the system" while abandoning its early attempts at creating positive alternatives of grassroots, decentralist organization.

The politics of the New Left and its heirs is frequently attributed to the "crisis of legitimacy" of the modern state.[12] This "legitimation crisis"[13] is seen by some theorists as a generalized problem in the advanced technological societies where bureaucratic manipulation by the state and political parties has resulted in mass apathy and alienation from the political process. In the United States this phenomenon was apparent in the early development of the New Left and articulated most vividly in the *Port Huron Statement* of SDS. It was complicated in America by the history of racial segregation and the exclusion of blacks from the electoral process. It was the specific character of the problem of racism that made the "legitimation crisis" of the sixties so unique in America. The history and direction of the American New Left and its relation to the system of electoral democracy was largely determined by the black political agenda.

Seymour Martin Lipset, writing in the late 1950s, made an unintendedly prophetic judgment which says much about the decade of the sixties that was to erupt in such unexpected ways. He wrote: "Political systems which deny new strata access to power except by revolution also inhibit the growth of legitimacy by introducing millenial hopes into the political system."[14]

In the 1960s, two social groups that had been denied power in the United States--blacks and students--were politicized in significant numbers around the issues of civil rights, the Vietnam war, and student powerlessness. When the existing political mechanisms failed to grant power to blacks, and when America's imperial policy in Southeast Asia proved unresponsive to protest, increasing numbers of blacks and students were radicalized and came to believe that the system of electoral democracy itself was so deeply tied to capitalist domination, expansionism and racism that it could not be changed and must be overthrown. Throughout that process, black leadership made decisions that were crucial for the rest of the movement--decisions that shaped the history of the American left and American politics for two decades.

Unlike the Old Left of the American Communist Party, the New Left did not begin by dismissing the American system of electoral democracy as a fraud. The Communist Party had engaged in electoral activity, but always regarded "capitalist democracy" as a tool of class rule. By contrast, the New Left began in fact by involving itself in massive voter registration drives of blacks and only came to regard electoral democracy and the two-party system as unproductive because of the experience of black civil rights activists who challenged the racism of the Democratic Party. It was the negative black experience of testing electoral politics rather than a theoretical or ideological analysis of capitalist democracy that led the New Left out of the electoral system.

In 1964, disillusioned black activists began to lead important segments of the black civil rights movement and the pre-dominantly white student left out of the Democratic Party and the two-party electoral system. In 1984 and 1988 black activists (most prominently the Reverend Jesse Jackson) led important segments of the black community and the American left back into the Democratic Party and reinvolved them in the liberal electoral process. Those events may prove to mark the boundaries of an era in American political life, an era in which the black community and the issues it raised set a political agenda that determined much of the direction of left politics in America. It was an agenda that tested the ability of the system of electoral democracy to integrate the black community into the institutions and processes of mainstream political life. In the course of events, other groups, communities and constituencies were also awakened and engaged in struggles for identity, equality, and full enfranchisement. Women, Native Americans, Latinos, Asian-Americans, gay men and lesbians challenged policies and prejudices that excluded and demeaned them. All of their struggles were of great importance, but the particular history of black Americans--slavery and then apartheid--made their struggle, their voices, and their decisions a special catalyst for all the others.

In August 1964 a black delegation, called the Mississippi

Freedom Democratic Party, challenged the conservative and racist Democratic regulars at the party's national convention. Lyndon Johnson's political managers proposed a "compromise" to seat two representatives of the MFDP as at-large delegates. This strategy was supported by the moderate civil rights leader Martin Luther King, Jr. of the Southern Christian Leadership Conference (SCLC), and opposed by the increasingly radical activists of the Student Nonviolent Coordinating Committee (SNCC), who had inspired and helped organize the MFDP. When the black delegates rejected the compromise, some of them were forcibly ejected from the hall, and the all-white delegation was officially seated. This event represented a major defeat for the electoral strategy of the civil rights movement, and led many blacks to reject electoral politics and the Democratic Party as hopelessly racist and corrupt.[15] Within two years, SNCC had embarked on the separatist path of "Black Power." Furthermore, the largest organization of the American New Left, the Students for a Democratic Society (SDS), sided increasingly with radical blacks in their opposition to liberal democratic politics and the Democratic Party. This opposition on the part of the white New Left was the result of more than the failures of the political system to respond to the demands of black people. It was also a direct response to the fact that the United States government had embarked on a truly genocidal war against the peoples of Southeast Asia. In fact SDS never made a formal decision regarding participation in electoral politics, but as opposition to the war intensified, support for participation in electoral politics largely disappeared in the New Left and SDS without significant debate.

No doubt the movement of SDS toward a position antagonistic to liberal electoral politics accurately reflected the growing frustration of the student and anti-war movements. It did not, however, answer the question of how a decentralist democratic movement might address the processes of representative electoral democracy. For lack of a more meaningful strategy, the position of either/or won out and led to the bloody and disastrous confrontation with the Chicago police at the Democratic convention in 1968. The New Left voted with its feet to the effect that liberal electoral politics was not in its eyes an effective instrument for social and political change.

Although some of its members have been galvanized by Jesse Jackson's Rainbow Coalition, large numbers of the "baby boom" generation of the New Left have never since participated in the institutions of representative democracy. They rebelled in the 1960s against authoritarianism and dehumanization of the multiversity, against racism and sexism, and against the war and the draft. Because of the alienation and disarray of the 1960s, they have not been integrated into the institutions of liberal electoral democracy. Their political voice has been heard in the national electoral arena only in the presidential bids of Eugene McCarthy, George McGovern, Jesse Jackson and, more faintly, Gary Hart. Their issues are feminism, gay liberation, decentralization, disarmament, peace, ecology, and post-scarcity economics. Their sensibilities are ecotopian and spiritually heterodox. Some have totally succumbed to a hedonistic materialism, but most long for a better, safer, more democratic and saner world. In the 1960s they were the first generation of young Americans who identified massively with the Indians instead of the cavalry, and they have not found a way to re-identify with America since. Perhaps it will take a new New Left to involve them meaningfully in politics.

The history of the New Left is a history of broken dreams; the interpretation that follows is largely an attempt to shed light on that brokenness so that the survivors may move on and those who have come after may learn and dream anew of democracy and rebirth. The democratic dream is different from all others. It is a vision of community, equality, and justice situated within a framework of freedom. It must have limits and form (which the New Left learned too late) to save itself from the twin evils of chaos and rigidity. There is no formula that can ensure the success of the democratic enterprise. But the experience of the New Left has important lessons for those who might renew its work.

Part I

Foundings:

Democracy Is From The Heart

CHAPTER 1

THE TURNING:

The Cultural Revolution of the Beat Generation

> . . .again at last the possibility of prophetic poetry.[1]

> Allen Ginsberg

> As a poet I hold the most archaic values on earth. They go back to the late Paleolithic; the fertility of the soil, the magic of animals, the power-vision in solitude, the terrifying initiation and rebirth; the love and ecstacy of the dance, the common work of the tribe.[2]

> Gary Snyder

In the decade following World War II, American society evolved a form of "liberal technocracy" bolstered by the Cold War ideology of aggressive anti-Communism. Political dissent was systematically stifled while the blandishments of the warfare-welfare state sedated an increasingly apathetic and conformist public. The disintegration and defeat of the Stalinist "Old Left" and the integration of the majority of the labor movement into the new liberal-technocratic consensus meant that there was no effective voice of political opposition in the country as the apparatus of the "National Security State" was consolidated. For the majority of Americans, this new national consensus became embodied in the dream of material prosperity and middle-classness built on the assumption of an endless upward spiral of power and progress.

There were two major determinants that conditioned the new political and cultural outlook that blossomed in the 1960s: technological overkill and imperial domination. In the United States, the full effects of the industrial-technological revolution and the triumphs and costs of world empire were experienced at the same time in the decade and a half following World War II. Geopolitical mastery and technocracy triumphed simultaneously in America to produce Pentagon capitalism and the national security state in the same breath. It was both of these aspects of mastery--domestic and foreign--that would be challenged by the Movement of the 1960s.

It was only through a slow and experimental process that a new cultural and political opposition to this megalith of technocratic manipulation and materialistic affluence was organized and articulated. The language, style, and critique of the Old Left were grossly inadequate to the task of criticizing and challenging the new American order. And as voices of a new style of opposition did appear, the Old Left was largely deaf to their relevance and meaning.

✦ The Spiritual Revolt

A new sensibility emerged in the 1960s that marked a turning point in the history of the United States. It involved a shift in values from the ethos of domination and expansionism that had guided the development of the imperial republic to a new outlook that prized peace, equality, and ecological sanity. It was a spiritual and cultural turning that began to set limits to the aggressive drives which had made America the most powerful economic and military force on earth at the cost of destroying that other American dream, democracy. In the process of this new awakening, all of the historical layers of domination that had constituted American power were exposed and challenged: slavery, Jim Crow and racism; economic expansion and imperialism; patriarchy and sexism; economic exploitation and classism; homophobia and heterosexism; and the rape and destruction of this land and its native peoples.

Beyond the factors specific to American society and history, this cultural and spiritual turning was a reaction to the mature development of that modern technological society which was the highest achievement of the Western world and had been described by the French Christian anarchist writer Jacques Ellul in *The Technological Society*.[3] It was an awakening to the fact that such a society--with its inherent drives toward domination, bureaucratization, and massification--was headed for disaster and that it was both collectively and individually undesirable. The prophets of that awakening in the United States were the poets of the Beat Generation. Its political harbingers were the radical pacifist draft resisters and peace activists, and its political catalysts were the activists and community organizers of the Students for a Democratic Society (SDS) and the Student Nonviolent Coordinating Committee (SNCC). These groups do not begin to encompass the variety and numbers of that gathering and outpouring of the sixties which called itself "The Movement." But understanding them and their experience is crucial to understanding the 1960s and the New Left because they turned their backs on the best that the system could offer and chose instead compassion, simplicity, justice, peace, community, and love. Somehow in America at the zenith of its power, expansionist technological society and the materialistic values of the modern world crash-landed in the hearts and minds of the young and some of them began to seek another way.

Central to the spirit of the Movement of the 1960s was a gestalt switch. Human happiness or fulfillment was no longer equated in the hearts of increasing numbers of (especially young) people with the accumulation of wealth and power. Instead, fulfillment was envisioned as a function of community, justice, decency, spiritual wholeness, and an ecologically sane lifestyle. The roots of these new attitudes were in the cultural movement surrounding the Beat Generation poets and in the small but soon-to-be influential libertarian and nonviolent decentralist left. Sometimes these sources were intermingled, sometimes not. But together they were the seedbed of many of the cultural and political trends of the 1960s.

The cultural movement that began with the Beat Generation writers in the 1950s was a revolt *against* consumerism, advanced technological societies, militarism, patriarchal domination, and sexual repression. It was a movement *for* simpler, more natural lifestyles, peace, ecological sanity, feminization, and erotic (including homosexual) liberation. It was also opposed to the modern state and in favor of democratic decentralist or anarchist social organization. The revolt against advanced technological society was originally expressed in poetry and prophecy, in cultural and spiritual questing.

The dominant vocabularies of modern politics--liberalism and Marxism--are based on a secular materialist outlook. Both the Beat Generation writers and the radical pacifists were influential in bringing notions of spirituality back into political life. They were key contributors to the creation of what we might call a post-modern spiritual-political-moral discourse.

Spirituality and *spiritual* are words loaded with heavy cultural baggage. The effort to find a meaning for those concepts that is not tied to religious sectarianism and obscurantism has been a difficult task. Traditional Western dualism, with its opposition of "spirit" and "matter" has given spirituality the sense of "other-worldness," the "supernatural." An important aspect of the Movement of the 1960s was an attempt to make spirituality, and the values associated with it, part of the everyday life of politics and culture. This trend was an integral part of the civil rights, anti-war, and counter-cultural movements. It produced a flowering of spiritual expression, often of Eastern inspiration but drawing also on sources as disparate as the Judeo-Christian tradition and Native American shamanism. It often had no connection with organized religion and it developed new forms of expression. It included "Human Be-Ins" and the new youth music, leading one observer to assert that "Rock was the organized religion of the Sixties."[4]

It is important in approaching the 1960s to understand this shift in meaning. Undoubtedly a major reason for the new popularity of non-Western spiritual traditions was that they offered a way to break with Western dualism. This was probably true of the popularity of Buddhism, the spiritual tradition of choice of the Beat Generation. "It should always be remembered that Buddhism does not recognize a spirit opposed to matter," as one contemporary Buddhist monk and scholar puts it.[5] Buddhism, a non-theistic spiritual path, hardly even qualifies as a "religion" in the eyes of the monotheistic Judeo-Christian tradition. The terms spiritual humanism or mystical humanism are sometimes used to describe its teachings.

More than just Western dualism was being rejected. It was the whole tradition of egocentric individualism in the West that seems to find its support in the Hellenized Judeo-Christian tradition. Alan Watts put it this way:

> Westerners are not the only people who feel that they are disconnected individuals, out there on their own. But they are the only people who brag about it, and this is because the isolated style of individuality has a highly positive value in their religious and philosophical traditions. Hebrew and Greek attitudes have combined through Christianity to nurture and exaggerate this particular sensation of personal identity.

He went on to say, "any suggestion that there is some inner level at which, as in Hinduism, God and man are identical, at which 'thou art That,' is dubbed *pantheism*--as if this anathema simply ended the matter then and there."[6]

Why then did the spiritual revolt against technological society not take the form of Christian renewal? For many young people, the answer was painfully obvious: Christianity and the whole Hellenistic Judeo-Christian tradition were part and parcel of the culture that spawned the will to domination over nature and gave birth to modern science and technology. St. Francis, with his love of nature, was an anomaly in Christianity whereas his teaching and poetry seem quite at home in a Taoist, Buddhist, or Hindu setting. There was certainly precious little one could turn to in 20th century Christianity that was not implicated in the bureaucratic technological world.

The following characterization of the state of religious life in the West, though written by Alan Watts in the early 1970s, could easily have been applied to America at the end of the Eisenhower era:

> Christianity . . . impresses the modern Westerner as the most impossibly complicated amalgamation of odd ideas, and though it is his spiritual birthright and the faith of his father, it is very much easier to help him understand Buddhism or Vedanta. . . . Furthermore, he is apt to find something indefinably embarrassing about the emotional atmosphere generated around clergymen and churches. . . . It is the

plainly identifiable stink of piety.
    Still more important, it is quite obvious to the canny observer that
most Christians, including clergy and devout laity, do not believe in
Christianity.[7]

Watts went on to argue that "today the Western world is
post-Christian." It was an idea propounded with increasing
frequency in the 1960s, an updated American version of
Nietzsche's dictum, "God is dead." Institutional Christianity was
seen as petrified and spiritually defunct. "The churches," Watts
argued, "are huge, prosperous organizations, and, aside from
expanding their membership and building new plants, their chief
concern is the preservation of family ties and sexual mores. Their
influence on major problems of domestic and international
politics is minimal."[8] But it was not just institutional morbidity
that Watts was condemning; it was spiritual death that he saw in
the institutional churches. "Outside Quaker meetings and Catholic monasteries," he wrote, "there is hardly the slightest concern
for the inner life, for the raising of human consciousness to union
with God--supposedly the main work of religion. Their politicking
and lobbying is largely preoccupied with the idiotic sumptuary
laws against gambling, drinking, whoring, selling contraceptives,
procuring abortions, dancing on Sundays, getting divorced or
practicing homosexuality."[9]
    In fact, there were important currents of change in the world
of institutional Christianity that Watts ignored. Christian existentialism, as in the theology of Paul Tillich, had brought new life to
Protestant thought, while Vatican II profoundly altered the face of
Roman Catholicism and later led to the development of liberation
theology. More importantly, the political-spiritual awakening in
black churches in America was providing the seedbed for the civil
rights movement, a political revolution unthinkable without the
dedication of black Christian ministers and lay people.
    For many thinking Americans, however, organized Chris-
tianity in the 1950s and early 60s seemed a pious fraud tied to the
most reactionary or the most insipid values and institutions of the
society. For secular liberals and Marxists, this development
appeared as part of a progressive secularization of thought--the
"end of an illusion" to borrow Freud's phrase. For others it was a
sign of a spiritual vacuum, a vacuum that would be filled with an

amazing diversity of spiritual searching and expression in the 1960s and later.

In the mid-1950s, at the height of the American Era presided over by the fatherly general become president, Dwight Eisenhower, the Congress of the United States added the words "under God" to the Pledge of Allegiance. It was, of course, inspired in part by the holy McCarthyite crusade against "Godless Communism." But it also had the feeling of an ideological reflex--a compulsive need to substitute words for belief to cover up the gaping hole in the actual spiritual life of the American people. It was out of that void and against that hypocrisy that the Beat Generation emerged.

◆ Gary Snyder and Buddhist Anarchism

The group of writers that came to be associated with the term "Beat Generation" did not begin with a common political outlook. Allen Ginsberg, whose mother had been a Communist, thought in his early years of becoming a labor organizer. Jack Kerouac, who christened the Beat Generation, was largely apolitical until his later years of alcoholic decline when he professed anti-Communist sentiments. Kenneth Rexroth and others in the San Francisco area had well-developed left libertarian politics and were members of the Anarchist Circle in that city. Gary Snyder, the most politically profound of the Beat poets, developed a politics that drew on the anarcho-syndicalism of the American IWW, the spiritual tradition of Buddhism, and an ecological awareness that was nourished both by his Buddhist practice and his intensive study of Native American cultures.[10]

In the *Dharma Bums* Kerouac described his encounter with Buddhism, and his joyous meeting with fellow Dharma follower Gary Snyder, a future Pulitzer Prize winning poet. He painted a portrait of Snyder in the fictional guise of the Japhy Ryder:

Japhy Ryder was a kid from eastern Oregon brought up in a log cabin deep in the woods with his father and mother and sister, from the beginning a woods boy, an axman, farmer, interested in animals and Indian lore so that when he finally got to college by hook or crook he was already well equipped for his early studies in anthropology and later in Indian myth and in actual texts of Indian mythology. Finally he

learned Chinese and Japanese and became an Oriental scholar and
discovered the greatest Dharma Bums of them all, the Zen lunatics of
China and Japan. At the same time, being a Northwest boy with
idealistic tendencies, he got interested in oldfashioned IWW anarchism
and learned to play the guitar and sing old worker songs to go with his
Indian songs and general folksong interests.[11]

Writing in the summer of 1961 for a new publication, *The
Journal for the Protection of All Beings*, Gary Snyder produced a
manifesto of sorts entitled "Buddhist Anarchism"[12] (later revised
and reprinted in his book of collected thoughts on ecological
politics called *Earth House Hold: Technical Notes and Queries to
Fellow Dharma Revolutionaries*). In three short pages, he
outlined a moral, political, and spiritual viewpoint that condemned the direction of the modern world and declared: "No one
today can afford to be innocent, or indulge himself in ignorance
about the nature of contemporary governments, politics, social
orders. The national politics of the modern world exist by nothing
but deliberately fostered craving and fear--the roots (both socially
and psychologically, if you trace back far enough) of human
suffering." Arguing that the consumer society that had developed
in the United States represented a prime example of this
"deliberately fostered craving and fear," he wrote that "[m]odern
America has become economically dependent on a fantastic
system of stimulation of greed which cannot be fulfilled, sexual
desire which cannot be satiated, and hatred which has no outlet
except against oneself or the persons one is supposed to love."

The problems were not limited to America by any means.
"The conditions of the cold war," Snyder argued, "have turned all
modern societies, Soviet included, into hopeless brain-strainers,
creating populations of 'preta'--hungry ghosts--with giant appetites
and throats no bigger than needles. The soil, and forests, and all
animal life are being wrecked to feed these cancerous mechanisms."

Snyder had become convinced through his spiritual questing
and studies of other societies that human nature did not dictate
destructive social orders:

A culture need not be mindless and destructive, full of contradictions,
frustration, and violence. This is borne out in a modest way by some of
the findings of anthropology and psychology, One can prove it for
himself through Buddhist practice. Have this much faith--or insight

and you are led to a deep personal commitment to some form of essentially non-violent revolutionary action.

Snyder, who was studying Zen Buddhism in Kyoto at the time, gave the following account of his adopted spiritual tradition:

Buddhism holds that the universe and all creatures in it are intrinsically in a state of complete wisdom, love, and compassion, acting in natural response and mutual interdependence. The point of being a "Buddhist"--or a poet, or anything else for that matter--is to follow some way of life that will bring about personal realization of this from-the-beginning state, which cannot be had alone and for oneself--because it cannot be fully realized unless one has given it up, and away, to all others.

Snyder went on to outline the failure of traditional Buddhism to deal with the social problems that contribute to human suffering:

In the Buddhist view, what obstructs the effortless manifestation of this natural state is ignorance, fed by fear and craving. Historically, Buddhist philosophers have failed to analyze-out the degree to which human ignorance and suffering is caused or encouraged by social factors, and have generally held that fear and craving are given facts of the human condition.

As a result of this view, Snyder believed, "The major concern of Buddhist philosophy is epistemology and 'psychology' with no attention paid to historical or sociological problems." And although Buddhism

has a grand vision of universal salvation and boundless compassion, the actual achievement of Buddhism has been the development of practical systems of meditation toward the end of liberating individuals from their psychological hangups and cultural conditionings. Institutional Buddhism has been conspicuously ready to accept or support the inequalities and tyrannies of whatever political system it found itself under. This is death to Buddhism, because it is death to compassion. Wisdom without compassion feels no pain.

Snyder believed he had found in Buddhist practices a path to a new kind of non-repressive, nonviolent community based on the rejection of consumerism. He was careful to distinguish his vision from Puritanism, Eastern or Western:

The disaffiliation and acceptance of poverty by practicing Buddhists becomes a positive force. The traditional harmlessness and refusal to take life in any form has nation-shaking implications. The practice of meditation, for which one needs "only the ground beneath one's feet" wipes out mountains of junk being pumped into the mind by "communications" and supermarket universities. The belief in a serene and generous fulfillment of natural desires (not the repression of them, a Hindu ascetic position which the Buddha rejected) destroys arbitrary frustration-creating customs and points the way to a kind of community that would amaze moralists and eliminate armies of men who are fighters because they cannot be lovers.

Snyder signalled what he saw as the relationship between Western political engagement and Eastern wisdom:

The mercy of the west has been rebellion; the mercy of the east has been insight into the basic self. We need both. They are both contained, as I see it, in the traditional three aspects of Buddhist practice: wisdom (prajna), meditation (dhyana), and morality (sila). Wisdom is knowledge of the mind of love and clarity that lies beneath one's ego-driven anxieties and aggressions. Meditation is going into the psyche to see this for yourself--over and over again, until it becomes the mind you live in. Morality is bringing it out in the way you live, through personal example and responsible action, ultimately toward the true community (sangha) of "all beings."

Finally, he concluded with a general appeal to realize these moral insights in political action, a call for a nonviolent revolution. In the original version of the essay Snyder described this change as "a kind of committed disaffiliation: Buddhist Anarchism," which included "the sexual revolution" and "true communism." In the slightly revised version entitled "Buddhism and the Coming Revolution" Snyder changed the concluding section to read:

This . . . means for me, supporting any cultural and economic revolution that moves clearly toward a free, international, classless world. It means using such means as civil disobedience, outspoken criticism, protest, pacifism, voluntary poverty and even gentle violence if it comes to a matter of restraining some impetuous redneck. It means affirming the widest possible spectrum of non-harmful individual behavior--defending the right of individuals to smoke hemp, eat peyote, be polygynous, polyandrous or homosexual. Worlds of behavior and custom long banned by the Judeo-Capitalist-Christian-Marxist West. It means respecting intelligence and learning, but not as

greed or means to personal power. Working on one's own responsibility, but willing to work with a group. "Forming the new society within
the shell of the old"--the I.W.W. slogan of fifty years ago.

The traditional cultures are in any case doomed, and rather than
cling to their good aspects hopelessly it should be remembered that
whatever is or ever was in any other culture can be reconstructed from
the unconscious, through meditation. In fact, it is my own view that the
coming revolution will close the circle and link us in many ways with
the most creative aspects of our archaic past. If we are lucky we may
eventually arrive at a free-form marriage, natural-credit communist
economy, less industry, far less population and lots more national
parks.[13]

Why *Buddhist Anarchism*? What was it that made this
formulation one of the clearest expressions of the political
implications of the Beat Generation? It is important to note that
all of the targets of the Beat revolt that Snyder summarizes are
characteristics of the world we associate with the masculine ego as
constituted since the rise of patriarchal civilization: namely, the
nation state, militarism, excessive aggression and competition, and
materialistic values. Traditional manhood and the values and
institutional forms that sustain it--domination, hierarchy, authori-
tarianism--were challenged by the Beat movement. The Beats did
not begin with a feminist analysis per se but with a challenge to
traditional concepts of masculinity. In particular, they challenged
one of the keystones of American masculinist culture and
masculine character formation--the taboo on male homosexuality.
If masculine sexuality is based on "the oppression of women,
competition among men, and homophobia,"[14] then the central
importance of the theme of homosexual love in the Beat
movement called into question the very essence of the American
definition of masculinity.

Imperial manhood had been the adjunct of the imperial
republic since the Founding Fathers opted for a centralized and
expansionist constitution as opposed to a limited decentralized
republic. Just as the nation set its course of domination and
expansion at Philadelphia, so too was the mold cast for the
masculine character type in America that would equate manliness
with ruthless individualism, racial chauvinism, domination and
conquest--the strain we find in American literature from James
Fenimore Cooper through Ernest Hemingway and Norman
Mailer. There had been male voices of protest against the

dominant American ideal of masculinity--Thoreau, Melville, Whitman--and many female opponents of sexism, but not until the Beat Generation were the icons of mainstream masculinity so thoroughly challenged and repudiated. In some ways, the cultural history of the 1960s can be seen as the struggle between the John Wayne legend of heroic conquest with his Marine Corps imitators, and the Allen Ginsberg image of a gay Beatnik poet with his bands of long-haired, loving flower children. Certainly the central role of Allen Ginsberg, America's first openly homosexual poet, was crucial to the development of this challenge to traditional masculine values.

Ginsberg, whose father was a poet and school teacher and whose mother was a political activist, came to grips with his homosexuality in a way no other American poet ever had. He eventually "married" his lover, Peter Orlovsky, and they became America's most celebrated gay male couple.[15] He also struggled mightily with the relationship of his sexuality to his spirituality and his poetry. Once, as a student, he was imprisoned in a mental hospital for his unwitting role in a drug bust. At another point, in Harlem, he was awakened by a vision in which he heard the voice of the poet William Blake speaking to him.

William Carlos Williams wrote, in an introduction to Ginsberg's most famous poem, *Howl!*:

> It is the poet, Allen Ginsberg, who has gone, in his own body, through the horrifying experiences described from life in these pages. The wonder of the thing is not that he has survived but that he, from the very depths, has found a fellow who he can love, a love he celebrates without looking aside . . . .
>
> Poets are damned but they are not blind, they see with the eyes of angels. . . . He avoids nothing but experiences it to the hilt. He contains it. Claims it as his own--and, we believe, laughs at it and has the affontry to love a fellow of his choice and record that love in a well-made poem.
>
> Hold back the edges of your gowns, Ladies, we are going through hell.[16]

Ginsberg experienced a spiritual transformation at the same time his fame as a poet grew. This process eventually brought him to a commitment to Buddhism, as it had other Beat poets. Thomas Merrill describes this development:

By 1961 Ginsberg had become an internationally recognized poet and he once more traveled to France, Morocco, Greece, Israel, India, Vietnam, and Japan. In the Orient his commitment to Buddhist beliefs galvanized an event documented in Indian Journals: March 1962-May 1963 and in "The Change: Kyoto-Tokyo Express.". . . This was a decisive point in Ginsberg's spiritual development, for it marked his abandonment of the gods, devils, and angels that had haunted his vision since the Harlem Blake experience fifteen years before. It is important to acknowledge Ginsberg's spiritual shift here from a theistic Judeo-Christian to a nontheistic Buddhist base. . . . In 1972 Ginsberg made a formal commitment to the Buddhist faith.[17]

✦ Ecological Politics and Spiritual Values

The Beat revolt also took the form of a renewed interest in "primitive" cultures. The disastrous direction of technological society raised the question whether the whole project that we call civilization had been worth it. The dream of returning to a (somewhat modernized) version of a confederation of neolithic towns and villages is a decentralist or anarchist vision that emerges in reaction to the nightmare of modern society and the centralized bureaucratic national state. It was, of course, the same line of questioning with which Rousseau had initiated modern democratic political theory. In a penetrating essay, "Poetry and the Primitive," Gary Snyder suggested that "one of the most remarkable intuitions in Western thought was Rousseau's Noble Savage: the idea that perhaps civilization has something to learn from the primitive."[18]

Rousseau asked whether human beings had not been better off in primitive society than in modern civilization, and decided that they probably had been. The modern political question for Rousseau was whether democracy on a decentralized basis was possible. He thought it was not in the modern world.[19]

When human beings confront the speciocidal direction of modern society they ask two questions. First, were human beings ever happy and self-governing? And second, if so, is it possible for them to retrieve such a possibility out of the increasing wreckage of the modern world? The question quickly devolves into an argument about human nature: are people basically good or bad, capable or incapable of living together in harmony?

Gary Snyder's answer in "Buddhist Anarchism" seems to be

that with the decentralization of power and a culture that nurtures our basic goodness rather than our egotism, we can find positive solutions. One clear reason for the attachment to Buddhism was that it offered a view of human nature compatible with decentralist politics. The belief in the necessity of a strong centralized state is closely tied to a pessimistic view of human nature. It is the view propounded by Thomas Hobbes in *Leviathan:* that in a "state of nature" without a strong centralized state, human life was "solitary, poor, nasty, brutish, and short."[20] Hobbes believed that humans were basically "desire machines" driven by competitive individualism in a "warre of all against all."[21] For Hobbes, unbridled desire was absolutely basic to human character. For Buddhism, desire is a problem that developed along with a fixed ego, but there are more fundamental aspects of the human psyche that are referred to as "Buddhamind" or "original (Buddha) nature," meaning the latent capacity for compassionate wisdom that is fundamental to our nature.

Beat generation spirituality was an expression of the conviction that "we all have Buddhamind, whether we like it or not." That is to say, the sources of wisdom and compassion--of goodness--in human beings are stronger and deeper than their propensities for malice. Gary Snyder's Buddhist Anarchism was a repudiation of the Hobbesian tradition, both its view of human nature and its concomitant commitment to the state. "Decentralize and work on yourselves!" Such might be an appropriate slogan for Snyder's "Buddhist Anarchism." In other words, "decentralize self and society." The two go necessarily together since the success of a decentralized society depends in part on the transformation of our competitive selves, at once more earthy and more spiritually alive.

Snyder's cultural agenda was not a political program as such. He recognized the failures of his adoptive spiritual tradition in social and political thought. Institutional Buddhism has probably as bad a record as institutional Christianity when it has come to caving in to existing political regimes. But Snyder was aware of that pitfall, and he tried to remedy it in thought and action. He does not argue that Buddhism explicitly proclaims a politics, but he does argue that it implies a politics of decentralization based on nonviolence in the post-modern world.

"As a poet," Snyder wrote, "I hold the most archaic values on earth. They go back to the late Paleolithic: the fertility of the soil, the magic of animals, the power-vision in solitude, the terrifying initiation and rebirth, the love and ecstacy of the dance, the common work of the tribe."[22] He was not attempting to romanticize primitive societies but to make a point about human communities. "We all know," he pointed out, "what they *do* have is this knowledge of connection and responsibility which amounts to a spiritual ascesis for the whole community." And he went on to say, "Monks of Christianity or Buddhism, 'leaving the world' (which means the games of society) are trying, in a decadent way, to achieve what whole primitive communities--men, women, and children--live by daily; and with more wholeness."[23]

In searching for a cultural and political alternative to the direction of modern technological societies, Snyder sketched out, in an essay called "Why Tribe?" a "synthesis of Gandhian 'village anarchism' and IWW syndicalism." "After World War II," he wrote, a new generation "looked at Communist rhetoric with a fresh eye and saw that within the Communist governments (and states of mind) there are too many of the same things as are wrong with 'capitalism'--too much anger and murder." Out of this perception grew the "suspicion that the whole Western Tradition, of which Marxism is but a (Millenial Protestant) part, is off track." This led people like Snyder to the study of other civilizations--India and China--and to the encounter with the Buddha Dharma, "a long, gentle, human dialogue--2500 years of quiet conversation--on the nature of human nature and the eternal Dharma--and practical methods of realization."[24]

This quest led Snyder and others to realize that the "journey to the East" was not a geographical displacement--"that the 'truth' in Buddhism and Hinduism is not dependant in any sense on Indian or Chinese culture; and that 'India' and 'China'--as societies--are as burdensome to human beings as any others; perhaps more so." Furthermore, "it became clear that 'Hinduism' and 'Buddhism' as social institutions had long been accomplices of the State in burdening and binding people, rather than serving to liberate them. Just like the other Great Religions."[25]

This realization of the failures of institutional religion led Snyder (and his fellow seekers) to the discovery of what he calls "The Great Subculture" that is opposed to the "Civilization Establishment." "It has taught," he wrote, "that man's natural

being is to be trusted and followed; that we need not look to a
model or rule imposed from outside in searching for the center;
and that in following the grain, one is being truly 'moral'."
However, he is careful to point out that this tradition has not
simply relied on spontaneity but requires a culture of psychological and spiritual discipline. "It has recognized that for one to
'follow the grain' it is necessary to look exhaustively into the
negative and demonic potentials of the Unconscious and by
recognizing these powers--symbolically acting them out--one
releases himself from these forces. By this profound exorcism and
ritual drama, the Great Subculture destroys the one credible claim
of Church and State to a necessary function."[26]

This Great Subculture "is the tradition that runs without
break from Paleo-Siberian Shamanism and Magdalenian cave-
painting; through megaliths and Mysteries, astronomers, ritualists,
alchemists and Albigensians; gnostics and vagantes, right down to
Golden Gate Park." It has been made up of small but influential
heretical and esoteric movements and has included "peasant
witchcraft in Europe, Tantrism in Bengal, Quakers in England,
Tachikawa-ryu in Japan, Ch'an in China." This Great Subculture
"transmits a community style of life, with an ecstatically positive
vision of spiritual and physical love." Snyder points out the
obvious:

> All this is subversive to civilization, for civilization is built on hierarchy
> and specialization. A ruling class, to survive, must propose a Law: a
> law to work must have a hook into the social psyche--and the most
> effective way to achieve this is to make people doubt their natural
> worth and instincts, especially sexual. To make "human nature"
> suspect is also to make Nature--the wilderness--the adversary. Hence
> the ecological crisis of today.[27]

Snyder links this critique of civilization and the reevaluation
of "the primitive" to a revolution in consciousness. "Nationalism,
warfare, heavy industry and consumership," he writes, "are already
outdated and useless. The next great step of mankind is to step
into the nature of his own mind--the real question is 'just what is
consciousness?'--and we must make the most intelligent and
creative use of science in exploring these questions."[28]

From its beginnings in the poetry and the spiritual quest of
the Beat Generation prophets, the new culture which emerged in

the 1960s combined the demand for decentralist democracy and spiritual rebirth. Snyder thus epitomizes the "gestalt switch" referred to earlier. In his view of human nature and his opposition to the politics of domination, centralization, and state power, and his emphasis on recovering the "archaic" values of nature, spirituality, and community, Snyder represents the articulation of the major outlines of a new paradigm of political, social, and cultural thought.

✦ Coda for Kerouac

Gary Snyder's vision of a non-repressive, spiritually informed, and nonviolent decentralism represents a politics that incorporated the values of many of the Beat Generation. The leading figures of the Beat movement did not become uniformly integrated into the world of political activism in the first half of the 1960s. They were mainly poets, not political organizers. Between the start of the civil rights sit-ins in 1960 and the beginnings of massive anti-Vietnam war protest in 1965, several of them spent time outside the country, some studying spiritual traditions in the East. The situation of Jack Kerouac, their leading figure, was different.[29] By 1960 Kerouac's struggle with self-revelation and the unconscious, aggravated by his long years of difficulty in finding an outlet for his work, had become a losing battle in which alcohol abuse began to dominate his life. The "journey to the East," movingly portrayed in *The Dharma Bums*,[30] which the Beats undertook in earnest and which produced real personal and spiritual growth for people like Gary Snyder and Allen Ginsberg, seems to have been only partially helpful for Kerouac. He was one of the first to study Buddhism seriously; he undertook meditation, wrote commentaries on sutras, and for a time seemed to experience some inner peace. But he never found a discipline that could sustain him through the terrors of grappling with the unconscious. If part of the spiritual journey of the male Beat poets was an expression of their search for a way to shed American hyper-masculinity and come to terms with a "feminine" side of themselves, then Kerouac failed to find a reliable path to the receptive self. The breakdown that he began to experience in late 1960 and which, with the proper guidance or discipline, might have led to transformation and growth, led instead to alcoholic suicide--a long process of self-destruction ending with his death in October 1969. In the course of his deterioration, Kerouac became politically reactionary and, on occasion, even disavowed his long friendship with Ginsberg. Despite the real ugliness that at times warped his disintegrating personality, he remained a true hero to Ginsberg and others who never returned his spitefulness. An enduring testimony to their fondness for the once warm and loving presence that had done so much to free and nurture their souls and talents is the Jack Kerouac School of Poetics at Naropa Institute, a Buddhist center in Boulder, Colorado, where the Beats and others still teach writing workshops and hold poetry readings.

Kerouac and friends had pioneered cultural breakthroughs of enormous importance for the Movement of the sixties, but tragically their most innovative guide lost his way and left others to benefit from the psychological risks he had taken. Kerouac's biographer, Dennis McNally, expressed this dismal paradox in *Desolate Angel*:

> In cultural realms far beyond writing styles, the Beats had been forerunners of a major American societal shift in the late 1960s and early 1970s that rejected traditional "masculinity." The resistance to the liberal-rational world view was embodied in the departure from private psychoanalysis to public, confessional, consciousness-raising and encounter groups, a turning away from "logic" in a mad world to values born of emotional openness and sensitivity in suprarational disciplines like Zen, yoga, meditation, astrology and the occult. By the time it happened, it was too late for Jack.[31]

Certainly Kerouac had played a key role in opening up the American male psyche to exploration and change. In the end, this warm and sensitive man was unable to resolve the conflicts created by his own conditioning to a traditional model of masculinity and the inhibitions of his sexually repressive Catholic upbringing. He opened up more spiritual and psychological territory than he was able to integrate.

Rather than reducing art to a "superstructure" built on an economic "base" (as materialist philosophy attempts to do), it is important to recognize poets and artists in their prophetic role. They are the sensitive precursors of change and to them falls the dreadful task of articulating needs, perceptions, and desires that are still preconscious for the vast majority of people. Their lives and their works are the true frontiers of the human spirit. Such was the role of the Beat Generation in America. Some flourished on that frontier; some perished. But in the end and because of their courage, we were all profoundly changed.

CHAPTER 2

POLITICS AS MORALITY:

The Nonviolent Revolution of the

Radical Pacifists

 . . .my devotion to Truth has drawn me into
the field of politics; and I can say without the
slightest hesitation, and yet in all humility,
that those who say religion has nothing to do
with politics do not know what religion
means.

Mohandas K. Gandhi[1]

The cultural movement catalyzed by the Beat Generation
poets was not the only force shaping the new politics that was to
emerge full-blown in the 1960s. Traditional views of manhood and
the political roles expected of men were also being challenged in
another arena--warfare and the state. The growth of a radical
pacifist movement in the United States had its roots in the draft
resistance movement during the Second World War. The defiance
of the state through nonviolent direct action, the central theme of
the radical pacifists, was to have a great influence on the
philosophy and tactics of the Movement of the sixties. Furthermore, the radical pacifist milieu contributed many important
leaders and organizers to both civil rights and anti-war groups. Its
leaders had made very serious commitments to working for social
change and had engaged in many years of activism. Their political
experience in and out of prison made them an extremely valuable
resource for young New Leftists. More than any other group on

the American left, they had a reputation for moral integrity and courage of conviction. Unlike the Marxist Old Left, they were not compromised either by the horrors, manipulations, and lies of Stalinism that produced the moral bankruptcy of the U.S. Communist Party, nor by collusion with the anti-Communist crusade that had corrupted the social democrats.

Additionally, the men among them who had engaged in draft resistance served as valuable role models for young men in the 1960s who opposed the Vietnam war. Refusing the demand of the state to serve as cannon fodder involved a serious encounter with one of the oldest institutions of manhood: warriorship. To refuse service in the military was tantamount to rejecting the dominant model of masculinity. In American society it was sufficient evidence that one might be "queer." The refusal of warriorship implied a reevaluation of masculine values and the possible creation of alternative models of manhood.

Beyond their contribution to the cultural critique of traditional masculinity, the radical pacifists made a profound contribution to the creation of a dialogue about democratic decentralist politics. There have always been some young men who had the good sense not to fight in wars that only served the interests of their masters. The radical pacifists, however, turned that kind of individual decision into a political stance and statement. They were not simply draft evaders; they were morally and politically motivated "war resisters" and social activists.[2]

The leading journal of the radical pacifists, *Liberation* magazine, which began publication in 1956, was perhaps the most creative and provocative left-wing publication in the United States. Writers for *Liberation* had a distinct advantage over most other leftist publicists in that their minds were not smothered by the stultifying discourse of Marxism and Marxism-Leninism. They were thus free to see social and political reality afresh and able to respond imaginatively to concrete situations. They brought a breath of fresh air into the turgid atmosphere of left-wing politics.

Above all, these decentralist leftists brought back together the questions of morality and politics. In their personal lives and political actions they inspired a belief that politics should be moral and morality political. They represented, in an odd way, the return to the classical viewpoint of Aristotle that "politics" is a branch of ethics. That notion put them at odds with the dominant political discourses of the modern world, liberalism and Marxism. It began with their personal challenge to the power of the state in the name of moral principle, and it set the framework for a new activism in which politics as morality would be a major theme.

♦ A.J. Muste and the Growth of Radical Pacifism

If the life of any one individual exemplified the development of radical pacifism in the United States, it was Abraham Johannes (A.J.) Muste. The product of a conservative Dutch Reform family and education, Muste was ordained a minister in his denomination in 1909, but quickly moved in the direction of a more socially activist ministry.[3] Before and during the First World War he became a socialist and pacifist, with a growing commitment to the beleaguered labor movement. He left the formal ministry in 1918 and worked as part of a commune of activists oriented toward political nonviolence. He was involved in the 1919 Lawrence textile workers' strike and became director in 1921 of Brookwood Labor College. At Brookwood, Muste played a key role in educating scores of organizers for the labor movement which had become the primary focus of his life. Muste became convinced that a new initiative was necessary for organizing industrial unions in the United States, and in 1929 he called for the establishment of a new organization, the Conference for Progressive Labor Action, which was designed to "create . . . unity among those advocates of industrial unionism who might offer a middle way for the American labor movement, a way between the reactionary AFL (American Federation of Labor) and various communist forces."[4]

During the 1920s at Brookwood, Muste's politics were deeply influenced not only by the desperation of American workers, but by events in the Soviet Union. By 1929 he was on the road to becoming a Marxist-Leninist, abandoning his earlier pacifism in favor of revolutionary violence. His political convictions were, however, strongly anti-Stalinist, and he became an admirer of Leon Trotsky. Muste's trajectory in the early 1930s led him to the formation of the American Workers Party (AWP) in December 1933. An alliance with the "official" Trotskyist organization, the Communist League of America (CLA), led in 1934 to a merger and the short-lived Workers Party of the U.S. Opportunism and manipulation quickly destroyed that organization and disillusioned Muste with the Marxist left. During a trip to Europe in late 1936 Muste had a profound spiritual experience in Paris which convinced him that the basic reality of the universe was love. He returned to the United States with a refound faith in Christian pacifism that remained the core of his convictions for the rest of his life. It was, however, a pacifism that was deeply political and decidedly radical.

During World War II, Muste exerted a decisive influence on the development of the radical pacifist movement. The war faced young men with the imperative of the draft. It was not an easy war to say "no" to, harder than World War I, which radical workers in the IWW had called "a bosses' war" and which, until the mobilization in 1917, many Americans had thought of as "the Kaiser's war." Eugene Debs, head of the American Socialist Party, had opposed that war, gone to prison for his oppositional activity, and while in prison received a million votes for the presidency in the election of 1920. In the 1940s, however, it took enormous courage of conviction to refuse to fight in the "war against fascism" and face the opprobrium not only of the nationalistic right but most of the American left as well (Communists flip-flopped on the issue, first opposing the war effort during the period of the Stalin-Hitler alliance, then joining the cause after Hitler's invasion of the Soviet Union in 1941).

Despite the popularity of the war effort, significant numbers of young men resisted the draft during the Second World War.[5] The resisters soon divided into two tendencies. On the one side were those who took traditional religious pacifist positions of opposition to all wars and refused to fight, but who cooperated with the government. Most of these men were sent to Civilian Public Service camps, operated on behalf of the government by religious organizations, where they were effectively neutralized. Another group, small at first but increasing in size over time, came to be known as "non-cooperators." They were men who took the position of total non-cooperation with the state on moral or political grounds, and most of them ended up in federal prisons. As the war dragged on, growing numbers of those who had entered the CPS camps with the intention of cooperating with the government were increasingly politicized and became non-cooperators. In all, some 50,000 men refused military service as

conscientious objectors and over 6,000 served prison sentences for
non-cooperation. (By contrast, in World War I only about 450
non-cooperators were jailed.)[6]

It was from the group of non-cooperators that the ranks of
radical pacifism and the philosophy of revolutionary nonviolence
were to grow. Among their numbers were Dave Dellinger, future
editor of *Liberation*, chairman of the National Mobilization to
End the War in Vietnam, and one of the "Chicago Seven"; Bayard
Rustin, later to become Executive Secretary of the War Resisters
League, an activist in the Congress on Racial Equality (CORE),
and assistant to Martin Luther King, Jr.; James Peck, CORE staff
member and 1961 Freedom Rider; Igal Roodenko, War Resisters
League organizer and Freedom Rider; and many others who were
to be key actors in the civil rights and anti-war movements of the
1960s.[7]

A.J. Muste devoted a great deal of his time and energy as
Executive Secretary of the pacifist organization, the Fellowship of
Reconciliation, to counseling and encouraging non-cooperators
during and after the war. It was with them rather than with
"individualistic" pacifists who did not develop a politics of radical
opposition to the capitalist war system that his true sympathies lay
(although he did support all those who refused the draft for
whatever reasons of conscience).[8]

♦ Radical Resisters and Direct Action Politics

Within this milieu of draft resisters and other opponents of
war there developed a new brand of American radicalism that was
communitarian, libertarian, and decentralist and which stressed
the philosophy and practice of active nonviolence. Some of these
activists had been strongly influenced both spiritually and
strategically by the study of Gandhian nonviolence in the late
1930s and 1940s. In brief, Gandhi's brand of nonviolence
"emphasized building decentralized communities grounded in
truth, justice, and mutual aid, and encouraged the use of mass civil
disobedience and non-cooperation when the state interfered with
the constructive program."[9]

Of the various colonies, or ashrams, in the United States
inspired by Gandhi's example, the Newark Commune (1939-1944),

founded by Dave Dellinger and others from the Union Theological Seminary, was one of the largest and most successful. It involved over sixty people who lived in the heart of the Newark ghetto, and served as a cultural center for black and white children. Members organized a buying cooperative and a communal farm in Chester, New Jersey. They were not involved in utopian withdrawal from the world, but rather emphasized a commitment to nonviolent social and political activism. They organized "the Essex County Equality League, which picketed and sat-in at restaurants and movie houses that discriminated against blacks." They also engaged in direct action for "improved welfare, neighborhood improvement, an end to police brutality, free hot lunches in the schools, and community participation in decisions" that affected it. Among their other activities were the "organization of a People's Peace Committee which picketed the U.S. capitol in Washington, leafleted factory gates, and held poster walks in half a dozen cities." In addition, they "protested the saturation bombing of German cities, the U.S. refusal to open its doors to Jewish refugees, and the unconditional surrender policy that prolonged the war."[10]

Dave Dellinger, who was imprisoned twice for non-cooperation with the Selective Service system, wrote later that the Newark Commune

> along with the Catholic Worker and other small but ambitious centers of communal economics, local organizing, and national actions, served as a bridge from the Old Left radicalism of the Thirties to a complex of ideas and actions that later gained prominence in the civil rights movement, the New Left, and other later movements.[11]

After the war Dellinger and some others from the Newark Commune "helped organize the Glen Gardner (New Jersey) Commune and the Libertarian Press, a workers' cooperative where *Liberation* magazine and other publications were printed." In December 1945 a new journal of militant nonviolence, *Direct Action,* was founded. Dellinger served as one of the editors. In February 1946, the Committee for Nonviolent Revolution (CNVR) was formed by Dellinger and other World War II draft resisters. It was a loosely structured organization that opposed all wars and militarism and supported a democratic, decentralist form of socialism.[12]

Direct Action and the CNVR were attempts to articulate and organize a movement for a democratic and decentralist libertarian socialism in the United States, a movement that based itself on a philosophy and practice of militant nonviolence. Although neither the journal nor the Committee lasted long, the members remained energetically involved in political activism and their politics had a widespread influence on the groups and movements that would constitute the New Left in the 1960s.

While the Old Left fell victim to both its own deceits and government repression, and while the leaders of the labor movement bought into business unionism, radical pacifists were practically the only vital and active opposition remaining in the United States. Their direct action campaigns against nuclear weapons and the militarization of American life and policy kept them in the forefront of radical politics in the late 1940s and 1950s. And with the Supreme Court decision *Brown v. Board of Education* in 1954, and the subsequent mushrooming of the civil rights movement, radical pacifists played a vital role in creating bonds of unity between blacks and whites in the struggle. Dr. Martin Luther King, Jr. stated that without A.J. Muste "the American Negro might never have caught the meaning of nonviolence."[13] And on the occasion of Muste's eightieth birthday, King paid tribute to the man in stirring language:

> You have climbed the mountain and have seen the great and abiding truth to which you have dedicated your life. Throughout the world you are honored as our most effective exponent of pacifism. You have been a great friend and inspiration to me and the whole nonviolent movement. Without you the American Negro might never have caught the meaning of true love for humanity.[14]

✦ Dorothy Day and the Catholic Worker Movement

Not all of the radical pacifists were draft resisters; many were women. Indeed no account of the development of a nonviolent decentralized movement in the United States would be complete without mention of the work of Dorothy Day and the Catholic Worker Movement. Founded in 1933 by Day and her mentor Peter Maurin, a Catholic lay activist from a French peasant background, the Catholic Worker was a newspaper, a movement and a network of "houses of hospitality," rural communes, and experiments in decentralist activism and community living. Strongly influenced by the school of Christian personalism around Emmanuelle Mournier in France and the decentralist political theories of Jacques Maritain,[15] the Catholic Workers represented a startling departure from the conservatism of the Roman Catholic Church in the United States, which had overwhelmingly sided with the dominant ethos of American individualism and capitalism.[16]

Dorothy Day and her associates dedicated themselves to living the Christian life in imitation of Jesus, accepted lives of voluntary poverty, and worked among the poor and oppressed. Their politics grew out of their lived participation in the mystical Body of Christ, the realization of which through active love they believed to be the essence of Christian faith. They sometimes referred to themselves as "anarchists" or designated their political viewpoint as "Christian Communism." They were opposed to totalitarian collectivism and favored "radical decentralization and the delegation to smaller bodies and groups what could be done far more humanly and responsibly through mutual aid, as well as charity."[17]

Dorothy Day spelled out clearly her opposition to centralized forms of socialism or collectivism on the Marxist model. Her vision was of a society based on "worker ownership of the means of production and distribution as distinguished from nationalization." The strategy for accomplishing this involved the creation of "decentralized cooperatives and the elimination of a distinct employer class."[18] Her radical vision led her to call into question those forms of trade unionism that promoted accommodation within the existing system. She wrote critically of the Association of Catholic Trade Unionists which was founded in 1937. In an article in *The Catholic Worker* of February 1949, she was to say of them,

> All they want, what they will settle for, is a share of the profits, instead of a share in the ownership, and the decentralization of the physical business of factories and production, and not a decentralization of control by widespread ownership.[19]

This decentralized political perspective was wedded to an ideal and practice of active nonviolence. Dorothy Day and the Workers took a stand directly in opposition to the doctrine of "just wars" that had dominated the thinking of the Catholic Church since the fifth century. Day became "the leading voice in American Catholic circles for militant pacifism."[20] She spoke up on behalf of conscientious objection when conscription was instituted in 1941, and *The Catholic Worker* carried articles during the war that defended a radical pacifist stand.

In the 1950s Dorothy Day worked closely with other advocates of active nonviolence in the Ban the Bomb movement and was arrested in New York City for refusing to take part in civil defense drills. Her overall influence on the development of a radical Catholic left in the United States is almost immeasurable. In November 1965, when five men burned their draft cards in Union Square in New York City to protest the Vietnam War, two of them were Catholic Workers, and Dorothy Day was one of the speakers, declaring that she "opposed the war and encouraged noncooperation with conscription and war on taxes." Later she was active in the Delano, California farmworkers strike and in the summer of 1973 (at the age of 75) was arrested and sent to prison for picketing with Cesar Chavez and the United Farmworkers Union.[21]

◆ A "Tract for the Times"

The founding in 1956 of *Liberation* magazine was a milestone in the development of the radical pacifist or nonviolent movement. Its first issue, in March 1956, carried an editorial statement, "Tract for the Times," which laid out the theoretical perspective of the founding group. It was signed "the Editors," and the five of them were listed as Dave Dellinger, A.J. Muste, Bayard Rustin, Roy Finch, and Charles Walker. It was an important statement of the political insights that activists and thinkers of a decentralist, nonviolent persuasion had gained over the prior decade and a half.[22]

The statement begins with an assessment of the state of political radicalism. "The decline of independent radicalism and the gradual falling into silence of prophetic and rebellious voices," they write, "is an ominous feature of the mid-twentieth century." They link this decline to a bankruptcy of ideas:

This failure of a new radicalism to emerge is an indication, it seems to

us, that the stock of fundamental ideas on which radical thinking of
recent times has been predicated is badly in need of thorough
reappraisal. Much of its inspiration appears to be used up.

Specifically they pinpoint the inadequacies of Marxism and
liberalism. "Old labels--principally in the Marxist and liberal
traditions--simply do not apply any more, and the phrases which
fifty years ago were guideposts to significant action have largely
become empty patter and jargon." Neither "reshuffling power"
nor an alteration of the "forms of property relationships which are
oppressive and destructive of true community" are worthwhile if
the results of these changes are that "the average individual finds
his life as dull and empty as ever and the enslavement of his hours
just as great." They assert their view of what is needed: "a
post-Soviet, post-H-bomb expression of the needs of today and a
fresh vision of the world of peace, freedom and brotherhood in
which they can be met."

That vision can only be created by a careful reexamination of
past political thought--"especially the two great dominant traditions of liberalism and Marxism" and a reaffirmation of spiritual
and moral values by a "return in part to root traditions from
which we derive our values and standards." These root traditions
are four: 1) "the ancient Judeo-Christian prophetic tradition," 2)
the American traditions of liberty, equality, and popular consent,
3) the "heritage of libertarian, democratic, anti-war, socialist,
anarchist and labor movements of Europe and the United States,"
and 4) the "traditions of pacifism or nonviolence," exemplified
worldwide by many religious teachers, in particular Gandhi who
"stands in this tradition, not as an example to be slavishly
imitated, but as a pioneer who in a series of great political and
social experiments joined nonviolence and revolutionary collective
action."

It should be noted that this statement of allegiance to
tradition is not narrowly religious while it does, however, make
clear that the "values and standards" that the authors regard as
absolutely essential to a renewal of radical political thought are in
part rooted in spiritual traditions. The appeal to the "ancient
Judeo-Christian prophetic tradition" is couched in the language of
the theology of the Social Gospel. It "gave men a vision of human
dignity and a reign of righteousness, equality and brotherhood on

earth." Furthermore, they write, it "taught them that building such an order of life was their task, and that a society of justice and fraternity could be built by justice and love and not by other means." Appeal is made, however, to a broader spiritual legacy "of great teachers and saints throughout the centuries and in many parts of the world." In addition, the American democratic tradition and the best in the libertarian, socialist, anarchist, and labor movements are named as sources of inspiration.

This statement of the derivation of values and standards from the root traditions is followed by two "critiques" of liberalism and of Marxism. In criticizing the tradition of liberalism, the authors state that

> the greatness of liberalism has been its emphasis on humaneness and tolerance, its support of the liberties of the individual and its insistence on the free and inquiring mind and rejection of fanaticism and dogmatism.

However, the weakness of liberalism has been "its failure to come to grips with war, poverty, boredom, authoritarianism and other great evils of the modern world." Even more importantly, "liberalism has tried to diagnose our problems without going to fundamentals--the inequalities and injustices upon which our present social order is based and which no 'goodwill' can wish away."

Liberalism is seen by the editors as "often shallow, hypocritical and dilettantish."

> Essentially the liberal accepts the existing order and wants to exploit it and share in it as much as the next man. At the same time he is troubled and wants the good conscience of repudiating its wrongs. Liberalism thus becomes a fashionable pose.

It makes the liberal "an easy prey of opportunism and expedience."

What is needed, they argue, is "a new quality of seriousness and personal honesty," "not political liberalism but political fundamentalism," i.e., a politics that goes to "fundamentals." They profess a preference for "concrete situations" over "rhetorical blueprints" and an interest in "individual lives" rather than "global historical forces which remain merely abstract." Finally they state:

> What matters to us is what happens to the individual human
> being--here and now. We will be just as flexible as the liberal, but we
> will strive to be more searching, and we will insist on spelling out
> things in terms of daily consequences, hour to hour, for everyone.

This appraisal is followed by a "Critique of Marxism" in which
the editors discuss the importance of some of Marx's insights
while emphasizing the grave failures of the Marxist tradition and
its inadequacy as a basis for a humane radical politics. Marxism's
"fundamental demand for economic justice and its attack on the
problem of poverty are permanently valuable," they write. "It
touches the source of much that is wrong in exposing the property
nerve." However, they add,

> many of its attitudes are those of the outmoded bourgeois epoch
> which it tried to repudiate. Marx was to a much greater degree than he
> himself realized a spokesman for nineteenth century thought patterns,
> now hopelessly out of date.

In particular they argue:

> His historical determinism, built up by analogy from now out-moded
> science, is an example. So also is the tendency to sacrifice the present
> for the future, so that human beings of today are regarded as pawns
> for bringing about something better in a tomorrow that never comes.

They then go on to deliver their most important theoretical
criticism of Marxism, its failure to understand the power of the
state, war, and political oppression:

> The most serious weaknesses of Marxism, however, are its omissions
> and its reactionary "realism" in respect to the instruments of
> revolution. Marx, for all his brilliant analysis of economic power, failed
> to analyze with equal profundity the questions of military and political
> power. Hence he underestimated the seriousness of the growth of the
> state and its emergence as an instrument of war and oppression. In
> trying to liberate mankind from economic slavery, he failed to see the
> looming horror of political slavery.

The failure of Marx to comprehend the problems of state
power, war, and political tyranny are closely linked in the authors'
minds to "Marx's inability to realize that social betterment cannot

be brought about by the same old methods of force and chicanery characterizing the regimes which had to be overthrown precisely because they embodied such evils." They then draw on a particularly American philosophical tradition, Pragmatism, to expand on this criticism of Marx's shortsightedness about methods of change:

> It is an illuminating insight of pragmatism that means and ends condition each other reciprocally and that ends must be built into the means. It is not sound, therefore to expect to achieve peace through war, justice through violence, freedom through dictatorship, or civil liberties through slave labor camps. Such instruments create the social attitudes and habit patterns which they are ostensibly designed to remove.

Having laid out their insistence on the necessary relationship between ends and means in the struggle for social and political change, they decisively reject anything resembling the Marxist "dictatorship of the proletariat."

> Dictatorship in any form, as well as spy systems, concentration camps, military conscription, restrictions on travel and censorship of books, papers and political parties must all be decisively rejected. What this means is that a truly radical movement today--if it does not want to fall into the trap which the Russian Communist movement has fallen into--must take these ethical problems much more seriously than many nineteenth century thinkers did, and must commit itself to an essentially democratic and non-violent strategy.

The writers then present an outline of what they call the "politics of the future." In order to overcome the fact "that many people are fed up with politics" (i.e., "the whole machinery of political life") they insist that "politics must discover its ethical foundations and dynamic." They go on to spell this out by arguing, "the politics of the future requires a creative synthesis of the individual ethical insights of the great religious leaders and the collective social concern of the great revolutionaries."

At this point they offer a clear definition of what differentiates them from all statist or centralist viewpoints:

> It follows that we do not conceive the problem of revolution or the building of a better society as one of accumulating power, whether by legislative or other methods, to "capture the State" and then

presumably, to transform society and human beings as well. The national, sovereign, militarized and bureaucratic state and a bureaucratic collectivist economy are themselves evils to be avoided or abolished. Seizure of the war-making and repressive machinery of the state cannot be a step toward the transforming of society into a free and humanly satisfying pattern. It is the transformation of society by human decision and action that we seek. This is a more complex and human process in which power as ordinarily conceived plays only a minor part.

The editors suggest that "community and cooperative experiments in many lands" (including the "Land Gift Movement in India") are included in a new conception of political action. And,

new political alignments in the narrower sense of the term may emerge from basic ethical and social changes, but preoccupation with or dependence upon the machinery of politics, or the violent seizure of power, are evils always to be avoided, and never more so than in the present system.

This caution about the "violent seizure of power" and "dependence on the machinery of politics" extends, in the attitude of the *Liberation* editors, to the whole direction of technological society. "Similarly," they write, "we reject the faith in technology, industrialization, and centralization *per se*, characteristic of both the contemporary capitalist and communist regimes."

Our emphasis is rather on possibilities for decentralization, on direct participation of all workers or citizens in determining the conditions of life and work, and on the use of technology for human ends, rather than the subjection of man to the demands of technology.

They go on to argue for a "new attitude toward utopianism" based on the "synthesis of the ethical and the political," and suggest that Marx will be understood as a visionary and utopian thinker once the "outmoded 'scientific' aspect of nineteenth century Marxism" disappears. They insist later (in a reply to criticism of the tract by George Woodcock) that the

utopianism to which the "Tract for the Times" referred is not the static concept to which Mr. Woodcock refers but an experimental attitude which "represents the growing edge of society and the creative imagination of a culture."[23]

Finally, they are concerned with the impact of thermonuclear war and "war-based prosperity" on the political future of the human race. "The problem of war," they write, is of special gravity.

> It may be argued that for personal ethics there is no distinction between a war in which a few persons are killed at a time and one in which multitudes are wiped out. But from a sociological view, the H-bomb and what it symbolizes--possible extinction of the race itself--presents mankind with a new situation. War is no longer an instrument of policy or a means to any rational end.

This new situation makes "withdrawal of support for the military preparation and activities of both the dominant power blocs a central part of any radical movement." In addition, "war and war preparation in the hands of any other power or group of powers is not a deliverance either." They express their support for groups "in non-committed areas" that are

> seeking to deal with the problems of economics and politics in a broader way and at a deeper level. They seek to build not another Military Force but a Third Camp or Third Way. They are striving not only to avoid war but to build a socio-economic order and culture different from both communism and capitalism.

As examples of these attempts to find a Third Way they cite "the Asian Socialist parties, the Gandhian Constructive Workers, and the Boodan movement of Vinoba Bhave in India" as well as "the non-violent responses to Colonialism in Africa" and the "June 1953 workers' revolts in East Germany."

♦ Dwight Macdonald, Decentralism, and Anarchism

The theme of decentralism, both as a political practice and as a long-range political, social, and technological goal would be one of the defining characteristics of the politics of the American New Left of the 1960s, and one of its clearest articulations was found in the journal *Politics* founded and edited by Dwight Macdonald in 1944. Macdonald had been a Trotskyist for two years (1939-41) although he never became a dogmatic convert to Marxism.

"I remember reading Marx and Engels intensively in the

summer of 1939," he later wrote, "in an effort to find out whether
I was a Marxist or not. I could never really make up my mind." He
went on to say that "the critical side attracted me, and also the
protest against capitalist injustice," however, "the dogmatism and
the insistence on explaining everything by one system of thought
repelled me (as did the moral callousness)." Macdonald left the
Trotskyist Socialist Workers Party in 1941 after opposing the
Russian invasion of Finland (1939) as "imperialist aggression,"
arguing for "a more democratic party," and having been rebuked
by Trotsky himself.[24]

Although Macdonald was not a traditional anarchist, his
exploration and development of decentralist ideas placed him
squarely in the left libertarian tradition of anarchists, anarcho-
syndicalists, and libertarian socialists as opposed to Marxist and
Marxist-Leninist centralism. *Politics* magazine evolved along the
lines of its editor's own political development. In Macdonald's
words, "after the first two years [1944-46]," it "forsook the true
Marxist faith to whore after the strange gods of anarchism and
pacifism." In a pivotal article, "The Root is Man," published in
the magazine in the spring of 1946, Macdonald outlined his newly
evolved political viewpoint. It was a prophetic prelude to the
politics of the New Left of the 1960s. He later described this
article in these terms:

> This was partly a demonstration that Marxism is no longer a reliable
> guide to either action or understanding, partly a discussion of the
> problem of values in politics and the limitations of the scientific
> method, partly some rather desperate suggestions for a new kind of
> radical approach--individualistic, decentralized, essentially anarchist.[25]

Macdonald's views on the outdated nature of the Marxist
framework as a basis for radical politics became increasingly
specific as his anarchist views matured, and he came to believe

> that anarchism gave a better answer to the real modern problem, the
> encroachment of the State, than did Marxism, which was revolutionary
> only about bourgeois private property (not a real issue any more) and
> was thoroughly reactionary on the question of the State. . . . The
> revolutionary alternative to the status quo today is not collectivized
> property administered by a "workers' state" whatever *that* means, but
> some kind of anarchist decentralization that will break up mass society
> into small communities where individuals can live together as

variegated human beings instead of as impersonal units in the mass sum.[26]

When Macdonald spoke of the relative unimportance of "bourgeois" property, he was not dismissing the capitalist nature of American society but emphasizing the point so frequently misconstrued by Marxists and liberals that *corporate capitalist ownership and control* had displaced *bourgeois family ownership* as the primary economic and social force in advanced capitalism. Furthermore, his identification of anarchism with "the individual and the community" was not a call for a return to rampant individualism but an appeal for the possibility of a society organized on the basis of face-to-face human communities where true individuality could flourish as it could not in mass society controlled by the state, be it corporate capitalist or authoritarian state socialist. In an article in *Partisan Review* (1950), Macdonald wrote:

> So long as the dominant areas of the world are organized in vast super-states, whose economic base is large-scale industry and whose political base is tens of millions of helpless "citizens," I see no hope of significant improvement. Nor do I see any signs that any considerable number of my fellow men are now in a mood to break up such monstrosities into *communities human in scale.*[27] [My emphasis.]

Interestingly, he wrote that it was "the emphasis on morality that caused the most scandal." Macdonald's emphasis on the primacy of values in political life was explicit although he was not a traditional religionist. He defined "religious belief" as a traditional theistic "belief that God exists," and avowed that "I just don't seem to have the knack for religious experience." He went on, however, to qualify this by adding: "although in surprisingly many ways I find myself agreeing more with contemporary religious-minded people than with the 'secular radicals.' God, attractive though the idea is from an intellectual standpoint, simply does not engage my feelings or imagination." Then on a revealing note he continued:

> This is all the more a pity since I have lost confidence in the dominant non-religious social tendency in this country today: the Marx-cum-Dewey approach represented by Sidney Hook (pure), the liberal weeklies (debased), the Reuther brothers and Senator Humphrey

("grass roots"), the Americans for Democratic Action (official) and
Partisan Review (highbrow). This seems to me to have failed
politically, culturally and even scientifically.[28]

Macdonald's dilemma was that of many non-theistic radicals
of a decentralist or anarchist persuasion who insisted on the
primacy of values but who had no other spiritual framework than
theism in which to present their convictions. Macdonald declared
that "although when I read Tolstoi and Gandhi I see the logical
convenience of the God-hypothesis, it does not move me
emotionally; nor do I feel a spiritual need for it." Without
explaining what he meant by this crucial category of "spiritual
need" nor considering the possibility of a non-theistic spiritual
framework like Buddhism, Macdonald propounded a conviction
that could have fit easily into a philosophy of spiritual humanism:
"I can believe that man is an end and not a means, and that to
love one another is the greatest duty and pleasure, without giving
this belief a religious [read theistic] basis."

His shocked former colleagues on the editorial board of
Partisan Review wrote that "Macdonald's notions about politics
are advanced under the banner of morality; actually they are
neither political nor moral, being a peculiar hodge-podge of
both."[29] This criticism prefigured similar attacks by both Marxists
and liberals on the young radicals of the New Left in the 1960s.
Interestingly, the label that Macdonald attached to this new breed
of political dissent was "Radical" in contradistinction to the
"Progressive" rubric being vaunted by the post-war Old Left. He
wanted to distinguish himself clearly from "Marxists [who] still
hold fast to the classic Left faith in human liberation through
scientific progress."[30]

Writing in 1957, Macdonald presented an excellent, concise
summation of the history of American radicalism, a view sharply
at odds with the "official" Stalinist version of the Old Left:

The last time in American history that radical ideas have had any mass
appeal was just before the First World War, when the Socialists
published half a dozen daily papers, elected Congressmen and almost
defeated Gompers with their candidate for the presidency of the
American Federation of Labor, and when that strange and unique
contribution of America to anarcho-syndicalism, the 'Wobblies'
(officially the Industrial Workers of the World, or IWW, also called I
Won't Work), organized great masses of unskilled workers and led

strikes in the New England textile mills, the Minnesota iron mines and the Pennsylvania steel industry that were as much social rebellions as economic conflicts. During and immediately after the war the Government, by the use of quasi-legal force and violence, permanently destroyed the Wobblies and the more militant section of the Socialist Party.

The radical tradition never came back, except among the intelligentsia. Not even at the lowest point of the depression, in 1932-33, were the Communists or the Socialists a serious political force.[31]

It was precisely this *American radical tradition* that was to reemerge clothed in the language of participatory democracy as the New Left of the 1960s, and Dwight Macdonald had framed much of the intellectual and moral problematic of its rebirth in the pages of *Politics*. In terms of the language he employed there was this one major difference: Macdonald eschewed the language of democracy that was central to the discourse of the New Left because, as he said, words like "'democratic' and 'scientific' came under increasing suspicion because of their abuse by the industrialized mass society that had produced the atomic bomb."[32] It would remain for the new radicals of Students for a Democratic Society to reclaim democracy in the name of a revitalized American radical tradition.

◆ *Beatniks, Anarchists, and Pacifists*

The framework laid out in the "Tract for the Times" that informed the editorial direction of *Liberation* magazine through the 1950s and 1960s, together with the work of anarchists like Dwight Macdonald, nourished the "new radicalism" in America in the post-World War II era. While the radical pacifists did not always share the cultural elan of the Beat Generation poets who were their contemporaries, they were close in spirit and their work overlapped in many areas. In San Francisco in October 1955, just as the first issue of *Liberation* was in the planning stage, a cultural event of tremendous significance took place that illustrates the close relationship between the cultural revolt and the movement of nonviolent radicalism. Perhaps it happened in San Francisco because the atmosphere was different and an alternative radicalism had been nourished there. In the words of Dennis McNally, Jack Kerouac's biographer,

San Francisco had not experienced the Stalinist/Capitalist New York
political split of the Cold War, because from World War II on it had
an active Anarchist Circle that welcomed draft resisters from the
Waldport, Oregon [CPS] camp and never succumbed to the rigidity
characteristic of the East Coast.[33]

In the Waldport Civilian Public Service camp, a small group
of war resisters had set up an artists' and writers' project in order
to engage in creative work while they were incarcerated. One of its
leaders was the poet William Everson, who later as "Brother
Antoninus" became an important Beat poet. Everson, along with
Kenneth Rexroth, Robert Duncan, and Philip Lamanthia--all
members of the pacifist Anarchist Circle--organized a poetry
reading at the Six Gallery in San Francisco on October 13, 1955.[34]
Those reading were Allen Ginsberg, Michael McClure, Philip
Lamanthia, Gary Snyder, and Philip Whalen. Kenneth Rexroth
served as master of ceremonies. Ginsberg sent out postcards
reading, "Six poets at Six Gallery. Remarkable collection of angels
. . . serious poetry, free satori . . . charming event."[35]
    The history-making moment of the evening was Allen
Ginsberg's reading of his long poem *Howl!.* The event was
responsible for launching the "San Francisco Renaissance," which
made San Francisco the leading center of American avant-garde
culture, and for casting the Beat poets in the national limelight. It
also signalled the fact that the new culture and the new politics
would grow together in powerful and unexpected ways.
    These two movements, the Beat Generation poets and the
radical anarcho-pacifists, represent what was new in American
political and cultural radicalism on the eve of the 1960s. They
shared a common opposition to the increasing power of the state
and its militarization. They were searching to find a decentralist
and democratic political alternative. They refused to accept the
separation of the spiritual, the moral, and the political, seeking
instead to create a vision that included all those elements. Either
through the teachings of Gandhi or the direct adoption of
Buddhism, they were influenced by Eastern spiritual thought,
although some like Muste remained committed to a politically
radical and nonviolent interpretation of the Christian gospel,
while others like Snyder rejected the whole tradition of what he
called "the Judaeo-Capitalist-Christian-Marxist West."[36] In both
cases, their spiritual vision was close to the (Quaker) notion of

"God in everyone" or the universality of a "Buddhanature." This optimistic view of human nature and its grounding in spirituality distinguished them from the materialist traditions of liberalism and Marxism. Finally, their spiritually benevolent view of human nature informed their decentralist political viewpoint and their opposition to the state and all centralized dominative forms of power like those described by Allen Ginsberg in *Howl!*:

> Moloch! Moloch! Nightmare of Moloch. Moloch the
>   loveless!
>   Mental Moloch! Moloch the heavy judger of men!
> Moloch the incomprehensible prison. Moloch the
>   crossbone soulless jailhouse and Congress of
>   sorrows! Moloch whose buildings are judgement!
>   Moloch the vast stones of war!
> Moloch the stunned governments![37]

For Allen Ginsberg, it was a new time when there was to be "again at last the possibility of prophetic poetry."[38]

These, then, were the elements of a turning--away from the dynamics of domination toward the decentralization of power. The "revolution" that the poets, anarchists, and pacifists were talking about did not involve the "seizure of state power" but rather the deconstruction of the very kind of power represented by the state and other institutions of exploitation and control and the substitution of decentralized "communities human in scale" where the human spirit and human individuality could flourish and bloom.

CHAPTER 3

BLACK AND WHITE TOGETHER:

SNCC and the New Activism

Once a great people's movement has become a thing of the past, it is easy to forget or dismiss the spirit which gave it life and provided the inspiration that moved its participants to acts of faith and courage. Like a corpse seen as a "dead thing," a movement can be dissected by historians, sociologists, or political theorists without ever discovering what made it live and breathe, what gave it hope and daring.

It was the spiritual depth and power of the civil rights movement that made it a soul-shaking force for change in American society. And it was the spiritual vision of nonviolence as the basis of a politics of compassion, redemption, and love that moved black people and their white allies to dare to struggle for a society freed of segregation and racial prejudice. It was the spiritual conviction that love is stronger than hate that made it possible for civil rights activists to imagine that a redemptive community of faith could overturn, through active nonviolence, a social order based on racism, the vilest and most violent of all human creeds. The notion of "black and white together" was the result of spiritual belief, not of materialist analysis. Too much academic scholarship has troubled itself with the dissection of the "dead thing" in an effort to dismiss the reality of the lived spirit.

The civil rights movement brought a new life and spirit to American politics that had been lacking for a long time--perhaps since the defeat of the Populist movement in the late 19th century. There came alive in the land a feeling that America could be fundamentally healed and radically changed by removing the deepest division and the ugliest scar in American political and social life--racism. This hope and belief released an enormous reservoir of human energy and imagination. It also opened deep wells of hatred, bitterness, and rage. The central drama of the civil rights movement revolved around the question of whether the spiritual force of nonviolence could control and overcome the power of rage, violence, and revenge. This drama was fundamental to the birth, growth, and demise of the New Left.

Active nonviolence as practiced by the civil rights movement was based primarily on Gandhi's philosophy of Satyagraha, which literally means "clinging to Truth." But Truth (Satya in Sanscrit) was only one of three principles of Gandhi's spiritually-informed politics of nonviolence. The other two were Ahimsa, which means non-injury to other beings or nonviolence, and "self-suffering" or the willingness to endure suffering in the practice of nonviolence. In the words of one of Gandhi's disciples:

> The far-reaching assumption involved here is that suffering, self-imposed and borne in the spirit of sacrifice, is the most potent of appeals. . . . Born of sacrifice, suffering is the human power which produces desired ends and defeats evil.[1]

Thus, "activities undertaken in the spirit of sacrifice, consequently, result in a veritable spiritual force."[2]

These three principles interact dynamically to create the political power of Gandhi's politics of nonviolence. In the words of one observer, "the source of Satyagraha's power is the spiritual force generated by self-suffering resulting from 'clinging to Truth'."[3] Gandhi himself explained it in the following terms:

> Satyagraha . . . is a case of appealing to the reason and conscience of the opponent by inviting suffering on oneself. The motive is to convert the opponent and make him one's willing ally and friend. It is based on the idea that the moral appeal to the heart and conscience is . . . more effective than an appeal based on the threat of bodily pain or violence.[4]

Thus Gandhian nonviolence depended on two crucial factors: the effectiveness of a moral appeal to the heart and conscience of one's opponent, and a willingness on the part of the practitioners to make the sacrifice of self-suffering. These tenets of nonviolence were to be tested to their limits in the American South.

It is important to note that this particular formulation of active nonviolence is not the only possible understanding of the subject. Furthermore, it is crucial to ask whether it represents a repressive philosophy of spiritual growth. It is clearly possible to interpret self-suffering as a rationale for martyrdom and masochism; and it was precisely this ambiguity that made it difficult to reconcile Gandhi's version of nonviolence with the emerging spirit of the new movement of the 1960s.

The Work of Martin Luther King, Jr.

There is no easy way to describe the relationship between the work of Martin Luther King, Jr. and the New Left. Surely, King and his associates in the Southern Christian Leadership Conference (SCLC) set the stage for the civil rights movement and provided an important part of its leadership and direction. King, more than any other single person, was responsible for the credibility and prestige that Gandhian nonviolence gained in the southern black movement in its formative years. And yet, King was not a radical "small d" democrat and his leadership style was not decentralist. Nor did he identify himself with the ideas of participatory democracy. King and his staff were not, in fact, an integral part of the New Left, and their relationship with New Leftists was uneasy and often contentious. Over all, the conflicts between King and the New Left were unproductive and divisive and, because there was little open political debate, the issues remained murky and ill-defined.

Martin Luther King, Jr., was the son of a southern black Baptist minister and grew up in the shadow of his father's church, the Ebenezer Baptist Church in Atlanta, Georgia. He was a sensitive, gifted child who became a brilliant student, entering Morehouse College in Atlanta at the age of fifteen and graduating four years later with a degree in sociology. From Morehouse, he went to Crozer Seminary in Pennsylvania in 1948 to study for his

Bachelor of Arts in divinity, obtaining the degree in 1951 as valedictorian of his class. King then chose to pursue his Ph.D. in systematic theology at Boston University's School of Theology.[5]

King's studies at Crozer and Boston University had a profound impact on his thinking. He became a firm believer in the Social Gospel of Walter Rauschenbusch and broke with the fundamentalism of his background to become a theological modernist. At Crozer he was exposed to Gandhi's teaching and he "embraced Satyagraha as the theoretical method he had been searching for." Despite the obvious differences he saw between the Indian political situation under British colonialism and the conflicts between blacks and whites in the United States, "King was convinced that Gandhi's was the only moral and practical way for oppressed people to struggle against social injustice."[6]

During his doctoral studies at Boston University, King deepened his appreciation of Gandhi's insight that true pacifism was not "nonresistance to evil, but nonviolent resistance to evil." It was, in King's own words, "a courageous confrontation of evil by the power of love, in the faith that it is better to be a recipient of violence than an afflictor of it."[7] He also rejected all war and believed that nonviolent alternatives were essential to the survival of the contemporary world.

In his political thinking, King had developed a critique of Communism as early as his undergraduate days at Morehouse College where he preached a sermon on "The Challenge of Communism to Christianity" and expressed the concern that "Communism may be in the world because Christianity hasn't been Christian enough." This criticism of Communism was not, however, intended as an apology for the status quo. Rather, it "only intensified his dislike of capitalism. In truth, he thought Marx correct in much of his criticism in *Das Kapital*, which underscored for King the danger of constructing a system on the sole motive of profit." For King, "capitalism fostered a materialism just as evil as Communism."[8] Beyond this, it is difficult to determine what King's political ideas were when he entered the civil rights struggle. Perhaps he is best understood as a Protestant liberal imbued with the Social Gospel but also profoundly influenced by the teachings of Gandhi and open to the more radical implications of both doctrines. It would not, however, seem possible to describe him as a political radical in any of the usual senses of the word.

One further thing does stand out about his theological perspective--and theology had been the central focus of his graduate work. King's studies led him to a profound belief in a personal God as he sought a reconciliation between the relativism and idealism of the philosophers whom he read. He felt he found a synthesis in the "philosophy of personalism, which held that a personal God operated in and on every human life." "Personal idealism," King said, became his "basic philosophical position." "Personalism's insistence that only personality--finite and infinite--is ultimately real, strengthened me in two convictions: it gave me metaphysical and philosophical grounding for the idea of a personal God, and it gave me a metaphysical basis for [my belief] in the dignity and worth of all human personality."[9]

When he finished graduate school in 1954, King turned his back on the immediate possibilities of an academic career and accepted a call to become pastor of the Dexter Avenue Baptist Church in Montgomery, Alabama. It was the same month, May, 1954, when the Supreme Court decision *Brown v. Board of Education* overturned the legal basis for segregated education in the South, that King first mounted the pulpit as the new pastor of the Montgomery church.

Within a year, King was already playing an active role in the political life of Montgomery's black community. With the support of the Reverend Ralph Abernathy, a new-found friend who would become his closest male companion, King rose to prominence in the historic Montgomery bus boycott. Ignited by the arrest of Rosa Parks for her refusal to give her bus seat to a white man, and organized by the Montgomery Improvement Association (MIA), the boycott was the first successful mass action by blacks against the Jim Crow system to receive nation-wide attention. King emerged as the most eloquent spokesperson of the movement and it gave him the opportunity to test his faith in nonviolent direct action. He was forced to develop viable strategies and tactics that were consistent with the beliefs he had learned from his study of Gandhi. It was King's political baptism, and he was able to articulate the message of nonviolent resistance for a mass black movement in a way that had not been done before. The Montgomery movement made King an important national leader at the same time that it marked a crucial step in the black struggle against segregation. The bombing of his home together with his arrest and trial drew the attention of the national media to the Montgomery movement. And King spread the story across the country during national speaking tours. National media attention certainly played an important role in putting pressure on the federal government to act. Finally, in November, 1956, the Supreme Court "affirmed a decision of a special three-judge U.S. District Court in declaring Alabama's state and local laws requiring segregation on buses unconstitutional."[10] In early December, at an Institute on Nonviolence sponsored by the Montgomery movement, King outlined his views in a speech entitled "Facing the Challenge of a New Age." In it he gave a succinct summary of his understanding of the power of Satyagraha as it applied to black people in America.

> Our defense is to meet every act of violence toward an individual Negro with the fact that there are thousands of others who will present themselves as potential victims. Every time one school teacher is fired for standing up courageously for justice, it must be faced with the fact that there are four thousand more to be fired. If the oppressors bomb the home of one Negro for his courage, this must be met with the fact that they must be required to bomb the homes of fifty thousand more Negroes. This dynamic unity, this amazing self-respect, this willingness to suffer, and this refusal to hit back, will soon cause the oppressor to become ashamed of his own methods.[11]

This was the Gandhian message in American terms. Oppressed people united in a willingness to endure the sacrifice of self-suffering would create a spiritual force that would "speak to the heart and conscience" of the oppressor.

Soon afterwards, on December 20, 1956, the Supreme Court mandate banning segregation in buses finally reached Montgomery. It was a resounding victory, and by Christmas bus protests had been launched in three other Southern cities: Birmingham, Tallahasee, and Mobile. There was also white backlash and it was often brutally violent. On December 28, whites opened fire on buses all over Montgomery and instituted a reign of terror that lasted for days. At every step of the way, victory would mean the necessity of further struggle.

The idea of forming a new civil rights organization "designed around Dr. King's charisma"[12] was already in the mind of at least one black activist. Bayard Rustin had come to Montgomery to give his support to the movement and become a close advisor of King. Rustin had a long history of political activism as a radical pacifist that went back to his refusal to serve in World War II and his subsequent imprisonment for twenty-eight months for non-cooperation with the draft. After the war he was arrested many times for sitting in at the British embassy in Washington in support of the Gandhian independence movement. He spent six months in India in 1948 studying the Gandhian movement at the invitation of the Indian Congress party. He was politically sophisticated and close friends with the leaders of the radical pacifist movement. He served as Executive Secretary of the War Resisters League from 1953 to 1964.

Rustin was one of the founding editors, together with Dave Dellinger and A. J. Muste, of *Liberation* magazine which had begun publication in May of 1956.[13] King and other black protest leaders agreed with Rustin's plan to form a Southern-wide organization based on the leadership of black churches. The intensification of violence by whites only strengthened their resolve.

The original strategy meeting for the new organization was held in King's father's church, the Ebenezer Baptist Church in Atlanta on January 10-11, 1957. Bayard Rustin had written seven position papers analyzing the direct action mass movement and making suggestions about its future direction. It was decided to form a Southwide organization which was formalized as the Southern Christian Leadership Conference (SCLC).

There are basically two conflicting interpretations of the nature of SCLC. One sees it primarily as a symbolic organization centered around the person of Martin Luther King, Jr. This traditional view has predominated in studies of the civil rights movement and has promoted the idea "that SCLC was not a real organization at all, but simply the shadow of Dr. King."[14] Most studies have presented SCLC as though it were Martin Luther King, Jr.--a charismatic leader without a functioning base.[15]

A differing view has been presented more recently by the black sociologist Aldon D. Morris in his important book *The Origins of the Civil Rights Movement: Black Communities Organizing for Change*. Morris's work, which includes a study of the affiliates of SCLC presents a picture of a network of "movement centers" organized primarily in or around black churches, which functioned as the social base of SCLC and without which neither SCLC nor the ongoing civil rights movement would have been possible. Morris describes SCLC as "a Southwide organization of organizations." "It was the local movements that created the need for the SCLC. Local movement centers already in existence provided the SCLC with its initial affiliated structures." Morris further argues that "Dr. King was not merely a symbolic leader created by the mass media. His power, like that of other important leaders, stemmed from the fact that he and his colleagues were able to mobilize a variety of resources through community organizations."[16]

Morris goes so far as to make the suggestion that "it is useful, therefore, to think of the SCLC of that period as the decentralized political arm of the black church. The SCLC's leaders," he contends, "did not attempt to centralize the activities of its affiliates, because it was felt that centralization would stifle local protest. Rather, the role of the SCLC's local affiliates was to organize local movements and address grievances salient in local communities."[17]

These differing views may in part reflect the contrast between what SCLC was originally intended to be, an organization of movement organizations linked to the charismatic leadership of King, and what it later became, a staff organization or cadre of organizers around King that operated increasingly as an independent entity. It is this later development that seems to have caused the intense conflict between King and the New Left in the 1960s.

Even when it functioned more as an organization of organizations, SCLC was never truly democratic. Its structure always meant that its effective decision-making members were overwhelmingly black ministers who acted as representatives of their local churches and/or movements. Furthermore, the structure of black churches was highly authoritarian and rigidly patriarchal. Black women were always relegated to secondary roles. And the internal life of black churches was centered on the charismatic leadership of male ministers.

SCLC thus reflected in its own structure the roles and structures of southern black churches. It was this authoritarian, patriarchal, and fundamentally undemocratic character of SCLC

that--however well it served the movement in its initial stages-
-would conflict with and be challenged by the new student activists
beginning in 1960. Even though it was built on a decentralized
network, SCLC was never based on a decentralist approach to
structure or organizing. And, though it was unreservedly committed to serving a people's movement, it never operated on a truly
democratic theory or strategy of people's power. SCLC was far
more than "a shadow of Dr. King", but it was, nonetheless, a
reflection of both the strengths and weaknesses of southern black
religious life.

◆ New Left Activism

It is not by words alone, but also through acts that people
become political. Politics is public life, and it was precisely that
life which people build together through political activity that was
disappearing under the post-World War II liberal technocracy.
Government by expertise (including military technique) was
rapidly replacing whatever modicum of government by the people
had existed in America.[18] And the cosmetic Kennedy campaign of
1960 marked the reduction of liberal electoral politics to a branch
of the advertising industry.

It was in this depoliticized atmosphere of the declining
Eisenhower years and the emerging Kennedy-style liberalism that
the New Left was born. In the early weeks of 1960, the cultural
and spiritual rebellion of the Beat generation was augmented by a
new kind of political activism. The student led sit-ins at
Greensboro, North Carolina, set the stage for the new politics of
the 1960s. In January of that year, the month before the sit-ins
began, the student branch of a small social democratic organization, the League for Industrial Democracy (LID), had changed its
name to Students for a Democratic Society (SDS). When black
student leaders of the sit-ins met to form the Student Non-Violent
Coordinating Committee (SNCC, pronounced SNICK) in April,
they created the second important set of initials that would be
associated with the student movement. SDS and SNCC were the
organizational seedbeds of the New Left.

They were never the same and only loosely affiliated for a
time; but they became two expressions of the process of

politicization through activism that created the new student left, and they were the leaders and shapers of much of that process. The process came to be called "the Movement," and, whether individuals joined SNCC or SDS or other groups, they talked and thought about being part of "the Movement." It was no accident that one of the critics of the new activists would call them "The Mystical Militants."[19] It was a movement of faith, not of ideology. "Called to Be Human" became a slogan of the new existentialist thinking in university student circles. It seemed to be just such a call that moved students, black and white, to activism.

◆ Democratic Community and Student Activism

Democratic community implies as a minimum both formal equality and a commitment to values and goals that transcend the narrow egotistical interests of its members. Institutional racism remained, at the beginning of the 1960s, the greatest single obstacle to democratic community in the United States. It was even more profoundly anti-democratic and anti-communitarian in its implications than class structure, corporate power, and private accumulation of capital. That is why the civil rights movement represented a gigantic leap of faith in the direction of democratic community: it affirmed with sacrificial determination the will to equality and the willingness to transcend egotism. Although its success was only partial--the formal abolition of Jim Crow--its impact was immense.

The civil rights movement began with the hope of creating an interracial community--black and white together. That it ended with the dismantlng of legal segregation but more interracial bitterness than before was a tragic development. Outsiders simply underestimated the depths of black rage and pain and the resistance of the system to meaningful change and reconciliation. And yet, although the vision of "black and white together" did not endure, the contribution of civil rights activism to the development of the New Left and its vision of radical democratic change was essential. The developments that began with the student sit-ins brought about a reassessment of political life and a redefinition of the democratic vision that led, in turn, to the elaboration of the idea of participatory democracy.

How, one might ask, did the idea of participatory democracy develop in the American New Left? In his book on the subject, *"Democracy Is in the Streets"*, James Miller is careful to point out that the idea did not originate in the black civil rights movement.[20] It seems, however, that by relying on a narrow intellectual and biographical history of the term itself, Miller has missed the ways in which the context and impact of the civil rights movement, and particularly the experience of SNCC, nurtured radical democratic and decentralist ideas and gave concrete experiential substance to a phrase that might not have gained currency without this rich political background. The phrase "participatory democracy" was actually first coined by a professor of political philosophy, Arnold Kaufman, in a paper entitled "Participatory Democracy and Human Nature."[21] It was adopted by Tom Hayden and became central to the vocabulary of the *Port Huron Statement.* (See Chapter 4.) It is, however, important to understand that the phrase fell on fertile ground because a movement of student activists was looking for a language in which to express a new sense of radical democratic idealism that had been nurtured in the civil rights struggles.

There is no definitive theory of participatory democracy; there is no coherent body of writings on the subject. Different people meant different things by that phrase. It probably covered a spectrum of belief from radical democrats to anarchists and anarcho-syndicalists through democratic socialists and even some social democrats. It was easier to say what it excluded: the "Old Left", orthodox Marxism, Cold War liberalism, and those social democrats who had sold their souls to anti-Communism.

One reason the concept of participatory democracy was never fully clarified was that actions spoke louder than words in the early 1960s and theory came after the fact. The New Left was born out of activism, not out of political theorizing. No one, least of all the participants, would have predicted that a sit-in by four black college students at a segregated lunch counter in Greensboro, North Carolina, on February 1, 1960, would have sparked a wave of student political activism that swelled larger and grew increasingly militant over the next ten years. The students in Greensboro had no grand political theory for their action, nor did they conceive of it simply as a tactic in a larger strategy. It was a form of bold nonviolent direct action that broke through a political stalemate that had developed in the civil rights movement and created possibilities for further direct actions against racist segregation that were quickly imitated and further elaborated.

It was important that on the second day of the Greensboro sit-ins the original four students were joined by others and that the second sit-in ended with a prayer. It was also important that students were the actors and that on the third day at the Greensboro Woolworth store, the growing number of black students were joined by three white students.[22] The form of the sit-ins, nonviolent direct action accompanied by religious language and gestures, set the tone for the new Movement: put your body and soul on the line. That some whites joined in almost immediately was important because it nurtured a vision of an interracial community and demonstrated that at least some white students would act in solidarity with the black students. Students were important precisely because they were not generally the most oppressed in traditional economic terms and therefore spoke for a wide range of needs and demands--and because colleges and universities would provide the network through which the new activism reached into the larger society.

The news went out and the sit-ins spread like wildfire across the South. Soon northern students were picketing Woolworth stores in support of the southern activists. A new mood and a new political awareness began to stir on campuses nationwide.

Moral witness, sacrifice, commitment, and community: these were the basic elements that went into the new student activism and awakened America from her torpor, complacency, and dreams of power. From its beginnings, the Movement seemed born under the sign of the cross, as though its understanding and motivations were more religious and moral than traditionally political, and it seemed often to express itself best in religious or existentialist language.

The Movement was also democratic in a very direct and fundamental sense: the people who did the acting made the decisions. The activism which spread across the South, and later around the country, was not the decision or program of a political party or a central committee or a trade union bureaucracy. Students acted and took responsibility both for their actions and the effects thereof. Then they met and talked and made more decisions and acted together again. When the actions had begun to involve many people in different locations, they faced the need for coordination. And so they met, in Raleigh, North Carolina, on April 15-17, 1960, and formed a coordinating committee that came to be called just that: the Student Nonviolent Coordinating Committee. Now there was action plus structure. This dynamic nurtured the vision of participatory democracy: direct-action democracy from the bottom up, inspired by moral, spiritual, and political motives and fueled by love and compassion on the one hand, and anger and outrage on the other.

If theory is an interpretation of reality and political theory is an interpretation of political action, then a political theory appropriate to the new activism of the 1960s would have had to involve a new kind of spiritual-moral-political discourse. Only theory based in such a discourse could comprehend the actual nature of the activism--the quality of its consciousness, the character of its motives, and the complexity of its evolving goals.

✦ The SNCC Founding Statement

When the 250 student activists gathered at Raleigh, their first priority was the development of a founding statement that would express the philosophy, vision, and values of the new student movement that was sweeping across the South. The person primarily responsible for drafting the statement was James Lawson of the Nashville student group.[23] Lawson, a northern black, was the southern field secretary for the Fellowship of Reconcilation (FOR), a pacifist organization that promoted Gandhian nonviolence. Lawson had been a draft resister during the Korean War and had gone to prison rather than accept induction. He had been paroled to the Methodist Board of Missions and "spent three years as a missionary in India, where he studied Mahatma Gandhi's use of nonviolence to achieve political change." Lawson had led nonviolence training workshops in the South, including two in Nashville in 1958 and 1959. The second of those, at Vanderbilt University, catalyzed the formation of a group of activists that included Diane Nash, James Bevel, John Lewis, and Marion Barry, who all became activists in SNCC and were among the most important leaders of the civil rights movement of the 1960s. In the fall of 1959, they had in fact "staged test sit-ins" in

Nashville before the February 1960 actions in Greensboro. When the news of Greensboro arrived, they led "one of the most disciplined and sustained of the early protests."[24]

Lawson and his supporters had a decisive influence on the formation of SNCC--an influence greater than that of Martin Luther King, Jr. It was Lawson who insisted that a discussion of the philosophy of nonviolence precede consideration of political strategies and organizational goals, and it was his influence that seems to have determined the adoption of the language of the founding statement of the organization. The statement which was adopted contained only four short paragraphs:

> We affirm the philosophical or religious ideal of nonviolence as the foundation of our purpose, the presupposition of our faith, and the manner of our action. Nonviolence as it grows from Judaic-Christian traditions seeks a social order of justice permeated by love. Integration of human endeavor represents the crucial first step towards such a society.
>
> Through nonviolence, courage displaces fear; love transforms hate. Acceptance dissipates prejudice; hope ends despair. Peace dominates war; faith reconciles doubt. Mutual regard cancels enmity. Justice for all overthrows injustice. The redemptive community supersedes systems of gross social immorality.
>
> Love is the central motif of nonviolence. Love is the force by which God binds man to Himself and man to man. Such love goes to the extreme; it remains loving and forgiving even in the midst of hostility. It matches the capacity of evil to inflict suffering with an even more enduring capacity to absorb evil, all the while persisting in love.
>
> By appealing to conscience and standing on the moral nature of human existence, nonviolence nurtures the atmosphere in which reconciliation and justice become actual possibilities.[25]

Anyone familiar with the "Judaic-Christian tradition" and its uses in the justification of war and all manner of social violence is forced to think twice when confronted with these claims. What did Lawson intend by the phrase: "Nonviolence as it grows from Judaic-Christian traditions . . ."? Certainly, as a student of history and theology, he had heard of the doctrine of "just wars" developed by the medieval Church, of the Crusades, of the Inquisition, the wars of religion, the burning of witches. Certainly those great hymns, "Onward Christian Soldiers" and "The Battle Hymn of the Republic," had been part of his apprenticeship in the "Judaic-Christian tradition." Of course, he was aware of all that.

What James Lawson and his supporters were proposing was nothing less than a revolution in Christian theology: a fundamental reinterpretation of Judeo-Christian belief in the light of Gandhi's teaching of Satyagraha. Leo Tolstoy had laid the bases of modern pacifism in the late 19th century by stripping away St. Paul and the Old Testament and by basing his faith simply on the teachings of Jesus in the Gospels.[26] Gandhi had been influenced by Tolstoy and forged a universal doctrine of nonviolence with deep roots in Hindu spiritual philosophy and practice. Lawson was proposing that Gandhi's philosophy and political strategy become the basis for a radical new view of the whole "Judaic-Christian" tradition. This was to be the basis of the new spiritual-moral-political discourse designed to mold and guide the new movement. One is forced to ask: How well did it work?

Two things are striking in the "Founding Statement": the unequivocal commitment to nonviolence, and the use of the language of the "Judaic-Christian" tradition with its appeal to the activity of a personal God.

Three questions arise from reflecting on the statement. First, did it represent the true beliefs of most of the activists present at the founding SNCC conference? Secondly, why did it tie nonviolence so narrowly to the Judeo-Christian belief in a personal God? Thirdly, did it present a foundation that could serve a broad-based movement--or was it sectarian?

In fact, close examination reveals that the document could only receive the unqualified support of fairly orthodox Christians and, perhaps, some believing Jews. Was it the intent of the framers to impose a Christian (or "Judaic-Christian") framework of belief onto "the philosophical or religious ideal of nonviolence?" Why not have just rested on the "philosophical or religious" ideal without the reference to the "Judaic-Christian traditions"? Why not (in the third paragraph) have been satisfied with the assertion that "Love is the central motif of nonviolence" instead of insisting in addition that "Love is the force by which God binds man to Himself and man to man"? Why, in short, exclude the potential loyality of all manner of humanists (spiritual or secular) and confine the potential adherents to Judeo-Christian monotheists?

If founding documents are important, as I think they are, then there is reason to question the wisdom of this founding statement of SNCC, which tied the "philosophical or religious ideal of nonviolence" to the "Judaic-Christian traditions" and the belief in the actions of a personal God. It is all the more curious in that its chief proponent, James Lawson, had been a student of Gandhian nonviolence in India and had certainly been exposed to broader philosophical and spiritual frameworks than Judeo-Christian monotheism. The Eastern concept of God differs dramatically from the personal God of the Judeo-Christian-Islamic tradition. It was the Eastern concept, with its three aspects of being (sat), consciousness (cit), and bliss (ananda) that was the basis of Gandhi's spiritual convictions. He wrote:

> The word 'Satya' Truth is derived from 'Sat' which means being. And nothing is or exists in reality except Truth. That is why 'Sat' or Truth is perhaps the most important name of God. In fact it is more correct to say that Truth is God, than to say that God is Truth. But as we cannot do without a ruler or a general, names of God such as King of Kings or the Almighty are and will remain more usually current. On deeper thinking, however, it will be realized that 'Sat' or 'Satya' is the only correct and fully significant name of God.[27]

The religious sectarianism inherent in the language of SNCC's founding statement almost certainly guaranteed that it would not serve well as a statement of principle for many members of the organization or for most student activists of the 1960s. It is both moving in what it presaged in terms of sacrifices and marred by its parochialism, which meant it would not serve as a serious point of reference or a basis for discussion when SNCC organizers faced crises of faith and direction. Moreover, because it tied nonviolence to a religious tradition and framework that would not be shared by most activists, it inadvertently weakened the case for nonviolence morally, politically and spiritually. The statement certainly failed to take account of the alternative cultural, moral, and spiritual changes that were brewing in the land, particularly among college and university students. When the crisis of the New Left arrived later in the decade, the SNCC statement did not provide a firm foundation to which activists could return as a basis of unity and a ground for discussion. It had failed to provide a universal language that would sustain unity in the midst of conflict.

What it did provide was a statement of a radical theology of nonviolence that allowed SNCC to speak to people identified with the tradition it evoked. This was of great utility, especially in reaching out to black churches in the South. As Aldon Morris has demonstrated quite convincingly in his study on *The Origins of the Civil Rights Movement*,[28] it was black churches that provided the network of support which made it possible for the student sit-ins to spread so rapidly across the South and for the movement to be sustained in the face of adversity. This was particularly true of so-called "college churches"--those that were located near black institutions of higher learning and had large numbers of black students in their congregations. These churches were particularly powerful and influential when they were situated in "clusters" as they were in several major centers of sit-in activity.[29]

It has been a serious error on the part of most writers, Aldon Morris argues, to regard the years between the Montgomery, Alabama bus boycott in 1955-56 and the February 1, 1960 sit-in in Greensboro as the "quiescent period" of the civil rights movement. To the contrary, it was a period of intense ferment and extensive self-organization in southern black communities. Furthermore, this organizing took place primarily within the framework of the most important black social institution, the church. Black churches provided both the meeting place and spiritual center of community life for blacks of all classes in an increasingly urbanized South. Black male ministers provided charismatic leadership for their congregations; and church meetings, which were frequent, provided the forum for debate about the problems of the oppressed black community. Youth and other groups within the churches, often led by women, provided a complex and comprehensive framework of involvement and identification. The elaborate structure of committees and meetings furnished the training and experience needed for organizing a mass movement.

When the sit-ins started, black churches were able to mobilize support quickly and efficiently. Both money (for bail) and moral support were made accessible in a way otherwise unimaginable given the level of poverty among southern blacks. Clearly the image of SNCC as philosophically and spiritually linked to "Judaic-Christian" traditions could only help to bolster its support among black churches. Wherever SNCC organizers worked from 1960 through 1965, their very survival depended on the maintenance of an intimate and mutually supportive relationship with those institutions. It was, perhaps, knowledge of this fact that prompted James Lawson to frame the language of the SNCC "Founding Statement" in the manner described. However, this was a decision that rested on a contradiction. As the movement grew, more and more of the students who enlisted as full-time organizers came from backgrounds that made them uncomfortable with the language of Judeo-Christian theism. Many were motivated by values which they did not link to a belief in a god. They were humanists of one stripe or another--secular or spiritual--who did not share the beliefs of the typical southern black Baptist congregation. This produced tensions that led, unfortunately, to the discrediting of nonviolence within the organization.

In retrospect, it seems that the philosophy and vision contained in the original SNCC document would have been more enduring if the language had been less parochial. If the spiritual-moral-political discourse of SNCC's origins had not been tied to traditional theism it might have served as a ground for a more fruitful debate on the issues. Insofar as it prejudiced debate in the direction of conflict between believers and non-believers, the language of the "Founding Statement" certainly weakened the case for nonviolence. This led not to the deepening of dialogue but to the truncating of debate and the wholesale rejection of nonviolence by those who came to control SNCC in the latter half of the 1960s.

Interpreting Student Nonviolence

One of the results of this development has been the writing of the early history of SNCC in a way that entirely discredits the moral and spiritual basis of its political activism. Because, in the long run, spiritual and moral discourse was rejected in favor of a secular materialist vocabulary, the earlier vocabulary is dismissed as inauthentic and thus explained away. Both the philosophy of nonviolence and its moral and spiritual foundation are discarded as an expression of political immaturity.

There are interpretations of the early sit-ins that offer an understanding of the motives, beliefs, and experiences of the student actors that differs from the interpretation of the actors themselves. Instead of taking the religious symbolism, speech, and gestures as expressions of true moral commitment or spiritual belief, this approach reduces them to other motives. Thus, Clayborne Carson, a black activist-scholar, who has written the most important scholarly book on SNCC, places emphasis on the latent anger and rage inherent in the nonviolent phase of the movement. His book, *In Struggle*, creates the impression that the religious language of the early movement was a cover-up, a "rationale": "The protestors themselves, though usually peaceful, were engaging in a form of 'passively aggressive behavior--stepping over the line and waiting, rather than exhibiting overtly hostile or revolutionary behavior'."[30] He goes on to say that:

> Nonviolent tactics, particularly when accompanied by a rationale based
> on Christian principles, offered black students an appealing combina-
> tion of rewards: a sense of moral superiority, an emotional release
> through militancy, and a possibility of desegregation.[31]

In this interpretation, "Christian principles" have become a "rationale," presumably for nonviolent tactics that nobody belie-ved in but that served as a temporary expedient when it was impossible to exhibit "overtly hostile or revolutionary behavior."

This approach fits with Carson's larger interpretative strategy, which paints a portrait of SNCC's apparent progress from nonviolent civil rights struggles toward black power militancy. "In the first stage," he writes, "civil rights activists came together in SNCC to form a community within a social struggle. SNCC workers sought to create a rationale for activism by eclectically adopting ideas from the Gandhian independence movement and from the American traditions of pacifism and Christian idealism as formulated by the Congress of Racial Equality (CORE), Fellowship of Reconciliation (FOR), and Southern Christian Leadership Conference (SCLC)."[32]

Thus, Gandhian and Christian pacifist ideas are relegated to the category of "rationale for activism." They are not considered serious beliefs or ideas in themselves, nor are they regarded as seriously held by activists. Later, in describing the founding of SNCC, Carson asserts: "Students at the conference affirmed their commitment to the nonviolent doctrines popularized by King, yet they were drawn to these ideas not because of King's advocacy but because they provided *an appropriate rationale* for student protest." [My emphasis.][33]

Carson goes on to explain what seems to him to be the logical progression away from nonviolence "rationalized" by Gandhian, Christian, and pacifist ideas towards "secular, humanistic radicalism."

> As the thrust of SNCC's activities shifted from desegregation to political rights, its philosophical commitment to nonviolent direct action gave way to a secular, humanistic radicalism influenced by Marx, Camus, Malcolm X, and most of all by the SNCC organizers' own experiences in southern black communities.[34]

For Carson, whose viewpoint now predominates in the American left, nonviolence based on spiritual belief, whether Christian or Gandhian or other, was a primitive and naive response to the political situation in the early 1960s. One gets the impression that serious reflection led quickly to its abandonment and replacement by "secular humanistic radicalism." The next step involved the period following the defeat of the Mississippi Freedom Democratic Party's challenge at the August 1964 Democratic Party Convention (see pp. 12-13 above.) There is a new shift in the status of nonviolence in Carson's interpretation. Speaking of the period 1964-66, he writes:

> Over the next two years, they [SNCC staffers] looked inward, questioning whether the strategy they had followed could achieve the fundamental social changes they now viewed as necessary. Staff members debated whether southern black people could achieve lasting improvement in their lives while continuing to rely on appeals for white liberal support and federal intervention, and whether SNCC could continue to expand the black struggle while remaining tied to the rhetoric of interracialism and nonviolent direct action.[35]

In this presentation, "interracialism and nonviolent direct action" have been reduced to the status of "rhetoric," one step below "rationale." The third and final phase "involved the members' efforts to resolve their differences by addressing the need for black power and black consciousness" and was the period in which, after being elected chairman of SNCC in May 1966, "Stokely Carmichael popularized the organization's new separatist orientation, but he and other workers were unable to formulate a set of ideas that could unify black people." Black power and black separatism are made to appear as the logical outcome of the development from the practice of nonviolence based on moral and spiritual belief, through secular radicalism; but the destruction of SNCC was also part of the same "logic." Furthermore, the abandonment of nonviolence and interracialism brought with it the destruction of the unity and community of the Movement of the 1960s as a whole.

> As SNCC workers sought to increase black awareness of the range of available political and cultural alternatives, they became embroiled in bitter factional battles and failed to sustain local black movements in the South. Disagreements about the future direction of black struggles also divided black communities throughout the nation. Weakened by internal dissension, SNCC withered in the face of the same tactics of subtle co-optation and ruthless repression that stifled the entire black struggle.[36]

Might it not be the case, however, that the beliefs and values of morally and spiritually inspired nonviolence had been the most authentic expression of the Movement and its constituencies and the only coherent set of values that could hold a racially diverse political movement together? And that once those spiritual values had been downgraded to "rhetoric," the possibility of sustaining the measure of unity necessary to a functioning democratic political community had also been destroyed?

Even Clayborne Carson seems to present conflicting testimony. While assuring us that the students at the founding conference of SNCC were drawn to nonviolent doctrines because "they provided an appropriate rationale for student protest," he later reveals that the group of delegates from Nashville "would subsequently provide SNCC with a disproportionate share of its leaders." And who were these unusual black students? "Though coming from varied backgrounds," he writes, "the Nashville activists shared a commitment not simply to desegregation but also to Gandhism and to the Christian ideal of 'the beloved community'."[37] These were students who "had schooled themselves in the philosophical doctrines of the Gandhian passive resistance movement in India." According to Carson, "It was these Nashville activists, rather than the four Greensboro students, who had an enduring impact on the subsequent development of the southern movement."[38]

We have seen the vital role that James Lawson and his

co-workers had in the founding and development of SNCC. Clearly their convictions and commitment to nonviolence were not reducible to the status of "rationale" or "rhetoric" but represented true beliefs. An interpretation like the one I have been criticizing is hard to accept as a serious representation of the early actors in the sit-in movement and the formation of SNCC. It fits a pattern in which the later adoption of black nationalism or Marxist ideology in the New Left (and its concurrent factionalization) becomes the interpretive filter through which the original statements of the Movement are read and explained away. It is an effort to delegitimize spiritual and moral categories by explaining away their pervasiveness in the early New Left and reducing them to something else. This is a classic attempt to impose grand theory on the interpretation of a political movement and represents a failure to develop grounded theory which relies on the serious evaluation of what the actors said, what they did, and how they understood the meaning of what they said and did.[39]

Instead of developing a theoretical interpretation of its activism in the form of a spiritual-moral-political discourse that nurtured democratic power from the bottom up, the Movement of the 1960s eventually lost touch with its own potential self-understanding by adopting much of the ideological rhetoric of Marxism and various versions of the top-down organizational style of Leninism. However, when one rewrites the early history of the Movement as though this later development explains it, one betrays the actors themselves and distorts their history.

The interpretation that seeks to explain away a spiritually-inspired politics of nonviolence seems to be in part a reaction against its emphasis on love, compassion, and redemptiveness. Nonviolent radicalism is seen as a denial of the negative feelings of resentment, anger, hostility, and rage which form part of the inevitable emotional response of socially oppressed peoples to the insults, inequities, and injustices that they have suffered. Insofar as the political nonviolence of the early civil rights movement did not provide an adequate recognition of the deep anger of black people, it set the stage--in this interpretation--for the victory of the angry rhetorical stance of black nationalism and Marxism.

There is no logical reason why the theory and practice of nonviolence need exclude the recognition and expression of anger. However, any practice of nonviolence that is based on the repression of such anger is an almost certain formula for eventual outbursts of hidden rage. The trick seems to be finding nonviolent modes of expression that are both emotionally healing and politically constructive. There is a kind of Christianity that places a taboo on anger and thereby creates an underground stream of passive aggression and resentment. It seems to have also been true that Gandhi himself was prone to the repression of anger and that his version of nonviolence may have been based on the denial of negative emotionality. It is also the case that he was sexually very repressive. The repression of anger and sexuality was certainly not a workable formula for what was to become the Movement of the 1960s.

◆ *Decentralism in SNCC*

The configuration of political thought and action that I am attempting to describe--the gestalt of the early New Left--emphasized both moral and spiritual values and democratic organization. In the organizational sphere, it stressed a radical, grassroots and decentralized version of democracy rather than those forms of liberal representative democracy that mask the real nature of power in American society. The powerful attachment to decentralization in the early years of SNCC did not develop in a vacuum. It was a reaction, in part, to the existing organizational forms of the civil rights movement itself.

One of the problems that student activists in the early sit-in movement faced was the authoritarian organizational style of the black (mainly Baptist) churches which formed, as we have seen, the social backbone of the southern civil rights movement. Black churches were leader-centered and the leadership was comprised of charismatic male ministers. Martin Luther King, Jr., and the Southern Christian Leadership Conference symbolized and institutionalized this organizational style. When students reignited civil rights activism in early 1960, they did so without consulting their elders, and they were not disposed to accept the top-down leadership of the black clergy. They were a grassroots movement, and they needed an organizational form and style that fit with their radical democratic mood and conviction.

Decentralism as a mode of organization, and the implicit

theory thereof, were nurtured by an exceptional figure in the Movement. Her name was Ella Baker. The granddaughter of "a proud, rebellious slave minister," Baker was born (1903) and raised in the South. She graduated from Shaw University in South Carolina as class valedictorian. She lived and worked in New York City in the late 1920s and early 1930s and was exposed to the political debates of the left and the social ferment of Harlem. In the early 1930s, she became an organizer of consumer coopera- tives and gained important organizational and political experience. In 1941 and 1942, she held the position of National Field Secretary for the NAACP and in 1943 became Director of Branches for that organization. During this time she traveled widely through the South and developed a broad range of experience and contacts. She left the NAACP in 1946 and worked in the New York YMCA.[40]

Baker first worked for SCLC as Associate Director. There was a good deal of reluctance to name a woman to the top administrative position in the organization but she eventually became Executive Director. Later, she was to say, "I knew from the beginning that as a woman, an older woman, in a group of ministers who are accustomed to having women largely as supporters, there was no place for me to have to come into a leadership role. The competition wasn't worth it."[41] Baker had many differences with the black ministers who controlled SCLC. Aldon Morris describes the situation this way:

> During that era men in general, and many black ministers in particular, were condescending toward women and could not envision them as full-fledged leaders. This stance of the ministers was bound to generate friction with Baker, who was self-directed and did not feel that women should automatically defer to men.[42]

Baker "believed that movement organizations should not be built around a leader or a few leaders." Furthermore, she felt "that for people's movements to be effective, participants must encourage and build local leadership among the masses."[43] In her own words:

> Instead of the "leader"--a person who was supposed to be a magic man--you would develop individuals who were bound together by a concept that benefited larger numbers of individuals and provided an opportunity for them to grow into being responsible for carrying on

the program.[44]

"I have always thought," she said, "what is needed is the development of people who are interested not in being leaders as much as in developing leadership among other people."[45] Baker's critique of charismatic leadership was explicit and probing. "I have always felt," she told her interviewer in 1970, "it was a handicap for oppressed peoples to depend so largely upon a leader, because unfortunately in our culture, the charismatic leader usually becomes a leader because he has found a spot in the public limelight." Her analysis of the way in which such leadership was created reveals a keen grasp of a problem that plagued the Movement. "It usually meant," she went on, "that he has been touted through the public media, which means that the media made him, and the media may undo him. There is also the danger in our culture that, because a person is called upon to give public statements and is acclaimed by the establishment, such a person gets to the point of believing that he is the movement." As a result, "such people get so involved with the game of being important that they exhaust themselves and their time, and they don't do the work of actually organizing people."[46]

Baker's experience of the civil rights movement led her to question the role of Martin Luther King, Jr., and the leader-centered, top-down organizational structure of SCLC. She had the experience and genius to recognize the possibility and necessity of developing an alternative model of organization for the new Movement based on student activism. It was Baker who called for a "Southwide Student Leadership Conference on Nonviolent Resistance to Segregation" (April 15-17, 1960) out of which SNCC was born. Because of her fundamental differences with SCLC about the role of leadership, Baker was being terminated as the Executive Director. She was determined that the students not be subordinated to SCLC, and she was supported in her position by the Nashville student movement.[47] Her strong belief in decentralized leadership was articulated in the phrase "group-centered leadership."[48] It was this concept that guided SNCC's early development in the direction of a decentralist and democratic politics.

Despite Baker's insights and her guidance, there was a contradiction built into SNCC's organizational form. Unlike SDS,

SNCC was never a membership organization. That is to say it never had individual members who had voting rights on a mass basis. It did not develop chapters on college campuses, but only sought to coordinate existing groups. In fact, rather than becoming a mass-based democratic membership organization, SNCC became an organization of organizers. Thus, despite its apparently decentralist orientation, it became a *de facto* cadre organization. This contradiction--between radical democratic and decentralist principles and a cadre style of organization--is probably a major reason for its later, self-destructive direction. It is instructive to compare its development with SDS.

While SNCC moved quickly from its initial role as "coordinator of campus protest activities"[49] to an "organization of organizers," SDS followed an almost opposite line of evolution. Up to the winter of 1964-65, SDS was largely a group of activists held together on a friendship basis with a few dozen chapters on college campuses and a handful of community organizing projects. After the Free Speech Movement at Berkeley, beginning in September of 1964, had ignited campus protest, and after President Johnson escalated the bombing of North Vietnam in February of 1965, SDS quickly mushroomed into a mass student organization with hundreds of chapters and tens of thousands of active participants. In contrast, as Clayborne Carson describes it, "Although SNCC remained under the nominal control of student representatives on the Coordinating Committee, its policies, values, and image were shaped by the increasingly confident and knowledgeable full-time staff."[50] This contrast is instructive. It shows that although SNCC seemed to espouse a decentralist politics, its actual structure became more that of a cadre organization of full-time organizers. It may be that this structure contained within it the dynamics of SNCC's eventual downfall which seems to have resulted from its failure to remain tied to any organic base--whether in the Southern community organizing projects or on campuses. SNCC eventually became a more radical version of what it critized the more moderate SCLC for being, namely, a centralized leadership organization rather than a decentralized organic expression of grassroots organizing.

This centralized cadre structure for SNCC was promoted primarily by the headquarters office in Atlanta under the leadership of James Forman and was already established by April

1962 when SNCC held its third general conference.[51] However, it was never accepted by important segments of the staff, many of whom remained committed to a decentralist approach. These differences produced tensions and political struggles within the organization that were not finally resolved until the spring of 1966 when SNCC simultaneously ousted its white organizers, adopted an official centralized structure, and embarked upon its national "Black Power" campaign under the leadership of Stokely Carmichael. Those changes would finally sever SNCC from its ties to grassroots organizing in southern communities and lead rapidly to its demise as an effective political organization. Unfortunately, SDS would follow a similar path in 1968-69 and destroy itself in the process. In both cases, leaders in the national offices attempted to create a cadre organization of full-time radicals. In both cases, they lost touch with their social base.

Leaving aside for now these later developments, I want to ask what relationship there was between spiritual commitment and the issue of centralism versus decentralism.

◆ *Spirituality, Politics, and Decentralism in SNCC*

There seems to have been a close connection in SNCC between spiritual and moral commitment and the emphasis on decentralist participatory democracy. And, on the other hand, the development of a centralist perspective seems to have gone hand-in-hand with the rise of a combination of Marxist ideology and black nationalism in the guise of black power separatism. The abandonment of the slogan and spirit of "black and white together" coincided with the rejection of a morally- and spiritually-based politics of radical nonviolence and participatory democracy.

Something in this development gives one pause. SNCC began its life by rejecting the authoritarian, leader-centered organizational style of SCLC, Martin Luther King, Jr., and the black churches. At the same time it embraced a politics of radical nonviolence based on spiritual and moral values and principles with the stated goal of integration. Thus it rejected the traditional forms of the patriarchal, authoritarian practice of black churches while affirming another vision of a decentralized democratic movement based on spiritual and moral conviction.

It appears that the members of SNCC who remained in the South and continued to work in local areas doing grassroots organizing were mainly those whose politics were tied to spiritual and moral values--the wing of SNCC that had the deepest faith both in integration and grassroots democracy. And it does seem clear that the adoption of a politics of racial separatism based on secular, materialist theories led to the abandonment by Black Power advocates in SNCC of long-range community organizing work in the South.

To paint the spiritually and morally committed members of SNCC who believed in nonviolence as politically naive or inept and inflexible is simply unfair. When the tactics of direct action proved inadequate for sustaining the Movement in 1961, new political strategies were needed. The most important examples of new forms of action were the first attempts at a voter registration drive in McComb, Mississippi, and the desegregation movement in Albany, Georgia. In both instances, the key SNCC organizers involved were individuals with a deep commitment to nonviolence and spiritual values. Bob Moses, the initiator of the Mississippi voter registration project, was (and remains) deeply interested in mysticism, and Charles Sherrod, who with Cordell Reagon set up the SNCC office in Albany, Georgia, was a Baptist preacher.

What I am trying to say is that there was a new radicalism in SNCC which was intensely political and did indeed grow out of moral and spiritual values--and that this radicalism was non-authoritarian, democratic, and decentralist. Furthermore, this is precisely the politics that endured best in the South and in the nation. It is simply wrong to treat these people as apolitical. And it is incorrect to portray the centralist and secular strain in SNCC as the source of its political good sense and wisdom. The contrary seems to have been the case.

The re-writing of SNCC's history in a way that discredits or invalidates its early commitment to nonviolence and spiritual values seems to me to undervalue the real sources of strength in SNCC and to distort its political history. It also makes it virtually impossible to understand SNCC's relationship to the larger New Left and the eventual failure of both. Such an approach falls into the realm of ideology. If theory is designed for interpretation and understanding, ideology is designed for the organization of power--particularly power from the top down. Ideology is a discourse of power.

The faith that held the civil rights movement together from the sit-ins of 1960 to the Democratic Party Convention in 1964 was that somehow politics and morality could be brought back together through nonviolence and grassroots organizing. That faith was shaken by the failure of the MFDP challenge to the Democratic Party regulars. What was revealed in the encounter was that at its highest levels liberal politics had nothing to do with morality, that it was simply a system of power brokerage covered over with pious platitudes. It was, I think, this discovery of the basic hypocrisy of American liberalism as embodied in the Democratic Party in 1964 that broke the early faith of young activists in the viability of a politics based on moral principles and spiritual values. It also reinforced the skepticism of those who had distrusted spiritually-inspired values and doubted the efficacy of nonviolence from the beginning.

The disillusionment of SNCC organizers with electoral politics which ensued upon the refusal of the Democratic Party to seat the MFDP delegation was only one of the deficits of the Freedom Summer voter registration drive of 1964. Some of the worst fears of SNCC organizers had materialized during the summer campaign. The presence of hundreds of northern college students as volunteers in the South had indeed accomplished the major goals of drawing the attention of national media to the police-state conditions in the Deep South and forcing federal intervention. At the same time, the mere presence of large numbers of well-educated and highly articulate white students, mostly from middle or upper-middle class backgrounds, was inhibiting and disorienting for black grassroots leaders, and had a disruptive effect on SNCC's long-range dynamics as a community of organizers building a grassroots movement. The bad feelings sometimes generated by the presence of northern whites left a legacy of ill will that made many black SNCC organizers question the wisdom of continued interracial cooperation within their organization.[52]

A crisis of faith developed leading to a period of confusion and doubt among SNCC activists that lasted from the end of the Freedom Summer and the MFDP challenge until the emergence of the Black Power campaign in the spring of 1966. There were basically two tendencies which emerged in that period. On the one hand, there was a centralizing tendency around the national office in Atlanta, led by James Forman, which was increasingly committed to Marxist analysis and ideology and saw SNCC as a potential revolutionary vanguard based on a centralist model of cadre organization. Secondly, there was a decentralist tendency committed to some version of participatory democracy and beloved community and still wedded to nonviolence but unable to articulate a clear vision of democratic decentralism which could provide organizational direction and produce a political strategy.

Running through the whole debate and often cutting across the other lines of difference was the question of separatism-versus-integration. The issue of separatism would finally overwhelm other differences and produce a curious realignment in which racial questions obscured other political issues. A melange of Marxist centralism and "black power nationalism" emerged in 1966. It proved to be a dramatic tool for agitational purposes; but after the shouting was over, a once powerful moral and political force was scattered in disarray, torn by factionalism, and poisoned by bitterness and broken relationships.

CHAPTER 4

DEMOCRATIC IDEALISM:

SDS and the Gospel of
Participatory Democracy

While SNCC took the lead in the new student activism of the 1960s, others were quick to follow. In particular, the growth of the Students for a Democratic Society (SDS) was conditioned by the sit-ins and the emergence of SNCC in 1960. SDS, which was to become the largest organizational expression of the New Left, was given both tactical and organizational inspiration and models by SNCC. Nonviolent direct action and a decentralized approach to organization were directly derived from SNCC's experience and guided the early development of SDS. Furthermore, this fruitful interchange between the predominantly black southern student movement and the white northern student movement informed both the strategies and the political philosophy of SDS. The broad principles of the politics of participatory democracy that SDS articulated in its *Port Huron Statement* of 1962 were drawn in part from its symbiotic relationship with SNCC during the first two years of the decade. Thus the political theory of the New Left emerged in part from the grassroots experience of the student-led wing of the civil rights movement.[1]

◆ Northern Students and the Sit-in Movement

The nationwide effect of the sit-in movement in the South in the spring of 1960 was dramatic and far-reaching, particularly in regard to its impact on northern white students. By the end of the spring of that year, according to Kirkpatrick Sale's account in *SDS,*

> students at perhaps a hundred Northern colleges had been mobilized in support, and over the next year civil-rights activity touched almost every campus in the country: support groups formed, fund raising committees were established, local sit-ins and pickets took place, campus civil rights clubs began, students from around the country traveled to the South.[2]

As Aldon Morris puts it: "No previous actions of the Southern civil rights movement had generated this kind of widespread activism among whites across the nation. In effect, the 1960 sit-ins generated the activist stage of the modern white student movement."[3] It had been shown "that the typical [white Northern] student was affluent, excelled in scholarly pursuits, usually majored in the social sciences, and had liberal-to-radical political values."[4] Furthermore, "they were dissatisfied with the huge gap between America's democratic rhetoric and its actual practices." Morris goes on

> to answer the question of why that discontented group of affluent white students became involved in the politics of protest. That group entered into the politics of protest because the sit-ins dominated by black students provided them with a visible protest model, which demonstrated how they could proceed tactically and organizationally. It was an especially attractive model because the white student shared two important characteristics with the sit-in demonstrators: both were students, and both were young.[5]

In the North, the newly reorganized Students for a Democratic Society was profoundly affected by the sit-in movement and the development of SNCC. Both the tactic of nonviolent direct action and the decentralist organizational style of SNCC provided models for SDS and thus shaped the emergence of the New Left from its inception. SDS leaders like Robert Alan ("Al") Haber and Tom Hayden were taught the methods of nonviolent direct action by

black activists at conferences and workshops. Haber served as
liaison with SNCC and was influenced by SNCC leaders whose
top-level meetings he attended. He recalls that "Ella Baker
provided a bridge between the black student movement and the
emerging white student movement."[6] Morris points out that "SDS,
like SNCC, emerged as a loosely structured organization that
emphasized local autonomy and direct action rather than strong
centralized leadership. In this sense Ella Baker was the 'mother' of
both SNCC and the activist phase of SDS."[7]

Despite the importance of SNCC's example and inspiration
for SDS, it is, however, important to realize that SDS made its
own unique contributions to the Movement. Among these, none
was more important than the articulation of a new vision of
democratic radicalism in its famous *Port Huron Statement*. If
there was a single manifesto that shaped the language and thought
of the American New Left, it was this document prepared for
SDS's first real national convention in 1962.

✦ *Vision and Values*

The 59 young people who gathered at the United Auto
Workers' camp at Port Huron, Michigan, in June 1962, had all
been deeply influenced in their political development by the civil
rights movement. None had been more impressed by the
experience of SNCC than Tom Hayden, whose wife Sandra
"Casey" Cason was a SNCC organizer and a member of the SNCC
Coordinating Committee. The central concern of this national
convention of Students for a Democratic Society was the final
scrutiny, revision, and adoption of a document on which Hayden
had been laboring for several months. What was produced came to
be known as the *Port Huron Statement*, and it served not only as
a manifesto for SDS but as a founding document for the American
New Left as a whole. It contained, among other things, the
guiding principles of the political discourse which was SDS's most
enduring contribution to political life and thought in this country
and abroad, *the gospel of participatory democracy.*

However incomplete and ambiguous this presentation of the
concept of participatory democracy proved to be, it did accomplish
one vital task: it gave the emerging New Left a new language for

talking about politics and social change. By breaking with the stultified rhetoric of Marxism and the hollow platitudes of liberalism, it opened up the possibilities of thinking about political and social problems in new and creative ways. It opened the horizons of political thought to the potential of a new vision for democracy.

Tom Hayden's political ideas were not formed entirely by his experience in the civil rights movement. There was a complex interaction between Hayden's experiences as an activist and his intellectual quest as a student. Perhaps the most difficult part of his development to decipher is the way in which values came to occupy a central place in his political thought. It was this characteristic that suited him so eminently for the job of framing a manifesto for the New Left, because it was precisely this issue of the primacy of values that distinguished New Left political thought from its Marxist and liberal predecessors.

Hayden's political development was almost synonymous with the growth of the early SDS. When the organization changed its name from the Student League for Industrial Democracy to Students for a Democratic Society in January of 1960, its parent organization (the League for Industrial Democracy) hired Al Haber as Field Secretary. Haber was an older professional student of sorts in Ann Arbor, Michigan, who soon recruited Hayden, editor of *The Michigan Daily*, to the new organization. While Haber represented the tradition of Jewish radicalism which had been a dominant force in the Old Left (Haber's father was a well-known economist and labor arbitrator whose political sympathies lay with Norman Thomas and the Socialist Party),[8] Tom Hayden was the product of a distinctly different background--unconnected to the history of the American Marxist left and the labor movement. Thus Hayden was heir to neither the Stalinist nor social democratic wings of the Old Left (the Communist and Socialist Parties), nor was he weaned on the predominant discourse of the left-wing intelligentsia, Marxism.[9]

Hayden, born December 11, 1939, came from a conservative Catholic background in Royal Oak, Michigan, and was actually baptized by the right-wing priest, Father Coughlin, whose reactionary demagoguery was eventually silenced by the Church. There seems little doubt that Hayden's early values were deeply influenced by his Christian faith and his Jesuit teachers. By the time he entered the University of Michigan in the fall of 1957, he had, however, broken with his traditional Catholic upbringing and set out on an intellectual, spiritual, and political odyssey that would make him the key figure in shaping the discourse of the New Left. Hayden's search for a broader understanding of human values led him to the works of Albert Camus, and existentialism provided him a framework for the exploration of values in a non-theistic framework. The existentialist path was a way for many of Hayden's generation to reconcile their attachment to deep moral and spiritual values, which were often learned in a religious context, with the loss of their religious beliefs. It was a shaky undertaking, but it worked for a time for many young Americans who were to become activists in the New Left. It gave them some basis, other than the Judeo-Christian tradition, for justifying their moral convictions and for the expression of their humanistic values.

Existentialism was by no means the only intellectual influence at work in Hayden's life. The work of the renegade American sociologist, C. Wright Mills, played an important role in giving Hayden a sense of social theory couched in a language of native American radicalism. Mills recognized the importance of understanding Marxism but was not a doctrinaire radical and his leading works, *The Power Elite* and *White Collar*, provided a fresh look at American social structures and dynamics that was free of the dead hand of Marxist dogma.[10] Finally, in the area of political theory, Hayden seems to have been deeply influenced by what James Miller, in *"Democracy Is in the Streets"*, calls "the tradition of civic republicanism that links Aristotle to John Dewey."[11] While it is possible that Miller overplays this theme, it is vital to understand that Hayden's political ideas were indeed shaped by the classical tradition of political theory in the Western World which, beginning with Aristotle, had seen politics as a branch of ethics and made the issues of civic virtue and a virtuous citizenry central concerns of political thought. It was this tradition which modern liberalism and Marxism had largely displaced with their differing versions of "social science."[12] The central role of moral action and the privileged position of values in Hayden's thought clearly link him to this classical tradition.

Finally, it is difficult to judge how deeply Hayden was

influenced by the philosophy of the civil rights movement. Certainly a commitment to nonviolence is explicit in the *Port Huron Statement*, and there seems no reason to doubt the sincerity of Hayden's statement of that commitment. Whether he absorbed much of the philosophy of Satyagraha is unclear. It is, however, true that he was deeply impressed by his contact with the radical pacifists around *Liberation* magazine and took their ideas seriously.

In terms of the cultural currents of the times, Hayden was clearly affected by some of the Beat Generation writers. It was the reading of Jack Kerouac's *On the Road* that inspired him to hitchhike across the country in the summer of 1960 and led to his direct contacts with the radical activist community in Berkeley, California.

In assessing the influence of the civil rights movement in Hayden's political development, it is important to recognize that his direct involvement was the primary educative factor. Just as for most other young radicals of the 1960s, activism proved a more powerful force than books in the shaping of Hayden's life. His first engagement with the civil rights movement involved writing an editorial in *The Michigan Daily* (the University of Michigan's student newspaper) supporting student picketers in Ann Arbor who were organizing demonstrations of solidarity with the southern student sit-in movement. The idea was suggested to him by Al Haber, and it did not represent an activist stance on Hayden's own part. He was still in the role of supportive journalist.

Interestingly, it was an encounter with Martin Luther King, Jr., that seems to have most directly affected Hayden's attitude toward activism. After traveling to Berkeley in 1960 and meeting extensively with activists there, Hayden's West Coast itinerary then took him to the Democratic Party Convention in Los Angeles. There he met King in person. He later said:

> Meeting King transformed me. There I was with pencil in hand, trying to conduct an objective interview with Martin Luther King, whose whole implicit message was: 'Stop writing, start acting.' That was a compelling moment. It seemed so absurd to be a student writing about students taking action, as opposed to becoming more of a committed writer and thinker, with commitment coming first.[13]

Commitment (*engagement* in French) was one of the keywords of the existentialist vocabulary. It was natural that Hayden would use it to describe the gripping effect of this meeting with King. It forced the marriage of values and action. As such, it represented very clearly the moral tone of the new political activism.

On his return trip to Michigan, Hayden stopped at the University of Minnesota to attend the annual congress of the National Student Association. Al Haber was there, pushing successfully for the adoption of his position paper, "The Student and the Total Community," as an NSA policy statement supporting student activism. But, perhaps more importantly, Hayden came face-to-face with a group of students who were to represent for him the new ideal of existential commitment to radical political activism. They were the delegates from the newly formed Student Nonviolent Coordinating Committee. Along them was Sandra "Casey" Cason who would became Hayden's wife. Cason was a white woman from Texas whose political activism was informed by a deep religious faith. A student at the University of Texas in Austin, she had become active in civil rights work through the YWCA. But she had also become deeply involved with a radical Christian "intentional community" called The Christian Faith and Life Community, an offshoot of the Wesleyan (Methodist) Student Fellowship in Austin. Under the charismatic leadership of the Reverend Joseph Matthews, this group preached a form of Christian existentialism and political activism that emphasized both living in community and intense involvement in the world.[14] Cason and her colleagues in SNCC provided a powerful role model for Hayden on his road to activism.

Over the next two years, Tom Hayden became an example of what was to happen to thousands of other American students of his generation. For the first time in American history political activism became the central focus of student life. The ivy-covered walls between the "Ivory Tower" of academia and the "outside world" came tumbling down and a new vision of *the student as democratic citizen* was born.

After his return to the University of Michigan in the fall of 1960, Hayden's new enthusiasm for a commitment to radical activism was expressed in a series of editorials in *The Michigan Daily*. He took some of his cues from David Riesman's *The*

Lonely Crowd, Vance Packard's *The Hidden Persuaders,* and William Whyte's *The Organization Man,* three popular sociological portraits of mass society, bureaucracy, and manipulative consumerism. "In recent times," Hayden wrote, "spokesmen as disparate as Riesman and the existentialists have been concerned with the actual breakdown of dogma and tradition and the resultant society which seems directionless, decisionless, amoral."[15]

The real questions that seemed to be haunting Tom Hayden were: "How can one create a democratic theory of politics and society which places values and morality first?" and "How can one justify individual commitment to social justice and political action outside of a traditional religious framework if it is not a matter of narrow self-interest?" He saw the new political idealism as being nurtured eclectically by "Mill and classic liberalism," "Jefferson's attitudes on liberty," "Gandhi's principles of non-violent action," and "Camus's concept of the human struggle and commitment." Students were the forerunners of a "revolution that would reduce complexity to moral simplicity, that would restore emotion to religion, that would in fact give man back his 'roots'." Student activists had shown a "new willingness to take up responsibilities of the individual to the democratic order."[16]

Hayden also founded a student political party on campus. VOICE, as it was called, was directly modeled on the UC Berkeley's radical campus organization, SLATE, which Hayden had studied first-hand during his summer travels. VOICE joined national and campus issues and ran candidates for student government. Then, in February, 1961, Hayden had his first real experience of the southern civil rights movement. He traveled to Fayette County, Tennessee, and reported on the struggles of black sharecroppers who had been evicted because of their determination to register to vote. He had his first experience of dealing with a "mob" that chased him out of town. This experience and his increasing involvement with activist Sandra Cason drew Hayden further into the civil rights struggle.

Hayden was also being drawn, or dragged, into SDS. Susan Jeffrey and Bob Ross, SDS members at the University of Michigan who came from Jewish social democratic backgrounds (like Al Haber who was now busy working in the New York office) actively recruited Hayden despite his great reluctance to become involved

in any organization linked to the traditions of the Old Left. Of
Jeffrey and Ross, Hayden recalls:

> Their view was that things weren't happening unless you were signing
> up people to become card-carrying members of this organization-
> in-the-making, the SDS. My view was that things were happening very
> well, thank you, without any assistance from these groups out of the
> morbid traditions of the left centered in New York City.[17]

He was also being recruited, unsuccessfully, by Michael Harrington of the Young People's Socialist League. Hayden felt that the
use of the word "socialism" was unsuited to the American
political tradition and would alienate the American public.

Hayden finally opted for membership in SDS with its
nonsectarian democratic rhetoric and style. He was a vitally
important recruit in providing a link to constituencies beyond the
narrow social base which hampered the growth of other left-wing
student organizations. In addition, he married Sandra Cason
whose work with SNCC in the South had been a source of deep
inspiration to him. Hayden became SDS Field Secretary in Atlanta
where Sandra Cason worked with Ella Baker in the YWCA
office.[18] This strategic position brought Hayden into direct and
continuous contact with SNCC and exposed him to the radical
decentralist ideas of "group-centered leadership" which Ella Baker
had fostered in that organization.[19]

In August and September 1961, SNCC organized its first voter
registration project in McComb, Mississippi, under the leadership
of Robert Moses. It was a bold and dangerous move that was
immediately met with white vigilantism and violent repression.
Hayden traveled to McComb with Paul Potter, National Affairs
Vice President of the NSA and future President of SDS. It was a
baptism of fire. Arriving secretly on October 9, Hayden and Potter
were forced to meet clandestinely with Moses and other SNCC
organizers. Two days later, Hayden and Potter were dragged from
a car and beaten by a white assailant. An Associated Press
photograph of the incident went out over the wire service and
made Hayden an instant symbol of the new student activism.

This experience of risk, commitment, and violence led Hayden
to write his most important political articles up to that time.
Reprinted as an SDS pamphlet entitled "Revolution in Mississippi," Hayden's reflections on the transformative power of the

southern civil rights struggle reveal the deep changes which it had wrought in this young man. It seems clear that the Tom Hayden who would author the *Port Huron Statement* had been profoundly radicalized by this "revolution" of which he wrote and in which he had been a participant. "Revolution in Mississippi" ends with a quote from the anti-fascist Italian writer, Ignazio Silone, whose novel *Bread and Wine* was a Bible of political and moral thought for many thoughtful activists of Hayden's generation. Silone wrote:

> I am convinced that it would be a waste of time to show a people of intimidated slaves a different manner of speaking, a different manner of gesticulating, but perhaps it would be worthwhile to show them a different way of living. No word and no gesture can be more persuasive than the life, and if necessary, the death, of a man who strives to be free . . . a man who shows what a man can be.[20]

✦ *The Port Huron Statement*

Though there was a genuine effort to make the *Port Huron Statement* a collective undertaking, in fact it is largely the work of Tom Hayden. He was delegated the task of drafting a broad statement of principles and political direction for SDS in the winter of 1962. Over the ensuing months, Hayden read widely and produced preliminary drafts of the document. These were distributed to members for comment, and he intended to incorporate criticisms in his revisions. The process did not work well. In reality, the most important criticism, coming generally from critics of Old Left backgrounds, was directed at Hayden's opening section on values. It simply did not fit well into the mind-set of people who had grown up in the various versions of the Marxist tradition to begin a political manifesto with a statement of values.[21]

Hayden responded to this criticism by rearranging his text in such a way that the values section was placed less prominently towards the middle of the document. This attempt to appease the "materialist" bias of Old Left traditionalists backfired in June at the Port Huron Convention itself. There the overwhelming sentiment of the assembled representatives of SDS was in favor of Hayden's original plan, and the decision was made to restore the statement of values to its original place near the opening of the manifesto, immediately following a general introduction.[22] This turnabout was deeply revealing and crucial to the long-range success of the *Port Huron Statement*. It showed that the sensibilities of a representative group of SDSers were more like Hayden's original instincts than the position of his critics. Furthermore, it ensured that the *Port Huron Statement* would reach a wide audience and become what it was destined to be: the most popular and most influential articulation of the political aspirations of a new generation of young American radicals. Had the section on values been displaced by a traditional Marxist-inspired "materialist" analysis, the document would have probably joined a long list of left-wing manifestos read only by those already initiated into the esoteric language and world-view of the Old Left. By breaking with that tradition--by placing values first--the *Port Huron Statement* was able to stand as the foundation of a new political movement that still speaks to the hearts and minds of sensitive people in the late 20th century. It ensured that Students for a Democratic Society would, for a time, be a broad-based movement of grassroots democratic radicalism instead of another troublesome but irrelevant Marxist sect.

"A first task of any social movement," the *Statement* reads, "is to convince people that the search for orienting theories and the creation of human values is complex but worthwhile."[23] It goes on to say: "We are aware that to avoid platitudes we must analyze the concrete conditions of social order." But, having recognized the need for such analysis of "concrete conditions," the author then asserts the primacy of values and their *a priori* character. The next sentences read: "But to direct such an analysis we must use the guideposts of basic principles. Our own social values involve conceptions of human beings, human relationships, and social systems." (6)

It seems clear that the old order of social scientistic thought is being overturned. Instead of values being derived from the "materialist" analysis of society, prior values must be appealed to which are "the guideposts of basic principles." And what are these basic principles which are being appealed to? They are, I believe, a statement of the values of the kind of spiritual humanism which was beginning to flourish in America among the ranks of humanistic psychologists like Abraham Maslow and which would inform much of what came to be called the human potential movement. The succeeding paragraph spells out these spiritual humanistic values:

> We regard *men* as infinitely precious and possessed of unfulfilled capacities for reason, freedom, and love. In affirming these principles we are aware of countering perhaps the dominant conceptions of man in the twentieth century: that he is a thing to be manipulated, and that he is inherently incapable of directing his own affairs. We oppose the depersonalization that reduces human beings to the status of things--if anything the brutalities of the twentieth century teach that means and ends are intimately related, that vague appeals to "posterity" cannot justify the mutilations of the present. We oppose, too, the doctrine of human incompetence because it rests essentially on the modern fact that men have been "competently" manipulated into incompetence--we see little reason why men cannot meet with increasing skill the complexities and responsibilities of their situation, if society is organized not for minority, but for majority, participation in decision-making. (5)

Then comes the statement of human potential and goals:

> Men have unrealized potential for self-cultivation, self-direction, self-understanding, and creativity. It is this potential that we regard as crucial and to which we appeal, not to the human potentiality for violence, unreason, and submission to authority. The goal of man and society should be human independence: a concern not with image of popularity but with finding a meaning in life that is personally authentic: a quality of mind not compulsively driven by a sense of powerlessness; nor one which unthinkingly adopts status values, nor one which represses all threats to its habits, but one which has full, spontaneous access to present and past experiences, one which easily unites the fragmented parts of personal history, one which openly faces problems which are troubling and unresolved; one with an intuitive awareness of possibilities; an active sense of curiosity, and ability and willingness to learn. (5-6)

This powerful statement of the potential of a truly human individuality is followed by a short, but carefully worded paragraph designed to distinguish this vision from any notion of rampant individualism. "This kind of independence," it states, "does not mean egotistic individualism--the object is not to have one's way so much as it is to have a way that is one's own. Nor do we deify man--we merely have faith in his potential."

The *Statement* then goes on to present a set of ideals governing the conception of human relationships and human community.

> *Human relationships* should involve fraternity and honesty. Human interdependence is contemporary fact; human brotherhood must be willed, however, as a condition of future survival and as the most appropriate form of social relations. Personal links between man and man are needed, especially to go beyond the partial and fragmentary bonds of function that bind men only as worker to worker, employer to employee, teacher to student, American to Russian. (6)

But how are these "partial and fragmentary bonds of function" to be overcome? The answer lies in a spiritual as well as political transformation that transcends the socially fragmenting forces of the dominant materialism.

> Loneliness, estrangement, isolation describe the vast distance between man and man today. These dominant tendencies cannot be overcome by better personnel management, nor by improved gadgets, but only when a love of man overcomes the idolatrous worship of things by man. As the individualism we affirm is not egoism, the selflessness we affirm is not self-elimination. On the contrary, we believe in generosity of a kind that imprints one's unique individual qualities in relation to other men, and to all human activity. Further, to dislike isolation is not to favor the abolition of privacy; the latter differs from isolation in that it occurs or is abolished according to individual will. (7)

The realization of these spiritual ideals is to be achieved through the democratic transformation of social, political, and economic life. "We would," the *Statement* affirms,

> replace power rooted in possession, privilege, or circumstance by power and uniqueness rooted in love, reflectiveness, reason, and creativity. As a social system we seek the establishment of a democracy of individual participation, governed by two central aims: that the individual share in those social decisions determining the quality and direction of his life; that society be organized to encourage independence in men and provide the media for their common participation. (7)

This dramatic and poetic vision is followed by the basic statement of the meaning and principles of participatory democracy:

In a participatory democracy, the political life would be based in several root principles:

that decision-making of basic social consequence be carried on by public groupings;

that politics be seen positively, as the art of collectively creating an acceptable pattern of social relations;

that politics has the function of bringing people out of isolation and into community, thus being a necessary, though not sufficient, means of finding meaning in personal life;

that the political order should serve to clarify problems in a way instrumental to their solution;

it should provide outlets for the expression of personal grievance and aspiration; opposing views should be organized so as to illuminate choices and facilitate the attainment of goals; channels should be commonly available to relate men to knowledge and to power so that private problems--from bad recreation facilities to personal alienation--are formulated as general issues. (7-8)

This formulation of the politics of participatory democracy is striking chiefly because it is a bold and decisive restatement of the classical view of political life as formulated in the beginning of the Western tradition by the Greeks. Politics is once again seen as the art of creating the *polis*, of building the community of a shared life which is the "necessary, though not sufficient, means of finding meaning in personal life." This notion "that politics has the function of bringing people out of isolation and into community" is dramatically modern in its formulation and yet truly classical in its inspiration. Here again politics is "seen positively, as the art of collectively creating an acceptable pattern of social relations." Gone is liberal cynicism about the political realm: gone too is Marxist economic determinism. The "political" is restored to its central, creative role in the determination of human affairs without, at the same time, overwhelming the "personal" or making utopian claims that a democratic society will answer all the questions of humanity's search for meaning.

This declaration of the political principles of participatory democracy is followed by a statement of economic principles which are clearly subordinate to and derived from the preceding political values and ideals. This reversal of the traditional materialist subordination of politics to economics is essential to the meaning of the *Port Huron Statement*. It meant that economic questions would always have as their primary criterion of judgment the prior political principle of democratic participation.

In the words of the *Statement* itself:

> The economic sphere would have as its basis the principles:
>   that work should involve incentives worthier than money or
> survival. It should be educative, not stultifying; creative, not mechani-
> cal; self-directed, not manipulated, encouraging independence, a
> respect for others, a sense of dignity, and a willingness to accept social
> responsibility, since it is this experience that has crucial influence on
> habits, perceptions, and individual ethics;
>   that the economic experience is so personally decisive that the
> individual must share in its full determination;
>   that the economy itself is of such social importance that its major
> resources and means of production should be open to democratic
> participation and subject to democratic social regulation. (8)

This subordination of economic principles to democratic
political principles suggested that, at the level of economic
restructuring, SDS was searching primarily for a vision of
economic democracy rather than the traditional formulations of
socialism. The guidelines for economic change for the New Left
were to be "democratic participation" and "democratic social
regulation." This formula is vitally important because a vision of
economic democracy governed by these principles pointed in the
direction of decentralization and grassroots control rather than in
the traditional socialist direction of state ownership (nationalization) and centralization, and thus it reinforced the decentralist
tendency in the New Left which would be its most authentic
expression.

Hayden's choice of language was not based on naivete.
Though not from an Old Left background, he was well acquainted
by 1962 with the rhetoric and dogmas of the Marxist socialist
tradition. He regarded that language as stultified and increasingly
empty of content. The vision of socialism as a state-controlled
planned economy was far from the aspirations of the young
democratic radicals of the New Left who had seen the limits and
disasters of both state socialism and welfare state capitalism.
However, as we shall see later, SDS failed in the *Port Huron
Statement* to match its vision and values with a satisfactory
economic and political program.

The values section of the *Port Huron Statement* ends with the
assertion that just like "the political and economic ones, major
social institutions--cultural, educational, rehabilitative, and others

--should be generally organized with the well-being and dignity of man as the essential measure of success." Furthermore, it is unequivocal in its support of nonviolence, arguing that in

> social change or interchange, we find violence to be abhorrent because it requires generally the transformation of the target, be it a human being or a community of people, into a depersonalized object of hate. It is imperative that the means of violence be abolished and the institutions--local, national, international--that encourage non-violence as a condition of conflict be developed. (8)

These were "the central values" which were to move and guide the message of SDS to the growing constituency of student activists in the United States and even abroad. Many who read it were deeply moved. Its power and beauty lie in its successful presentation of democratic political ideals in a language of spiritual humanism that dared to speak of values long banished from the realm of political discourse. In so doing, it turned on its head the principles of political discourse established by Machiavelli and Hobbes, and by Lenin and Marx. It represented the covert triumph of *a philosophy of democratic idealism.*

♦ Towards American Democracy

While insisting on the priority of values in political thought and action, the *Port Huron Statement* offered much more than a spiritual and moral manifesto. It contained a detailed political, social, and economic analysis of the malaise of welfare-warfare state capitalism and the failures of American democracy, and stinging indictments of the concentration of wealth and economic power; the "hard-core poverty [which] exists just beyond the neon lights of affluence" (20); the "pervasiveness of Racism in American life" (36); the paralyzing role of anti-Communism in the domestic politics and foreign policy of the United States; the madness and waste of resources of the arms race and nuclear deterrence strategy; and the anti-democratic role America's foreign and economic policies had played in the developing world.

The analysis of what was wrong with American society was followed by a detailed, specific program for economic and political change. It is in the prescriptive sections of the *Port Huron*

Statement that we can see in embryo some of the fundamental ambiguities that were to plague the New Left throughout the decade of the 1960s. One way of framing these issues is to ask the question: "Was the domestic political program of the *Port Huron Statement* basically one of social democratic reform to curb the excesses of corporate capitalist society, or did it propose a truly radical democratic alternative?"

Phrased in these terms, the question elicits a fairly straightforward answer: the *Port Huron Statement* offers a basic set of social democratic reforms designed to expand government control of the economy through the enlargement of the (non-military) "public sector" and the expansion and improvement of the social programs of the welfare state at the expense of the warfare state. Insofar as this is true, the *Port Huron Statement* fails to develop a political program which realizes the radical democratic vision of participatory democracy and fails to make the values it espouses operational in its concrete programmatic proposals. Having said this, it is then necessary to point out that there is a second voice in the section on domestic programs which is radically democratic and decentralist but which is heard only intermittently and is much less fully developed than the dominant social democratic theme. Finally, it should be understood that there was a fundamental contradiction in the *Port Huron Statement* between these reformist proposals and the kind of radical democratic movement SDS was heralding and proposing to build. That movement, inspired by the kinds of vision and values Tom Hayden had elaborated, was the truly radical proposal of SDS at Port Huron, and, as it grew, it would be increasingly at odds with the social democratic reformism of its stated political program. But it is appropriate to pause here and explore the program briefly.

There are six points.

The first falls into the strategy called *realignment*-"America must abolish its political party stalemate." (46) Realignment was a political strategy strongly favored by the social democratic wing of SDS in New York. The argument was basically that Dixiecrats should be driven out of the Democratic Party to force a realignment of liberals and conservatives and to incorporate blacks into the Democratic Party. The Democratic Party would then become a left-liberal or social democratic party and the Republicans would develop into the truly conservative party. Not all of this argument was made explicit in the *Port Huron Statement*, but realignment was the basic strategy which was being proposed when it stated: "Two genuine parties, centered around issues and essential values, demanding allegiance to party principles shall supplant the current system of organized stalemate which is seriously inadequate to a world in flux." The demand is raised that the President "no longer tolerate the Southern conservatives in the Democratic Party" who are referred to as "racist scoundrels." (46-47)

The second proposal is: "Mechanisms of voluntary association must be created through which political information can be imparted and political participation encouraged." (47) Even realignment of political parties "would not provide adequate outlets for popular involvement." Something is needed to counter the "giant lobby interests of business." This is a call for the creation of institutions "that engage people with issues and express political preference . . . in national decision-making enterprise." Basically this is a blueprint for citizens' lobbies designed to encourage public participation and to offset corporate power in government. (47)

Thirdly, the domestic program argues: "Institutions and practices which stifle dissent should be abolished, and peaceful dissent should be actively promoted." (47) This is an appeal for the reaffirmation of the "First Amendment freedoms of speech, assembly, thought, religion and press" which are "guarantees, not threats to national security" and for the abolition of "institutions bred by fear and apathy," namely, "the House Un-American Activities Committee, the Senate Internal Security Committee, the loyalty oaths on Federal loans, the Attorney General's list of subversive organizations, the Smith and McCarran Acts." Abolition of these "blighting institutions is the process of restoring democratic institutions." (47)

The fourth point is strangely ambiguous in its wording: "Corporations must be made publicly responsible." (47) The sense of the proposal is that corporate power must be democratized, for, "It is not possible to believe that true democracy can exist where a minority utterly controls wealth and power." The interests and actions of corporations and industrial leaders "should become structurally responsible to the people." "A new reordering" is necessary which includes "changes in the rules of society by

challenging the unchallenged politics of American corporations."
Efforts at government "regulation," even if realized, "would be
inadequate without increased worker participation in management
decision-making, strengthened and independent regulating power,
balances of partial and/or complete public ownership, various
means of humanizing the conditions and types of work itself,
sweeping welfare programs, and regional *public* development
authorities." These suggestions are offered as "examples of
measures to re-balance the economy toward public--and indivi-
dual--control." (48) This hardly adds up to a program for
"socialism" (a state-controlled planned economy), nor is it a clear
blueprint for decentralized economic democracy. The obvious
ambiguities are only partially resolved in the two succeeding
points.

Point five asserts: "The allocation of resources must be based
on social needs. A truly 'public sector' must be established, and its
nature debated and planned." (48) The currently existing public
sector is largely the "permanent war economy" and "America
must return to other mechanisms of growth besides military
spending." (48) In addition, the "main private forces of economic
expansion cannot guarantee a steady rate of growth, nor
acceptable recovery from recession--especially in a demilitarizing
world." However, any proposal for "major intervention into
civilian production by the government" poses enormous issues:

A. "How should public vs. private domain be determined?"

B. "How should technological advances be introduced into
society?"

C. "How shall the 'public sector' be made public, and not the
arena of a ruling bureaucracy of 'public servants'?" (49-50)

In all three areas an attempt is made to assert public need or
interest over private interest or monopoly. It is a formula for a
mixed economy with a social democratic direction. Only in the
third area (C), do we get a glimmer of a decentralist alternative.
The problems of a "ruling bureaucracy" (which are inherent in
social democratic systems) are to be met by "steadfast opposition
to bureaucratic coagulation . . . . Bureaucratic pile-ups must be at
least minimized by local, regional, and national economic planning
. . . [and] by experiments in *decentralization*, based on the vision
of man as master of his machines and his society." (50)

These *important experiments in decentralization* are not

spelled out in great detail after having been accorded pride of place. The most daring suggestion is that our "monster cities, based historically on the need for mass labor, might now be humanized, broken into smaller communities, powered by nuclear energy, arranged according to community decision." (50) The decentralist vision of "blueprints in civic paradise" is unwittingly marred by faith in nuclear power. Nonetheless, the social democratic perspective does not prevail without this strong voice of caution about the need for decentralization.

The sixth and final point outlines a set of social programs. "America should concentrate on its genuine social priorities: abolish squalor, terminate neglect, and establish an environment for people to live with dignity and creativeness." (50) The specifics of such a strategy should include anti-poverty programs, civil rights legislation, model cities programs, more and better mental health and public health facilities, educational and prison reform and federal support for farmers cooperatives. Finally, "science should be employed to constructively transform the conditions of life throughout the United States and the world," and the imbalance in favor of military over non-military research corrected. (50-53)

In retrospect, the contrast between the *manifesto of democratic radicalism* with which the *Port Huron Statement* begins and the program for social democratic reform which follows is indeed striking and somewhat bewildering. It reflected the division in SDS between the philosophy of democratic idealism that seemed to be at the core of Tom Hayden's thinking, and the tradition of socialist or social democratic leftism that had survived from the Old Left and which was basically informed by Marxist analysis.

If the *Port Huron Statement* had ended with the programmatic sections described above, it would have been disappointing. This was, fortunately, not the case and some of the elan of the manifesto was recaptured in the final two sections: "Alternatives to Helplessness" (54-61) and "The University and Social Change." (61-63)

♦ *What Is To Be Done?*

Surveying the political landscape of America for signs of hope

and levers of change, the founders of SDS were less than sanguine
about the prospects. Before presenting the possibilities of political
organizing in the universities, the *Statement* examined each of the
significant social forces in the country and found them wanting.
First, the southern civil rights movement was heralded "as the
most heartening because of the justice it insists upon, exemplary
because it indicates that there can be a passage out of apathy."
This movement has instilled "a sense of self-determination . . . in
millions of oppressed Negroes," it has "challenged a few thousand
liberals to new social idealism," and it has won "a series of
important concessions . . . such as token school desegregation,
increased Administration help, new laws, desegregation of some
public facilities." However, "fundamental social change . . . has
not come." Instead, the "civil rights struggle has come to an
impasse" that has led the movement to enter "the sphere of
politics, insisting on citizenship rights, specifically the right to
vote." This "use of *political* means to solve the problems of
equality in America" is particularly important because "the moral
clarity of the civil rights movement has not always been
accompanied by precise political vision" or even by "a real
political consciousness" which makes "the new phase revolutionary in its implications." "Linked with pressure from Northern
liberals to expunge the Dixiecrats from the ranks of the
Democratic party, massive Negro voting in the South could
destroy the vise-like grip reactionary Southerners have on the
Congressional legislative process." (54-55)

Turning next to the "broadest movement for peace in several
years," the framers were highly critical of its isolation from power.
The peace movement was seen as operating "almost exclusively
through peripheral institutions" and "individuals interested in
peace have nonpolitical social roles." The social units of the peace
movement "have not been located in spots of major social
influence." "The results are political ineffectiveness and personal
alienation." This has meant that the "organizing ability of the
peace movement . . . is limited to the ability to state and polarize
issues." Furthermore: "As long as the debates of the peace
movement form only a protest, rather than an opposition
viewpoint within the centers of decision-making, then it is neither
a movement of democratic relevance, nor is it likely to have any
effectiveness except in educating outsiders to the issue." This

rather harsh indictment is followed by a suggestion that the peace movement might "prepare a *local base*, especially by establishing civic committees on the techniques of converting from military to peacetime production." (55-57)

The appraisal of organized labor reveals a New Left impaled on the horns of an old dilemma. On the one hand,

"Labor's presence today as the most liberal of mainstream institutions" is duly noted while, on the other hand, "it would be irresponsible not to criticize labor for losing much of the idealism that once made it a driving movement." This amounts to a somewhat tangential recognition that while organized labor exists as a social force there is no labor movement as a real force for change. This situation is recognized to be "only partly due to anti-labor politicians and corporations. Blame should be laid, too, to labor itself for not mounting an adequate movement." This failure stems in part from the fact that "Labor has too often seen itself as elitist, rather than mass-oriented, and as a pressure group rather than an 18-million-member body making political demands for all America."

There are "indicators . . . that labor might regain some of its missing idealism." These signs stem from "workers' discontent" with collective bargaining gains and "occasional splits among union leaders" on "nuclear testing or other Cold War issues." More importantly, the "permanence of unemployment, and the threat of automation" are creating these "feelings of unrest" as are "the growth of unorganized ranks in white-collar fields." Finally, there is "the tremendous challenge of the Negro movement" for labor's support.

There is a good deal of ambivalence in this assessment of labor's political future. The situation is seen as "a profound crisis: either labor will continue to decline as a social force, or it must constitute itself as a mass political force." One voice at Port Huron argues that "A new politics must include a revitalized labor movement," and that it is "the best candidate for the synthesis of the civil rights, peace, and economic reform movement." Another voice says that "the new politics is still contained; it struggles below the surface of apathy, awaiting liberation. Few anticipate the breakthrough and fewer still exhort labor to begin. Labor continues to be the most liberal--and most frustrating institution in mainstream America." (57-59)

It would have been more honest to admit the dilemma outright. The rather tortuous reworking of the "labor question" suggests real differences and real political struggles among the participants at Port Huron. If there is a lack of clarity about these differences, it is because a sincere effort was being made to contain somewhat conflicting viewpoints within a single document. By obscuring these differences, the framers produce positions lacking precision and clarity.

The survey of social forces includes a brief glance at the Democratic Party and the ill-fated "Liberal Project" of Wisconsin's Representative Kastenmeier--an attempt to create a "liberal force in Congress." The sheer brevity of the discussion of the Democrats at this juncture leads one to suspect that a lot was left unsaid. In fact, of course, there was relatively little evidence that the Democratic Party deserved to be listed among those "social forces" which stood as harbingers of change in America. (59) The political strategy that follows the assessment of social forces is basically another statement of "realignment." "An imperative task for these disinherited groups, then, is to demand a Democratic Party responsible to their interests." (60)

◆ The University and Social Change

The pessimism that seems to flow from this appraisal of the potential forces of change in America is countered in the final section of the *Port Huron Statement* by an assessment of the potential role of universities.

> There is perhaps little reason to be optimistic about the above analysis. True, the Dixiecrat-GOP coalition is the weakest point in the dominating complex of corporate, military, and political power. But the civil rights, peace, and student movements are too poor and socially slighted, and the labor movement too quiescent, to be counted with enthusiasm. From where else can power and vision be summoned? We believe that the universities are an overlooked seat of influence. (61)

Central to SDS's conception of the building of a New Left was its particular view of the university as an institution and students as actors. Students were "breaking the crust of apathy and overcoming the inner alienation that remain the defining charac-

teristics of American college life." (9) Furthermore, this awakening among students was taking place in an institution that had
become pivotal in American society. SDS was perhaps unique in
its grasp of the importance of this conjuncture of institutional and
social forces. No other group seems to have realized so early that
students and the university constituted in and of themselves a key
focus for social ferment and political change. Those gathered at
Port Huron may in fact have underestimated the power that the
university constituency would have in the emerging New Left, but
they certainly did grasp the centrality of its position and invested
great hope in its potential. Their vision of students and the
university was basically as catalytic agents that would energize
other sectors of the society. They almost certainly did not share
the same analysis of students and university-trained workers that
was later associated with notions of "the new working class."

The *Port Huron Statement* lists four reasons for the
importance of the university. First, it is "located in a permanent
position of social influence" and is a "crucial institution in the
formation of social attitudes." Second, "it is the central institution
for organizing, evaluating, and transmitting knowledge." Third,
"the extent to which academic resources presently are used to
buttress immoral social practice" (revealed through "defense
contracts," the use of social science as a "manipulative tool" for
modern corporations, and "motivational research" as a "manipulative aspect of American politics") demonstrates "the unchangeable
reliance by men of power on the men and store-houses of
knowledge." All this "makes the university functionally tied to
society in new ways, revealing new potentialities, new levers for
change." Fourth, it is "the only mainstream institution that is
open to participation by individuals of nearly every viewpoint."
"Social relevance, the accessibility to knowledge, and internal
openness . . . make the university a potential base and agency in a
movement of social change." (61)

This brief analysis is followed by a six-point declaration that
outlines the essential features that this new movement in
universities must display. First, "Any new left in America must be
. . . a left with real intellectual skills" and "the university permits
the political life to be an adjunct to the academic one, and action
to be informed by reason." Second, "A new left must be
distributed in significant social roles" which is the case of

universities. Third, "A new left must consist of younger people who matured in the post-war world" which makes universities "an obvious beginning point" for recruitment. Fourth, "A new left must include liberals and socialists, the former for their relevance, the latter for their sense of thoroughgoing reforms in the system" and universities are "a more sensible place than a political party" for dialogue between them. Fifth, "A new left must start controversy across the land" and "the ideal university is a community of controversy." Sixth, "A new left must transform complexity into issues that can be understood and felt close up by every human being." It must (in a paraphrase of C. Wright Mills) "give form to the feelings of helplessness and indifference, so that people may see the political, social, and economic sources of their private troubles and organize to change society." (62) (This challenge to link *the personal and the political* prefigured a major theme of the women's liberation movement later in the decade.[24]) Finally, there is a recognition that a new movement cannot rely solely on the old levers of economic deprivation to motivate people in the direction of change: "a new left cannot rely on only aching stomachs to be the engine force of social reforms." (62)

The *Statement* ends with a clear recognition that a new left movement in universities will not be sufficient in itself and must seek allies and build bridges to other constituencies "in labor, civil rights, and other liberal forces outside the campus." In long range terms, the "bridge to political power . . . will be built through genuine cooperation, locally, nationally, and internationally between a new left of young people and an awakening community of allies." On campuses there must be "national efforts at university reform by an alliance of students and faculty" that would "wrest control of the educational process from the administrative bureaucracy." Moreover, students and faculty "must make debate and controversy, not dull pedantic cant, the common style for educational life . . . and consciously build a base for their assault upon the loci of power." (62-63)

The *Statement* ends with this pronouncement:

> As students for a democratic society, we are committed to stimulating this kind of social movement, this kind of vision and program in campus and community across the country. If we appear to seek the unattainable, as it has been said, then let it be known that we do so to avoid the unimaginable. (63)

✦ An Open-ended Discourse

Not unexpectedly, the presentation of participatory democracy in the *Port Huron Statement* raised more questions than it answered. Its "creative ambiguity" was both a boon and a burden, for there were basically two different interpretations that could be given to that phrase and they were fundamentally irreconcilable. The ambiguity was further reinforced by the obvious disparity between the radical democratic vision of the first part of the document and its reformist program. This meant that there were many people who would be attracted to the radical potential of the ideal of participatory democracy when reading the first part of the *Port Huron Statement* but who would be dismayed or bored by the programmatic section. People like this would adopt the language of participatory democracy and begin to draw their own conclusions about its implications. This was how ambiguity became the basis for real political conflict in the New Left. Each side felt it represented the authentic interpretation of the vision of democratic participation.

On the one hand, there was a "liberal reformist" interpretation which could argue that the basic institutions of the liberal democratic capitalist order needed new mechanisms that would increase democratic participation in political processes and would facilitate further social and economic reforms. This position, whether its supporters liked the label or not, was basically "social democratic." Its logic implied that the proper direction for American political life was to build on the achievements of the New Deal welfare state and extend reforms in the direction of a full-blown social democracy. This position was more or less compatible with both "left-liberal" ideology and with reformist (or "revisionist") Marxism of the social democratic or "democratic socialist" variety. On the other hand, there was to be a "radical decentralist" interpretation which regarded the vision of a participatory democracy as basically incompatible with the centralized, hierarchical, and dominative institutions of corporate capitalism and the modern state. This second position led in the direction of radical decentralizing change in political, social, and economic life and emphasized anti-authoritarian or libertarian values and the importance of alternative, liberatory cultural values and experimentation. This second position was highly skeptical of liberal electoral politics and was likely to seek its historical inspiration in the decentralist, libertarian, anarcho-pacifist, or anarcho-syndicalist traditions. Since, however, relatively little was known in the United States about these traditions, the decentralist position was slow to articulate its differences from the left-liberal or social democratic positions.

These two interpretations were inherent in the problematic framed by the discourse on participatory democracy. The two positions are the logical outcome of raising questions about liberal capitalist democracy from a radical democratic viewpoint. And therein lay the dilemma: even if the intent of *some* of the framers of the *Port Huron Statement* was predominantly left-liberal or social democratic, the critique of liberalism inherent in the phrase "participatory democracy" led inevitably to radical democratic conclusions. This was the case because the demand for democratic participation implies that power should function from the bottom up, and liberal capitalist "democracy" perpetuates power from the top down. It was this dynamic which led to the fundamental distinction that New Leftists came to draw between "liberal" and "radical."

Thus, however much certain of the original members and leaders of SDS wanted to maintain the liberal reformist or social democratic perspective, they had adopted a document whose language had radical implications that would be explored and elaborated whether they liked it or not. Furthermore, participatory democracy was just the kind of concept that would attract increasing numbers of young democratic radicals with decentralist values and libertarian instincts and an aversion to the ideological baggage of all left-wing debates, whether Marxist or anarchist. Participatory democracy offered a new and exciting way to talk about radical democratic ideas and in so doing it created the opportunity for the rebirth of a genuinely American radicalism. The very open-ended character of this new discourse was an invitation to creativity, but it was also the seedbed of ambivalence and honest confusion. It was possible for people with fundamentally different political perspectives to believe that participatory democracy spoke for their different viewpoints. As the New Left grew during the 1960s, these differences would become increasingly apparent and shift the direction of SDS.

CHAPTER 5

THE NEW STUDENT LEFT

And The Berkeley Rebellion

If Tom Hayden created a political language for the New Left at the University of Michigan in Ann Arbor, then students at UC Berkeley wrote much of the ensuing script for the student movement. Politically aware people were conscious of the awakening on campuses that had begun with southern student sit-ins in 1960 and had spread North and West through support activities. But no one was quite prepared for the explosive eruption of students as a political force with their own issues and demands which occurred at the University of California's Berkeley campus in the fall of 1964. From that point on, Berkeley became synonymous with "the student movement," and most of its strengths and weaknesses could be seen there in microcosm.

♦ Students Beyond the Campus

Since Port Huron, SDS had become a student organization in search of a constituency. The declarations concerning "The University and Social Change" had gone largely unimplemented as SDS searched outside the campus for a social base in the "real" world. Despite its theoretical insistence on the social and political importance of universities, SDS was still taking its cues from the black civil rights movement. The hold which the black movement had on the minds and political imaginations of student activists is demonstrated both by what happened to SDS in 1963 and what occurred at Berkeley in 1964.

Although SDS continued to organize students into local chapters on campuses, by 1963 SDS activists felt increasingly compelled to define an organizing strategy beyond the walls of academia. They felt the burning need to develop a strategy that would correspond to the increasing vitality and power of black organizers--particularly SNCC organizers--in the South. It was this need to respond politically to the black movement that led some SDSers to formulate a bold and courageous organizing strategy under the rubric of the Economic Research and Action Project.[1] ERAP became for SDS what labor organizing had been for the Old Left in the 1930s--outreach toward a potential social base. The central idea in the ERAP strategy was to create "an interracial movement of the poor."[2] Basically ERAP's formulators argued that SDS should build a movement among poor people in northern urban ghettoes that would act as an ally to the movement of poor southern blacks being created by the civil rights struggle. The alliance of the unorganized poor, South and North, would be the political base for catalyzing an even broader off-campus movement.

This strategy was strongly contested within SDS and attacked by critics on the Left outside of SDS. Within the organization, opponents came mainly from the New York social-democratic/ left-liberal wing of SDS who supported the strategy of realignment and whose perspective involved working within the Democratic Party and forming an alliance with progressive elements in organized labor.[3] They were joined in their opposition by critics outside of SDS like Michael Harrington, social democrat (or democratic socialist) from the Socialist Party, who attacked the ERAP organizers as "Narodniks" (a reference to Russian populists of the 19th century). The split between the ERAP wing of SDS and the social democrats was a reflection of a difference in outlook between the vision of democratic idealism and a kind of reformist or revisionist socialism. The democratic idealism of the ERAP organizers implied idealist values (whether spiritually explicit or not) and grassroots decentralist structures. This democratic idealism was never articulated as a coherent political philosophy but was expressed in a radical democratic belief in the ability of ordinary people to control their own lives if given access to the knowledge and resources to do so.

✦ ERAP and Democratic Idealism

The ERAP projects embodied, perhaps better than any other New Left undertaking, two fundamental aspects of SDS's democratic idealism: compassion and democratic faith. The decision to organize among poor people had little to do with sociological analysis and much to do with the caring hearts of young American idealists. Marxists might dismiss the poor as "lumpenproletariat" and deride these efforts as glorified social work, but New Leftists in ERAP projects were moved by convictions much deeper than those ordinarily surveyed by "value-free social science." Just as important as their sense of compassionate solidarity with affluent America's most forgotten and oppressed was their democratic faith that ordinary people, even the most downtrodden and deprived, could put participatory democracy into practice and "make the decisions that affect their lives." Furthermore, the ERAP organizers set out to prove it. It is perhaps no accident that the same person who would later articulate the New Left's first manifesto of Gay Liberation, Carl Wittman,[4] was also the person who was responsible for some of the clearest statements of ERAP's philosophy and goals.[5]

Ten organizing projects in Northern ghettoes were launched by ERAP in 1964. The most successful were in Chicago, Cleveland, and Newark. These projects involved small groups of SDS activists moving into poor neighborhoods, living among the poor, and attempting to build community organizations of poor people around issues that directly affected their lives--housing, welfare, jobs, health care. Some of the projects also involved experiments in communal living among the organizers.

Organizers! That was a key word in the new projects. It created a mystique. SDSers were no longer just student activists; they were now becoming *community organizers*. It sparked a new vision of what student radicals might do with their lives after college and, at the same time, it reinforced the decentralist and communitarian tendencies within SDS. "Let the People Decide" became a favorite ERAP slogan which expressed the sense of radical democratic values embodied in these experiments in community building from the bottom up. This was SDS at work creating grassroots participatory democracy. It was also a step in the creation of a group of full-time committed radicals who saw their futures and their survival tied to long-range political work and the success of the Movement.

ERAP had repercussions on both SDS and the student movement that were far more important than the success or failure of the individual projects. My first experiences of national SDS were weekend visits I made with groups of my students from Iowa State University to the Chicago ERAP project called JOIN Community Union. The dedication of its organizers to work among the poor reminded me of the Worker Priest movement in France and formed some of my most important impressions of the meaning of "the Movement." Community organizing gave the student movement a sense of relatedness to the outside world and a chance to test its notions of participatory democracy in the larger society. But it also raised questions about the wisdom and effectiveness of student radicals trying to act as agents of change in a milieu drastically different from their own backgrounds. ERAP organizers felt they had to become something other than who they were--to live and become like poor people--in order to gain acceptance and achieve credibility. In this process they risked engaging in self-denial and even self-flagellation. What is more, they broke their ties with the student movement on campuses and, in some cases, began to view the student movement as unimportant or lacking substance. Poor people were being endowed with a mystique of authenticity while students were seen as "middle-class," even "sell-outs." This did not create a healthy relationship between the student movement and off-campus organizing but rather the opposite--a dynamic of self-denial and recrimination. ERAP projects moved further and further from SDS and eventually separated from the organization.[6]

The tendency of the civil rights movement to draw students away from campuses was also manifest in another arena--the South itself. SNCC organizers had begun to engage in voter registration projects in the fall of 1961 in Mississippi, and SNCC had, in fact, provided the model for students leaving the university to work full-time in communities. The SNCC experience had had an important influence on the formation of ERAP. But, in 1964, a new kind of involvement was to change the face of both the southern civil rights movement and the northern student movement.

In late 1963, Bob Moses of SNCC proposed a summer voter registration drive that would bring hundreds of northern white college students into the heart of the segregationist South. The strategy was simple: since the federal government would not provide protection for black organizers in the South, the presence of large numbers of white college students and the inevitable violence against them would force the federal government to intervene. Clayborne Carson described the dilemma succinctly:

> Despite their increasing suspicions about the motives of the Kennedy administration, most SNCC workers agreed that federal intervention was needed to overcome segregationist resistance in the deep South. . . . The Mississippi Summer Project was designed to force a confrontation between state and federal authorities and thereby to prevent the intimidation and violence that had stymied previous civil rights work in Mississippi.[7]

At first, some SNCC organizers were opposed to the Mississippi Summer Project. Their own organizing work in some of the toughest Southern communities had taught them the necessity of decentralized structure and local control. "Participatory democracy" was for them a matter of survival.[8] At the same time, they had grown increasingly mistrustful of Martin Luther King, Jr., whose centralized organization and charismatic leadership model were seen as destructive of long-term grassroots organizing. They were justifiably concerned that the influx of large numbers of inexperienced white college students on a short-term basis, would destroy the careful organizing work they had done in local communities. They felt that reliance on dramatic "campaigns," like those that SCLC had waged, often raised hopes and sometimes produced short-term results, but failed to lay the groundwork that would sustain a long-term movement. Many SNCC workers were also concerned that the influx of large numbers of white students would stifle the development of local black leadership.[9]

The Summer of 1964 project produced some startling results and some painful tragedies. The deaths of three young men in Mississippi, at the hands of white racists from the KKK, stunned the nation and seared the consciences of many northern middle-class liberals.[10] But the Freedom Summer also had unanticipated consequences for the student movement on northern campuses. Returning student volunteers from the South brought a heightened political awareness and a new spirit of assertiveness back to their campuses which helped to spark the Berkeley student revolt and a new chapter in the student movement as a whole.

◆ *Clark Kerr and the Multiversity*

Perhaps institutional change only becomes *politically* significant when it can be captured in a name. The term "capitalism" had been used before Karl Marx's time, but only he gave the word the significance that would make it a key concept in the socialist movement for more than a century. Profound changes in the structure of higher education in America had been proceeding ever since the end of the Second World War, but it was only when Clark Kerr codified this transformation in the term "multiversity" that the new student movement had a name for its institutional enemy.

Clark Kerr, President of the University of California at Berkeley, was invited to give the prestigious Godkin Lectures at Harvard University in 1963. He chose as his topic, *The Uses of the University*.[11] Kerr's analysis of what he called "the multiversity" was incisive and prophetic. He described the vast changes that had taken place in American higher education and foresaw a student revolt. It is no accident that his background as an expert in labor and industrial relations had led him into the job of chief administrator of the largest university in the most dynamic system of higher education in the world--the Berkeley campus of the University of California system. Nor is it surprising, given this background, that Kerr's primary metaphor for understanding the nature of this new type of institution would be drawn from industry: he called it "the knowledge factory." In his "Foreword" to the published version of the Godkin lectures, Kerr wrote, regarding the "new role" of the university:

> The basic reality, for the university, is the wide-spread recognition that new knowledge is the most important factor in economics and social growth. We are just now perceiving that the university's invisible product, knowledge, may be the most powerful single element in our culture, affecting the rise and fall of professions and even of social classes, of regions and even of nations. (v-vi)

Kerr went on to portray the close relationship between this central economic and social role in knowledge production and the changes in the U.S. university in the post-war world:

> The university is being called upon to educate previously unimagined numbers of students; to respond to the expanding claims of national service; to merge its activities with industry as never before; to adapt to and rechannel new intellectual currents. By the end of this period, there will be a truly American university, an institution unique in world history, an institution not looking to other models but serving, itself, as a model for universities in other parts of the globe. (86-87)

Kerr saw three historical strands in the development of American universities up through the 1930s--the humanistic, the scientific, and the professional--which have specific roots in the British, German, and American traditions of higher education. This had produced an odd amalgam:

> The resulting combination does not seem plausible but it has given America a remarkably effective education institution. A university anywhere can aim no higher than to be as British as possible for the sake of the undergraduates, as German as possible for the graduates and the research personnel, as American as possible for the sake of the public at large--and as confused as possible for the sake of the preservation of the whole uneasy balance. (17-18)

Kerr called this "unlikely compromise" the "multiversity" and he was explicit about its fragmented nature.

> The multiversity is an inconsistent institution. It is not one community but several--the community of the undergraduate and the community of the graduate; the community of the humanist, the community of the social scientist, and the community of the scientist; the communities of the professional schools; the community of all the

nonacademic personnel; the community of the administrators. Its edges are fuzzy--it reaches out to alumni, legislators, farmers, businessmen, who are all related to one of these internal communities. (18-19)

This multiplicity of communities produces an institution without a single animating principle and with a contradictory relationship to society at large, according to Kerr.

> It serves society almost slavishly--a society it also criticizes, sometimes unmercifully. Devoted to equality of opportunity, it is itself a class society. A community, like the medieval community of masters and students, should have common interests; in the multiversity they are quite varied, even conflicting. A community should have a soul, a single animating principle; the multiversity has several--some of them quite good, although there is much debate on which souls really deserve salvation. (19)

This complexity and inorganic diversity pose a problem of governance. The "city state of the multiversity," as Kerr called it, "may be inconsistent but it must be governed--not as the guild it once was, but as a complex entity with greatly fractionalized power." (20) The "competitors for this power" are the students, the faculty, public authority, "influences--external and semi-external," and the administration. Atop this unwieldy machine sits the university president, no longer the "giant" his predecessors once might have been but now "mostly a mediator." (36) The passing of the "giants" of the past is not mourned by Kerr so much as accepted--as a given in the general drift of society. "Instead of the not always so agreeable autocracy," he wrote, "there is now the usually benevolent bureaucracy, as in so much of the rest of the world." (33) In order for the institution to operate effectively, the "president must police its use by the constituent groups." But, danger lurks, according Kerr: "When extremists get in control of the students, the faculty, or the trustees with class warfare concepts, then the 'delicate balance of interests' becomes an actual war." (39)

The growth of the research focus has furthered the fractionalization of intellectual life in the multiversity. Professors are no longer part of a community of scholars. In fact, their primary identification is no longer with the institution in which they work.

"Faculty members are less members of the particular university and more colleagues within their national academic discipline groups." The new academic "may even become, as some have, essentially a professional man with his home office and basic retainer on the campus of the multiversity but with his clients scattered from coast to coast." (44)

This development is fueled primarily by two outside influences: the federal government and private industry. The first of these created "the federal grant university" which "responded to the massive impact of federal programs beginning with World War II." These programs (basically war-related contracts) produced a "vast transformation . . . without a revolution" in the course of which the "multiversity demonstrated how adaptive it can be to new opportunities for creativity; how responsive to money; how eagerly it can play a new and useful role; how fast it can change while pretending that nothing has happened at all; how fast it can neglect some of its ancient virtues." (45)

The second great transformative influence involves the imperative for the university "to merge its activities with industry as never before." Economic growth is now tied to education. "It has been estimated," Kerr writes, "that over the last thirty years nearly half our national growth can be explained by the greater education of our people and by better technology, which is also largely a product of the educational system." The "university has become a prime instrument of national purpose. . . ." and this is "the essence of the transformation now engulfing our universities." (87)

At the heart of this transformation is what Kerr calls the "knowledge industry . . . which is coming to permeate government and business and to draw into it more and more people raised to higher and higher levels of skill." (87) Kerr cites a study which contends that "29 percent of gross national product" is accounted for by the "production, distribution and consumption of 'knowledge' in all its forms." (88) Furthermore:

> Knowledge has certainly never in history been so central to the conduct of an entire society. What the railroads did for the second half of the last century and the automobile for the first half of this century may be done for the second half of this century by the knowledge industry: that is to serve as the focal point for national growth. And the university is at the center of the knowledge process. (88)

Kerr's statement about knowledge and society is curiously twisted. In fact, knowledge "in all its forms" has been central to the conduct of all societies and most important of all have been political and spiritual knowledge (for better and for worse). What Kerr has done is to equate knowledge solely with modern science and technology and their specific applications to the production processes of advanced technological societies. Given the centrality of technology in this transformation and the key role higher education had assumed in the development of technocracy, Kerr might well have called this institution the "*technoversity.*" It is the ties between the multiversity, industry, and the highly militarized state apparatus that make the "knowledge industry" so important. Kerr illustrates this linkage by arguing:

> An almost ideal location for a modern university is to be sandwiched between a middle-class district on its way to becoming a slum and an ultramodern industrial park--so that the students may live in one and the faculty consult in the other. M.I.T. finds itself happily ensconced between the decaying sections of Cambridge and Technology Square. (89)

This marriage of the multiversity and industry produces a new configuration of industrial development. "Universities have become 'bait' to be dangled in front of industry with drawing power greater than low taxes or cheap labor." Kerr cites "Route 128 around Boston" as a prime example of this development as well as "the great developing industrial complexes in the San Francisco Bay Area and Southern California" and "Sterling Forest outside New York City." The proof of the pudding lies in the fact that

> 41 percent of defense contracts for research in the fiscal year 1961 were concentrated in California, 12 percent in New York, and 6 percent in Massachusetts, for a total of nearly 60 percent, in part because these were also "centers of learning." (89)

Kerr is unwilling to write the equation *knowledge industry = multiversity + defense contracts*, but he is unstinting in his determination to show how this new industrial-educational-technological combine works. And it works best, of course, in sunny California where, Kerr announces, "*new industrial labora-*

tories were located next to two new university campuses before the first building was built on either of these campuses." (89) [My emphasis.]

The marriage of industry and multiversity is consummated in a variety of ways. "Sometimes," Kerr tells us, "industry will reach into a university laboratory to extract the newest ideas almost before they are born. Instead of waiting outside the gates, agents are working the corridors. They also work the placement offices." (89-90) But the courtship is pursued in both directions, for "the university, in turn, reaches into industry, as through the Stanford Research Institute." (90) This has vast consequences on the configuration of economic development. "The new connection of the university with the rise and fall of industrial areas has brought about an inter-university and interregional competition. . . . A vast campaign is on to see that the university center of each industrial complex shall not be 'second best'." (90)

The marriage also involves a merging of industrial and academic styles:

> The university and segments of industry are becoming more alike. As the university becomes tied into the world of work, the professor--at least in the natural and some of the social sciences--takes on the characteristics of an entrepreneur. Industry, with its scientists and technicians, learns an uncomfortable bit about academic freedom and the handling of intellectual personnel. The two worlds are merging physically and psychologically." (90-91)

New agglomerations of multiversities and industrial parks are being created that form great complexes of talent and power. "These clustering universities . . . have clustering around them scientifically oriented industrial and governmental enterprises. To match the drawing power of the great metropolis, there now arrives the new Ideopolis." (93)

This pattern of development is not, to be sure, the only possible one. "France and Russia," Kerr points out, "have not made their universities so central to the life of society. They have segregated their research institutes to a substantial degree and established separate institutions for much of their technical training." However, Kerr thinks that this alternative is "not as productive." (93) To be sure, "these national, industrial, and academic pulls" on universities have compromised the traditional

City of Intellect which stood somewhat apart. But, such a separation is no longer possible, and "the 'City of Intellect' of the modern university . . . must look outward and to reality; it cannot be 'a company apart'." (93-94)

The transformation that has created the multiversity has wrought great changes in the lives of both students and faculty. For the student, the "multiversity is a confusing place. . . . He has problems of establishing his identity and sense of security" amidst "a vast range of choices, enough literally to stagger the mind. . . . The casualty rate is high." (42)

Equally important is the change in the circumstances of faculty life since the "multiversity is in the mainstream of events." New faces abound. "To the teacher and the researcher have been added the consultant and the administrator." And then Kerr adds, *inter alia*, what was to become the crux of contention:

> Teaching is less central than it once was for most faculty members; research has become more important. . . . In one university I know, the proportions at the Ph.D. level or its equivalent are roughly one researcher to two teachers to four who do both. (42)

In this veritable revolution, the faculty "seems to sense a loss of unity--intellectual and communal unity" as they are pulled from their traditional tasks. Faculty members "are increasingly figures in a 'lonely crowd,' intellectually and institutionally" and Kerr feels it is "a sad commentary of the 'community of masters' when its elements come together in interchange only when they coalesce feverishly over a grievance about some episode related to a change of the calendar or a parking fee." (101) Alumni too are troubled by the transformation, which throws into sharp contrast their memories of "the spirit of the 'halls of ivy' as against the technological materialism of the federal grant university." (103)

No group has suffered as much from these changes as the undergraduates. And it is in the description of their plight that Clark Kerr proved to be most painfully prophetic.

> If the alumni are concerned, the undergraduate students are restless. Recent changes in the American university have done them little good--lower teaching loads for the faculty, larger classes, the use of substitute teachers for the regular faculty, the choice of faculty

members based on research accomplishments rather than instructional capacity, the fragmentation of knowledge into endless subdivisions. *There is an incipient revolt against the faculty; the revolt that used to be against the faculty* in loco parentis *is now against the faculty* in absentia. (103) [My emphasis.]

Kerr's failure lay, of course, in believing that the students would turn their discontent solely against their professors and miss the real centers of power and decision-making. Perhaps his experience in industrial relations had convinced him that American workers would always fail to attack the real causes of their misery. In any case, he did seem to realize that students were coming to experience themselves somewhat like disenfranchised workers. In a remarkable passage, he wrote:

If the faculty looks on itself as a guild, the undergraduate students are coming to look upon themselves more as a 'class'; some may even feel like a 'lumpen proletariat.' Lack of faculty concern for teaching, endless rules and requirements, and impersonality are the inciting causes. A few of the 'nonconformists' have another kind of revolt in mind. They seek, instead, to turn the university, on the Latin American or Japanese models, into a fortress from which they can sally forth with impunity to make their attacks on society. (103-104)

It is at this point that Kerr reveals the true limits of the managerial mind; for his prophetic vision seems myopic when compared to the real events that would unfold in the pathways and plazas of the multiversity. "If federal grants for research brought a major revolution," he wrote "then the resultant student sense of neglect may bring a minor counterrevolt, although the target of the revolt is a most elusive one." (104)

♦ Students As Citizens

The conditions that Clark Kerr described as characteristic of the new multiversity were only part of what motivated the student rebellion beginning in the fall of 1964. Regarding the purposes of higher education, Kerr had argued in his Godkin Lectures that the "ends are already given--the preservation of the eternal truths, the creation of new knowledge, the improvement of service wherever truth and knowledge of high order may serve the needs of man."

He underlined the point by adding: "The ends are these; the
means must be ever improved in a competitive dynamic environment."(43) But Kerr had missed the mark; for everything else in
his message demonstrated that the "ends" were not "there" but
increasingly elsewhere--not in the university itself but in government defense contracts and industrial research parks and giant
corporations. The university was being reshaped by ends that had
nothing to do with "the preservation of eternal truths" and
everything to do with the proliferation of power and profit. The
ends of the multiversity were not grounded in a concern with how
"truth and knowledge of high order may serve the needs of man"
but were based on the power drives of an increasingly militarized
federal government and the profit margins of the corporations.
The multiversity was an institution increasingly subordinate to the
ends of the imperial state and corporate capital. Kerr's own
analysis made this apparent in somewhat more elusive language. It
is characteristic of the instrumental rationality employed by liberal
technocrats like Kerr to obscure the issue of "ends" by confusing
ends and means. At one level, the student rebellion of the 1960s
was one vast effort at cutting through the veil of liberal
technocratic obfuscation in order to clarify the question of "ends."

This effort at deobfuscation erupted at Berkeley in the fall of
1964 over an alternative set of ends or goals that student activists
espoused. These ends involved the relationship of students to the
larger political society--their role as citizens. Berkeley students
had been active in their support of the black civil rights movement
since the beginning of the decade. And even before that they had
spearheaded a major campaign for political rights in their efforts
to abolish HUAC--the House Un-American Activities Committee.
Their long history of activism had made them one of the most
sophisticated political communities in the country. In many ways,
the Bay Area was displacing New York City as the center of
American radicalism. Both on and off the campus--in both
Berkeley and San Francisco--there were large communities that
nurtured radical politics and an experimental counter culture.
Bohemians, beatniks, and political radicals thrived in an atmosphere that was relatively free of the stifling sectarianism which
permeated the left-wing milieu of New York. It seemed, at least
for a time, a more open atmosphere in which a New Left might
flourish on its own terms. This is not to suggest that Berkeley did

not have a significant number of sectarian leftists. It did. But still
it was possible to have meetings which were largely made up of
new people with fresh ideas. In New York, by contrast, every
political gathering tended to be overwhelmed by representatives of
the remnants of Old Left factions, and every debate to degenerate
into a vituperative sectarian squabble.

It was in the Bay Area that the effects of a mass movement of
student citizenry were first felt. And the "minor counterrevolt"
which Clark Kerr had anticipated turned into a major uprising
with catalytic effects that swept across the nation.

✦ After Clark Kerr

It seems almost too simplistic to say that after Clark Kerr's
brilliant liberal technocratic analysis the student movement never
knew who or what it was. It might be more precise to say that it
was never able to improve sufficiently on his analysis to validate
itself on its own terms--self-validation being in the currency of this
"new age" the equivalent of "self-empowerment." It may be the
final truism of sociological insight that, as long as a group does
not know who or what it is, it is incapable of acting on behalf of
itself or anyone else in a meaningful way. Marxist and other
revolutionary ideologies have been struggling with attempts to
comprehend or dismiss this issue for most of a century, arguing
that a social group can be "objectively" revolutionary or radical
without "subjectively" fulfilling its historical role. The group in
question is said to have "false consciousness." This odd proposition seems to follow from the rather mechanical Marxist
assumption that politics are strictly determined by social-economic
conditions. If consciousness does not conform to the theory, then
it must be explained away.

In any case, it is somewhere in the vicinity of the Berkeley
campus revolt in the fall of 1964 that the question of political
identity began to cloud the mind of the New Left. And the New
Left seems never to have recovered despite its repeated attempts
to situate the student movement in an historical context that
would lead to a viable political strategy. The flailing about and the
confusion of identity that ran through the succeeding years of the
student movement were grounded in large part in this inability of

students to find a clear political strategy for dealing with the fundamental fact that their teachers were prostitutes of power and that they were betrayed day-by-day, inch-by-inch. Frustration turned to hatred and threatened to arouse the most self-destructive impulses. Finding a path of sanity out of this morass of betrayal was an almost impossible task. In the end, a leading segment of the student movement took the suicidal route and blamed themselves in an orgy of self-hatred, naming their suffering "White Skin Privilege."[12] The inner demons of guilt and masochism won out. But, for a time, there were more intelligent attempts to fight the sickness and heal wounds.

One such attempt to externalize the threat of self-hatred was a pamphlet by Jerry Farber called "The Student As Nigger."[13] It is easy to revile this polemic as a pathetic fallacy by analogy and in so doing fail to grasp the inner necessity which drove the argument to such extremes. But there was a reason for making the analogy between students and "niggers"--it lay in a confused attempt to create a common sense of identity and a sense of common oppression between disaffected groups who needed to support each other and to understand the meaningful integrity of each others' pain and confusion. Students and black people were the largest and most cohesive social groups involved in political rebellion in the 1960s and their political destinies had been linked ever since the first student sit-ins in Greensboro, North Carolina, in 1960 that gave birth to SNCC.

It is, however, true that the "student as nigger" thesis could not bridge the gap between the experience of students in the multiversity and of black people in segregated America. The resort to the analogy is indicative of how difficult it was to find a meaningful mode of self-definition for students.

◆ Alternative Suppositions

The search for alternative approaches to higher education began to activate the renewal of utopian and anarchist thought within the New Left in this period. At almost the same time that Clark Kerr was delivering his proclamation on the inevitable sell-out of the multiversity to the demands of corporate capitalism, a uniquely American anarchist writer, Paul Goodman, was presenting a visionary alternative for American higher education in a long essay called "The Community of Scholars."[14] Goodman made a libertarian and decentralist argument for the possibility of radically different options in the face of a seemingly predetermined future. His outlook was based on models of learning and community derived from an alternative interpretation of the past.

Goodman's interpretation grows in part from the historical work of Peter Kropotkin, the Russian Anarchist.[15] Kropotkin challenged the world-view constructed by both liberal and Marxist analysis that bourgeois capitalism, its science, technology and centralization, represents a "progressive" advance in human development. Both Marxism and liberalism see the development of capitalist industrialism and the modern state as "advances" over more "primitive" forms of social structure. Goodman's argument is a re-take of Kropotkin's conviction that not only capitalism but also the development of the state had subverted the basic decentralist and communitarian potential of the early revolts against capitalism in the 11th and 12th centuries. Kropotkin and others, like Goodman after them, were arguing that there existed a variety of realistic alternatives to the centralist models of the historical development of liberal capitalism and the Marxist model of "a state socialist future."

Goodman served as one of the editors of *Liberation* magazine[16] and was an important writer and activist in the radical pacifist movement. "An outspoken advocate of individual and sexual freedom," Goodman left his mark as a "writer, teacher, poet, and social critic." His "message was not so much ideology as a challenge to celebrate life and love, and to reject the American norms of military violence, sexual conformity, and racial hatred."[17] Perhaps his most influential work was *Growing Up Absurd*,[18] published in 1960 and one of the seminal works of the sixties Movement. Goodman was gay, married, and the father of three children. In an effort to clear up the ambiguity about the bisexual aspects of his history, he later simply described himself as "queer"--thus defying the efforts of political identity movements to make rigid labels the hallmark of radical political respectability. He called himself a "conservative anarchist" and argued: "In a society that is cluttered, overcentralized, and over-administered, we should aim at simplification, decentralization, and decontrol."

In his novel, *Making Do*,[19] he detailed what seemed a semi-autobiographical account of a love affair between an older male teacher and a young male student. His advocacy of the goodness of homosexual relationships extended into the realm of education. "As an erotic drive," he wrote, "teaching seems to be a projection of one's own ego ideal, seen as more possible in the young than in oneself; therefore it would tend to be homosexual, in both sexes; but in our culture, of course, not very physical, especially among the males."[20] When the Vietnam War became a major issue, he was a champion of draft resistance and one of the supporters of "A Call to Resist Illegitimate Authority," a manifesto of support for draft resistance from a large group of American intellectuals.[21] In the latter part of the 1960s, when the emerging gay liberation movement sought his support, he published an exploration of his homosexuality in *Win* magazine. He wrote:

> In essential ways my homosexual needs have made me a nigger. . . .
> In general, in America, being a queer nigger is economically and professionally less disadvantageous than being a black nigger, except for a few areas like government service, where there is considerable fear and furtiveness.

He went on to say, "My actual political attitude is a willed reaction-formation to being a nigger."[22]

Because of his anarchist ideas, and perhaps because of his Jewish background, Goodman, like the gay poet Allen Ginsberg, was a particularly troublesome figure for the largely Jewish, Marxist, and homophobic Old Left in New York. Like Ginsberg, he was able to transcend this provincial New York background and speak to the hearts of American youth across the nation. His influence on the New Left was enormous. As one former National President of SDS wrote in 1972 when Goodman died prematurely of a heart attack:

> Jewish Yankee
> citizen of a nation not yet born,
> . . . .
> Corrupter of youth, city's peripatetic,
> grim lover

tilting at office buildings,
cranky uncle who never approved

and had to be consulted,
who helped me grow up

a little less absurd.
It will not be a matter of disciples

more the original meaning of "gone to seed"
for the man who walked alone

dourly whistling a song I can't get out of my mind
even after he has vanished around the corner.

Todd Gitlin,
"Homage to Paul Goodman."[23]

On the issues of decentralization, sexual liberation, anti-militarism, and the freedom of human beings to explore new social options in a non-authoritarian mode, probably no one spoke more directly to the concerns of the new activist generation of the 1960s than Paul Goodman. He anticipated, in his life and writings, many of the fundamental concerns that still preoccupy America. There is little doubt that his deep involvement, both as client and lay therapist (and, finally as theorist)[24] in the rise of Gestalt therapy had a profound effect on his thinking and way of being. Goodman argued that Gestalt therapy was the most important development in Western psychology since Plato.

In the field of education, Goodman had a crucial impact. He added his own insights to the pioneering work of people like A. S. Neill, whose experiment in non-authoritarian education in England became widely known through his book *Summerhill*.[25] Goodman's ideas had enormous influence on the widespread experimentation with "free schools" in the 1960s and later. It is here, in the field of alternative education, that the term "libertarian" found one of its most genuine expressions in practice, not in the sense that pro-capitalist, laissez-faire advocates now use it, but in the more traditional left-libertarian meaning that Kropotkin intended when he wrote:

Throughout the history of our civilization, two traditions, two opposing tendencies have confronted each other: the Roman and the popular traditions; the imperial and the federalist; the authoritarian and the libertarian.[26]

It is important to note that Goodman did not advocate a simplistic anti-authoritarianism; he was not an opponent of all forms of authority and distinguished between legitimate and illegitimate, rational and irrational forms of authority. In this he appeared to differ from those tendencies in the anarchist tradition which were based on a blanket rejection of all authority, as seems to have been the case with Kropotkin and the Russian anarchist movement.

Goodman described himself as a "Jeffersonian anarchist" and it is difficult to extract from his writings a clear vision of the future. This was, perhaps, the source of Goodman's true strength as a social critic. One writer has described him as a "pragmatic utopian,"[27] a label that captures both the visionary and the earthy side of Goodman's thought, which created his unique appeal to youthful dissidents.

Goodman was by no means a slavish admirer of the young although he was their advocate. Of the "Youth Subculture," he wrote,

> In my opinion, this subculture is constructed by the active community of youth *against* the adults. It is a substitute to fill the soul. Its rudimentary contents, cars, games, sex, simple music, being popular, are things that are spontaneously attractive to adolescents, but they do not go far. Its motivation and style, however, are both against the adults and inevitably imitative of them. There is plenty of spiting, rebelling, and delinquent reaction-formation. But in cultural format and economic style, the youth culture is only an absurd imitation of an absurd adult culture; the youth craving for popularity is only a pathetic imitation of a bathetic adult sociality and craving for celebrity; and the youth sexuality is as bad as the grownups'. The tone of the whole is not improved, either, when the adults in turn imitate the youth. That is, there is nothing authentic in the youth subculture except its youthful vitality, its disappointment in being cut off from the adult world, and its spite against the adults' demands. Meantime, waiting and in the background, is the real world of the Organized System to which most of the youngsters will inevitably conform.[28]

In the field of higher education, Goodman's view was that universities had been constituted in the Middle Ages as self-governing "communities of scholars" and that the ideal solution to their problems was to reconstitute those communities. His position was the reaction of decentralist radicalism against precisely those developments that Clark Kerr described and accepted as inevitable. Goodman regarded the destruction of the "community of scholars" as a disaster for "teaching-and-learning" which he argued should be the central purpose of colleges or universities. He did not regard "bigness" as inevitable, but as inevitably destructive of a truly educative community and he tended to focus on the proliferation of administrative bureaucracy as a primary culprit in the subversion of higher education. He wrote that:

> It is iterated and reiterated that these factory-like and businesslike ways are inevitable under the modern conditions with which administration must cope. . . . Maybe. The fact remains that the administrators engage in a tooth-and-nail competition to aggrandize their institutions and produce these very conditions. *They* are among the major forces.[29]

Goodman stood clearly against everything that Clark Kerr and his myriad counterparts stood for. In this regard, Goodman was able to articulate the radical discontent of a whole generation of American students and, in a sense, to help legitimate the incipient student revolt.

He stated his outlook plainly:

> My argument . . . is a simple one. The colleges and universities are, as they have always been, self-governing communities. But the personal relations in such communities have come less and less to consist in growing up, in the meeting of veterans and students, in teaching and learning, and more and more in every kind of communication, policing, regulation, and motivation that is relevant to administration. The community of scholars is replaced by a community of administrators and scholars with administrative mentalities, company men and time-servers among the teachers, grade-seekers and time-servers among the students. And this new community mans a machine that, incidentally, turns out educational products.[30]

Paul Goodman's strategy for reforming the university can be summed up in one word: *secession.* He proposed that small groups of teacher secede from existing universities and establish colleges, perhaps near such institutions, and make them models of teaching-and-learning, restored communities of scholars. "The principles of college reform," he wrote, "are clear-cut: to get back to teaching-and-learning as a simple relation of persons, and to make the teaching-and-learning more committed, more for keeps."[31]

He felt strongly that part of the faculty of such new institutions should be made up of "veterans" of "real life" experience outside the academic world. "For the sake of *both* the university and the professions," he argued, "the professions must return and assume responsibility for the history and humanity of their arts by taking real places again on the faculty of the university." Despite the fact that "[r]esponsible teaching of the young is always teaching of the more ideal" and that "narrow practical teaching" is "too boring," he contended that "only real practice is believable and authoritative." "The university must," he said, "incorporate veterans so the teaching-and-learning can be for keeps." Goodman's secessionist colleges would not only include "veterans who have retired to it" but also "people who have a special calling for teaching." Furthermore, he felt too much emphasis was placed on the reform of curriculum. "The crucial question" in Goodman's judgment "is not what ought to be taught, but whether the teaching-and-learning makes any difference. Is it committed or merely 'academic'?" He believed that "the academic question is the following: how to teach what is practical and yet not make the university a trade school."[32]

Goodman's proposal really amounted to a strategy of "parallel institutions," a notion that was widely advanced by the more "decentralist" or "libertarian" elements of the New Left. It amounted to the creation of new and experimental institutions alongside the old with the conviction that change could be generated by creative example. Goodman's colleges as communities of scholars would have had ten teachers and 120-150 students in classes of 12 to 15. They would also, of course, have been self-governing, and by excluding administration, cheaper. He said he was proposing

> simply to take teaching and learning in its own terms, for the students and teachers to associate in the traditional way and according to their existing interest, but *entirely dispensing with the external control, administration, bureaucratic machinery, and other excrescences that have swamped out communities of scholars*.[33]

Goodman's vital contribution raises the question of the extent to which his "anarchism" was part of the New Left. He was one of the few writers of the period to specifically identify himself as "anarchist," a label despised by the Marxist social democratic wing of SDS and generally ill-defined within the American radical movement. Although Paul Goodman was often a critic of the New Left, his life and work became an integral part of the larger sixties Movement. The ideas for which he stood and which he helped to elaborate were certainly comprehensible within the vision of "participatory democracy"--and, furthermore, they helped to open the debate about what decentralist democratic ideals might imply for the future of the New Left. His attempts to relate the questions of "libertarian leftism" to issues of sexual liberation coincided with the cultural demands of the "Beat Generation" and the emerging "counter culture" even though he had many differences with that wing of the Movement.

My analytic impulse since the 1960s has been to make a distinction between "centralist" and "democratic decentralist" thought and to avoid the use of the terms "anarchism" or "libertarian socialism" unless they are accompanied by explicit definitions--although my politics are clearly rooted in the left-libertarian tradition, in the anarcho-syndicalist vision of democratic community and workers' control, and in anarchist opposition to the centralized, militarized, and bureaucratic modern state. This impulse is born of a conviction that a simple reversion to 19th century oppositions between "Marxism" and "Anarchism" will not further the political project launched by Tom Hayden in the first half of the *Port Huron Statement.* I still believe, as I think Tom Hayden did in 1962, that we need a new language and approach to political theory. And, I believe that such a discourse lies in the area of "democratic idealism" and what I have sometimes called "democratic decentralism"--a specifically decentralist version of "participatory democracy" based on spiritual values and idealist principles.

If the tone of the New Left changed during the Berkeley rebellion, if it became more acrid and vituperative, certainly part of the problem lay in the nature of academia and its supposed ruling body, the Faculty Senate. Never had so many adolescents been raised to the status of elders in a community without ever having passed through the realities of adulthood. Here in the multiversity were thousands of young students, graduates or undergraduates, being subjected to the guidance of men and women who had never really graduated from school. University faculties are replete with the ranks of professors drawn from a self-perpetuating process of perpetual immaturity. They are largely elder boys and girls teaching youthful boys and girls how to cope with a world that demands the talents and capabilities of mature men and women. It is little wonder that so few grow up in a university. There are so few grown-ups present to offer adult role models or a modicum of wisdom about how such a maturation process might take place.

The philosophy of this practice of infantilization was embodied in the credo known as *in loco parentis.* It might have better been called: *in lack of adulthood.* Higher education in America had became a further extension of the process Paul Goodman had named "growing up absurd."

◆ *Students As Students*

It was two years before SDS developed an adequate response to the Berkeley student revolt and its implications. SDS was not strong at UC Berkeley, and the FSM (Free Speech Movement) remained for most of the period 1964-66 the vehicle of the student movement and the forum for student radicalism on that campus. Elsewhere in the country, SDS became the primary bearer and beneficiary of the new phase of student activism that the Berkeley students had sparked.

Basic to the problems facing students across the country was the search for a definition of who they were in terms of the larger "Movement" throughout the society. The Berkeley rebellion had begun around the issues of free speech and the civil and political rights of students. But, it was linked directly to student involvement in support for the black civil rights movement. No one can question the connection of the Mississippi Freedom Summer of 1964 and the outbreak at Berkeley of the Free Speech Movement in the fall of that year.

Thus the FSM, although an expression of students' demands for their own rights, was born, in part, of political consciousness derived from the struggle for *other people's* rights. Herein lay the crux of a conflict that would plague the new student movement throughout the rest of the 1960s and be a major factor in its splintering and demise. The conflict was between two opposing viewpoints. The one saw students as the privileged ally of other people's struggles, a view which both denied the oppression of students as such and yet might well accord them a special leadership role as members of the "intelligentsia." The opposing view saw the majority of students in the multiversity as a new phenomenon born of the radical changes in American higher education and granted legitimacy to students-as-such as a particular constituency in the larger Movement. This second viewpoint even attributed a special relevance to the new student movement and its demands because students were involved at the cutting edge of the social transformations created by advanced technological society.

The first radical formulation of the new analysis of the student movement came in the form of a brief but major position paper prepared for the SDS National Convention in August of 1966 at Clear Lake, Iowa. Its author was Carl Davidson, a graduate teaching assistant at the University of Nebraska, soon to be elected (at Clear Lake) to the post of Vice-President of SDS with special responsibility for internal education. Davidson's paper was entitled "Toward a Student Syndicalist Movement, or University Reform Revisited."[34]

◆ *Carl Davidson and Student Syndicalism*

At this point in his career, I think it is safe to say that Carl Davidson was a new breed of anarcho-syndicalist. Born into a social stratum one rung above the industrial working class (his father was a gas station owner and mechanic in Aliquippa, Pennsylvania), Davidson epitomized an inner struggle for identity that was at the heart of the student movement. If one was not a member of the proletariat and yet was also not a member of the (petite or grande) bourgeoisie, then how did one identify oneself socially and politically? It was this inner tension, the product of his social background, which made Davidson the perfect person to bring a new point of view to the analysis of the student movement.

His special gifts and his training as a student of philosophy gave him the ability to formulate a series of documents that would begin to outline a new version of decentralist politics in SDS.

Davidson was an early cultural rebel. "I date my political awakening," he writes, "to Elvis Presley, James Dean, jazz music and rock and roll." He goes on to say:

> My dad and I had bitter fights over whether I could play that "nigger, jiggaboo" music in the house and whether I could have long hair like the "dagoes and wops." In fighting his authoritarian horseshit, I became more drawn to the beat and rebellious subculture. In 1959 I first read On The Road and Howl, lent to me by a guy in an Aliquippa pool hall, a real working-class beat, also my first contact with reefer. From there, it was an easy step to hanging out with the civil rights and peacenik crowd once I wound up at the university.[35]

Davidson made clear his identification with the historical tradition of anarcho-syndicalism in the United States by joining the small remnant of the IWW, which still had a small national office in Chicago. He carried the "Little Red Book" of the Wobblies with him on organizing tours and his favorite slogan was (and Davidson loved slogans) "Don't Mourn! Organize!"--the defiant words of the IWW poet and organizer, Joe Hill, as he faced the firing squad in Utah. His bushy mustache and scruffy clothes gave Davidson the appearance of a young Wobbly organizer from the nineteen-teens. "Actually," he writes, "Steve Weisman from FSM visited me at Penn State in 1965 and turned me on to syndicalism and the IWW. I declared myself an anarcho-syndicalist at Nebraska and tried to implement some of the ideas there in our Campus Freedom Democratic Party, which, obviously, also drew from Fannie Lou Hamer."[36]

Davidson's paper reflected a fundamental ambivalence towards the student movement. On the one hand, there was a positive assessment of organizing students as students on a radical decentralist "syndicalist" platform. On the other hand, there was a fairly negative evaluation of student roles both in the "knowledge factories" and in the larger society after graduation.

Davidson reviewed the failure of SDS, and students in general, to sustain a long-range movement for "university reform." He gave a brief summary of the radical understanding of universities and colleges that emphasized "the relation between the university and corporate liberal[37] society at large." He wrote that:

> Most of us are outraged when our administrators or their student government lackeys liken our universities and colleges to corporations. We bitterly respond with talk about a 'community of scholars.' However, the fact of the matter is that they are correct. Our educational institutions *are* corporations and knowledge factories. What we have failed to see in the past is how absolutely vital these factories are to the corporate liberal state.[38]

It has been argued that the most obvious commodity of these factories is "knowledge," which Davidson calls "the know-how that enables the corporate state to expand, to grow, and to exploit people more efficiently and extensively both in our own country and in the third world." However, Davidson takes a somewhat different viewpoint in assessing this analysis. "But knowledge," he writes, "is perhaps too abstract to be viewed as a commodity. Concretely, the commodities of our factories are the *knowledgeable*." Here he reveals his basic ambivalence towards students as a constituency in themselves. "AID officials, Peace Corpsmen, military officers, CIA officials, segregationist judges, corporation lawyers, politicians of all sorts, welfare workers, managers of industry, labor bureaucrats . . ."[39]--his list is a totally negative roll call of the agents of imperialism abroad and social control at home. Although he says that he "could go on and on," he actually names only those professions that play a socially conservative or reactionary roll in the service of the corporate liberal state. It will be interesting to compare this negative appraisal with the decidedly more optimistic assessment of students in the multiversity developed by this author and, more extensively, by the authors of the so-called "Port Authority Statement."[40] Davidson himself would later adopt a more positive approach in "The Multiversity: Crucible of the New Working Class," only to abandon it in an abrupt turn to Marxism-Leninism.[41]

Despite his exclusive emphasis at this point on the negative roles of (some) students, Davidson still believed that SDS should organize a mass "student syndicalist movement." It is hard to reconcile the apparent contradiction in his attitude, which is well expressed, but not resolved, in a brief paragraph.

It is in our assembly lines in the universities that they [the students] are molded into what they are. As integral parts of the knowledge factory system, we are *both the exploiters and the exploited. As both managers and managed,* we produce and become *the most vital product of corporate liberalism: bureaucratic man. In short, we are a new kind of scab.* [My emphases.][42]

When Davidson asks, "Who are the dehumanizers and oppressors?" of the "dehumanized and oppressive system" of "corporate liberalism," he answers that it is "our past, present, and future alumni: the finished product of our knowledge factories."

Given the gloomy picture Davidson paints of university graduates, it is difficult to imagine the reasons for organizing a student syndicalist movement in the first place. Once again it is important to emphasize the difference between Davidson's outlook at the Clear Lake Convention in August of 1966 and later "new working class" analyses.

Davidson's ray of hope and his rationale for organizing students lay in the possibility of changing the system of corporate liberalism by depriving it of the product he had described. The "assembly line that starts with children entering junior high school and ends with junior bureaucrats in commencement robes" could apparently be altered, according to Davidson's vision. He argued that "the rules and regulations of *in loco parentis* are essential rules along the assembly line." Furthermore, he claimed, "Without them it would be difficult to produce the kind of men that can create, sustain, tolerate, or ignore situations like Watts, Mississippi, and Vietnam."

It seems clear that Davidson's strategy of student syndicalism was designed to deprive the corporate liberal state of the personnel it needed to continue its expansion, domination, and profiteering. He reveals the core of his strategy when he suggests that "we ask ourselves what would happen if the military found itself without ROTC students, the CIA found itself without recruits, paternalistic welfare departments found themselves without social workers, or the Democratic Party found itself without young liberal apologists and campaign workers?" He means to suggest that political organizing on campuses can deprive corporate liberalism of its much needed personnel. "In short," he asks, "what would happen to a manipulative society if its means of creating manipulable people were done away with?"

It was a big question and a big order to deliver on, for the success of Davidson's strategy rested on a more or less complete takeover of America's institutions of higher education by students.

Davidson's ambivalence is not to be explained solely by his social background. The question of student identity ran through the entire student movement. Were students oppressors or oppressed? Were they "middle-class" or were they workers? Davidson's program for student syndicalism came down hard in favor of organizing students as students even if it gave a grim caricature of their social role. In this it differed both from the strategy of ERAP, which placed students in the role of organizers of the poor, and from the Marxist-Leninists who wanted to recruit them as cadres for organizing "the workers."

It remained for "new working class" theorists to redefine students and their movement in decidedly new terms. It is, however, important to recognize that Davidson's position paper and his election as SDS's Vice-President in charge of internal education marked a new recognition of the importance of the student movement as such and signalled a new direction for the New Left.

Part II

From Protest To Resistance

CHAPTER 6

RESISTANCE AND WAR:

Not With My Life, You Don't!

 . . . the real difference is not between the moral man and the political man, but between the man whose moral thinking leads him no further than his own "sinlessness." It is the difference between the man who is willing to go dirty himself in the outside world and the man who wishes to stay "clean" and "pure."[1]

Michael Ferber

Circumstances changed so swiftly in the late fall and winter of 1964-65 that it is difficult in retrospect to capture the immensity of the transformation. During the same months that the Berkeley rebellion was radicalizing the self-awareness of the student movement, the electoral process of liberal American democracy was producing a hoax of such gigantic proportions that its outcome would alter forever the trajectory of the New Left. Perhaps the most powerful symbol of this process could be seen in its effect on SDS.

In the fall of 1964, the Political Education Project (PEP) of SDS produced a slogan for the national presidential campaign. It was sold on buttons that read "Part of the Way With LBJ"[2]--a position of conditional support based on Lyndon Johnson's promise to keep the U.S. out of war in Southeast Asia. Only three months after the elections, on February 8, 1965, President

Johnson used the ruse of the "Gulf of Tonkin Resolution" as legal grounds for the bombing of North Vietnam. Barely two months later, on April 17, SDS was leading the first mass demonstration against the Vietnam War in Washington, D.C., with a march of twenty thousand angry activists. Although the PEP slogan represented only a minority position amongst the leadership of SDS, it still reflected a genuine ambivalence in the organization about its relationship to the liberal wing of the Democratic Party. However, the open split between the Movement and the Party, which dated from the Democrats' refusal to seat the Mississippi Freedom Democratic Party at the August 1964 Convention, would widen into an unbreachable gulf as Johnson's policy of escalation in Vietnam drove larger and larger numbers of young New Left activists "from protest to resistance." Deeply entwined in this process was a growing disaffection from the entire structure and practice of liberal electoral democracy, the basis of the American political system. In the long run, the increasing alienation of New Leftists from liberal electoralism drove them further and further towards adventurism and self-destruction. This fateful winter marked a turning point beyond which it would be increasingly difficult for the New Left to define a workable political strategy.

The immensity of this crisis was experienced almost in disguise within SDS. It emerged first as a breakdown of leadership, secondly as an absence of strategy, and finally as a crisis of analysis and theory. The leadership crisis was evident in the increasing inability of the Old Guard (as the early leadership came to be known) to present candidates for national offices who were sufficiently representative of the rapidly growing organization. This was partially due to to the fact that much of the early leadership had left SDS to work in the ERAP projects and no longer participated actively in the affairs of the organization. This aspect of the crisis was only resolved when the Old Guard was displaced by a new generation of leaders at the Clear Lake Convention in August 1966. In the prior year, 1965-66, the job of National Secretary, which was becoming increasingly the most important and powerful national position, was filled by four different interim officers. That same year, Jeff Shero, a member of the avowedly "anarchist" chapter at the University of Texas had been elected Vice-President although his work in the National Office was made difficult by the Old Guard. While the changing leadership at Clear Lake in 1966 was hailed as the victory of "Prairie Power," this misleading rubric masked the real nature of the transformation which involved the ascendency of a new decentralist and libertarian politics embodied in part in Carl Davidson's strategy for "student syndicalism."[3] (See Chapter 5.)

At the level of strategy, the Vietnam War required a program of opposition that was not satisfactorily achieved until the organization voted to support all (including illegal) forms of resistance to military conscription in December of 1966. The third issue of analysis and ideology was finally addressed by "new working class" theory in 1967, only to be rather quickly displaced by an abrupt shift to traditional "workerism," Marxism-Leninism, adventurism, the factionalization of SDS, and the implosion of the entire New Left.

◆ Resistance

Together with the student phase of the civil rights movement and the ERAP projects, the draft resistance and anti-war movements embodied the best of the spirit of the New Left. The assault on democratic values inherent in the war against Southeast Asian peasants was met with courage and moral conviction on the part of millions of American young people. They were joined by millions of their older countrymen as the traditional peace movement swelled its ranks with ever increasing numbers of middle-class participants. In addition, the issues of anti-war activists and draft resisters were espoused by the more progressive elements of the black civil rights movement. Finally, resistance spread to the ranks of the military itself as GIs and veterans, mostly from working-class and minority backgrounds, protested and organized to stop the draft and the war.

Stopping the war and conscription was, after all, the crux of the matter. If the Vietnam War had not become the overwhelming issue facing persons of conscience in America, the New Left might have experimented, grown, and matured into a long-range movement for political change. It is ironic that the issues of the war and the draft, which galvanized the energies of the New Left and brought inestimable numbers of activists into its organizations, also overwhelmed its perspectives for long-range grassroots organizing and altered its priorities. At the very same time that the Berkeley rebellion of 1964-65 was catalyzing the consciousness of the new student movement across the nation, the necessity of organizing to stop the war became the overriding issue of student activism. At Berkeley, this was evidenced in a shift in the organizational focus of political activity from the Free Speech Movement (FSM) to the Vietnam Day Committee (VDC).

Just at the point where students were beginning to revolt against the multiversity and develop their own self-awareness as a constituency, their attention was drawn to an imperial military adventure in a far-off land. It is revealing that Carl Davidson's position paper, "Towards a Student Syndicalist Movement," was presented to the annual SDS National Convention in August 1966 just five months before the quarterly SDS National Council meeting adopted the organization's comprehensive draft resistance manifesto in December of that same year. Throughout the period 1966-68, SDS and its new generation of leaders were constantly faced with the dual task of organizing anti-war resistance and trying to build a viable long-range New Left. They might have succeeded had they not been invaded by opportunists with their own political agendas--especially the Marxist-Leninist Progressive Labor Party (generally called "PL").

◆ SDS and the Anti-war Movement

From its inception, SDS was genuinely ambivalent about the traditional peace movement. The *Port Huron Statement* had criticized it forthrightly:

> The "peace movement" has operated almost exclusively through peripheral institutions--almost never through mainstream institutions. .
> . .
> The organizing ability of the peace movement thus is limited to the ability to state and polarize issues. . . . As long as the debates of the peace movement form only a protest, rather than an opposition viewpoint within the centers of serious decision-making, then it is neither a movement of democratic relevance, nor is it likely to have any effectiveness except in educating more outsiders to the issue. It is vital, to be sure, that this educating go on. . . .
> But in the long interim before the national political climate is more open to deliberate, goal-directed debate about peace issues, the dedicated peace "movement" might well prepare a *local base,*

especially by establishing civic committees on the techniques of
converting from military to peacetime production.[4]

The peace movement, even today, has built-in dynamics that
make it a difficult working partner for political radicals. It tends to
focus tenaciously on a single issue, peace, and to inhibit
aggressively the development of a multi-issue radical analysis and
a movement committed to political change. It exemplifies some of
the worst of that pious self-righteousness in American culture that
is probably a reflection of its Judeo-Protestant roots. In the
tradition of American Puritanism, the point of action tends not to
be *effective* political change but proving that its participants are
members of "the elect," of "the saved." This motivational dynamic
prejudices the peace movement in favor of demonstrations
(wherein better to prove one's sainthood) and evades long-range
grassroots organizing. These problems were greatest in the 1960s
in what is regarded as the "liberal" wing of the peace movement.
By contrast, the radical pacifists (see Chapter 2 above), especially
as exemplified by *Liberation* magazine and its group of associates,
were the focal point of much creative radical democratic thought
and action in the 1960s. Under the leadership of A. J. Muste, and
later of David Dellinger, radical pacifists provided much of the
direction for national mobilizations against the Vietnam War.
Unfortunately, even with the leadership talents of such a powerful
thinker and courageous activist as Dellinger, the narrow focus on
demonstrations limited the peace movement's effectiveness and
led to the very sincere complaints of New Left activists that it was
mired in an apolitical strategy of "symbolic moral protest."

It was less because of the inherent weaknesses of the peace
movement and more because of the divisive and frequently vicious
sectarianism of the New York-based left that SDS moved
temporarily into a position of leadership in the anti-war
movement in the late winter and spring of 1965. SDS was able, on
its own, to issue a call for the April March on Washington
because it had freed itself of entanglements with the Cold War
anti-Communism of the League for Industrial Democracy and the
squabbles of the New York Marxist sects. At its first National
Council meeting after the 1964 presidential victory of Lyndon
Johnson, SDS voted, in December 1964 in New York, to organize
a march on Washington, D. C., on April 17. The march would

exclude no one, not even organized Communists.[5] Ironically, SDS issued its call for the demonstration on the very day, Feb. 8, 1965, that LBJ began the bombing of North Vietnam.

Even the strongest critics of SDS have recognized the importance of its decision to call for the March on Washington.

> [O]n December 29, in New York City . . . a momentous event took place: the anti-war movement was born. . . . The body which brought it forth was not, as might have been supposed, one of the traditional peace groups but a relatively new organization, Students for a Democratic Society.[6]

Having provided the leadership for this first national demonstration against the war, SDS was not, however, prepared to abandon its effort to build a long-range New Left in favor of a role that it feared would sacrifice democratic grassroots organizing on the altar of national mobilizations. SDS has been roundly criticized for its "failure" to remain in the leadership of the national anti-war movement. Its critics fail to recognize the very legitimate *political* concerns underlying SDS's decision. SDS was opposed in principle to the manipulative potential inherent in the strategy of "mobilization." Mobilizations were typical of the tactics of Old Left groups whose goals were, first, ideological control of so-called "mass movements" (thus the endless haggling over *slogans*) and, secondly, recruitment of cadres to their centralist, Leninist sects. Traditional Marxist-Leninist organizations frequently attempted to restrict mobilizations to single issues because they opposed radicalization on broad democratic lines that would undermine their control.

The decision of SDS to withdraw from leadership of the anti-war movement was motivated, in part, by simple revulsion against all the manipulation and sectarianism. But, more importantly, its response was dictated by its commitment to a democratic, decentralist, grassroots perspective.

♦ Liberals, Radicals, and the Name of the System

A lot of confusion could have been avoided and a lot of name-calling prevented if the terms "liberal" and "radical," "liberalism" and "radicalism," had been more carefully defined and used more discriminately in the New Left. In his widely publicized speech to the 20,000 assembled demonstrators at the April 1965 March on Washington, Paul Potter, National President of SDS, stated very clearly the basic radical premise that the issue of the war could not be separated from the system that produced it. He said:

> The incredible war in Vietnam has provided the razor, the terrifying sharp cutting edge that has finally severed the last vestige of illusion that morality and democracy are the guiding principles of American foreign policy.

Then he asked:

> What kind of system is it that allows good men to make those kinds of decisions? What kind of system is it that justifies the United States or any country seizing the destinies of the Vietnamese people and using them callously for its own purpose? What kind of system is it that disenfranchises people in the [American] South, leaves millions upon millions of people throughout the country impoverished and excluded from the mainstream and promise of American society, that creates faceless and terrible bureaucracies and makes those the place where people spend their lives and do their work, that consistently puts material values before human values--and still persists in calling itself free and still persists in finding itself fit to police the world? What place is there for ordinary men in that system and how are they to control it, make it bend itself to their wills rather than bending them to it?

And then in words which rang long and loudly through the minds of New Left activists and still hang strangely in the political air of our time, Potter said:

> We must name that system. We must name it, describe it, analyze it, understand it and change it. For it is only when that system is changed and brought under control that there can be any hope for stopping the forces that create a Vietnam today or a murder in the South tomorrow or all the incalculable, innumerable more subtle atrocities that are worked on people all over, all the time. . . .
> I wonder what it means for us to say we want to end the war in Vietnam--whether, if we accept the full meaning of that statement and the gravity of the situation, we can simply leave the march and go back to the routines of a society that acts as if it were not in the midst of a grave crisis. . . .
> There is no simple plan, no scheme or gimmick that can be

proposed here. There is no simple way to attack something that is
deeply rooted in the society. If the people of this country are to end
the war in Vietnam, and to change the institutions which create it,
then the people of this country must create a massive social
movement--and if that can be built around the issue of the war in
Vietnam then that is what we must do. . . .

Here Potter laid out the difference that would divide New
Left radicals from others in the anti-war movement by qualifying
his statement with a grassroots organizing perspective.

But that means that we build a movement that works not simply in
Washington but in communities and with the problems that face
people throughout the society.[7]

This was the voice of an experienced SDS organizer who
worked in the Cleveland ERAP project and knew through the
lessons of frustration and pain just how difficult it was to "change
the system." It was, also, the voice of a segment of SDS's
leadership that was not directly in touch with the burgeoning
student movement on campuses. Potter was, of course, correct in
emphasizing the necessity of building a long-term social movement rooted in people's felt concerns in local communities. He
and others like him were justifiably wary of the "liberal" elements
in the anti-war movement who thought the war could be treated
as an isolated issue and who thought they could return home from
a demonstration to the peace and comfort of an America that was
otherwise "okay." He was also afraid of the outlook of those who
thought only in terms of building bigger and bigger demonstrations against the war at the national level but who would ignore
the difficulties of building a movement that could change the
system.

However, Potter and many of the very serious organizers like
him, were trapped in a system of their own. They had become
prisoners of the ERAP mystique and the dream of "an interracial
movement of the poor," and, because of their very deep and real
investment in that perspective, they were reluctant to face the fact
that the most dynamic constituency of the anti-war movement was
awakening on university campuses across the country and could be
organized both in its own right and, at the same time, would
respond energetically and militantly to the struggle against the

Vietnam War.

The "failure" of SDS in regard to the anti-war movement was due to the fact that many of its most lucid radical organizers were committed to a long-range political strategy that was out of sync with the fast-moving changes in foreign policy. This important segment of New Left leadership could not suddenly tear themselves away from the ERAP projects to turn their leadership talents back towards the campuses. They had, after all, left the strictly student movement for what seemed like serious, long-range political commitments. Probably more than anything else, this explains why the task of assessing the potential of the new student movement and developing the strategy of "resistance" appropriate to its involvement in the anti-war struggle fell to a second generation of SDS organizers. In fact, the new leadership in SDS was probably closer in its politics to ERAP organizers than the question of "agency" would lead one to believe. Many of the ERAP people, like Potter, shared a decentralist perspective similar to the so-called "Prairie Power" contingent and were closer in spirit to them than they were to the social-democratic wing of SDS.

While there can be little doubt that Paul Potter's viewpoint represented the perspective of a political radicalism that demanded fundamental social change in America, it is also true that his call to "name the system" without actually doing so created a disturbing ambiguity. Why did he not simply name it "capitalism" or "imperialism" as most radicals would today? In answer to this very question, Potter later wrote:

> I did not fail to call the system capitalism because I was a coward or an opportunist. I refused to call it capitalism because capitalism was for me and my generation an inadequate description of the evils of America--a hollow, dead word tied to the thirties.[8]

Because this was a landmark speech and a crucial event for SDS and the anti-war movement, it is important to realize the importance of Potter's decision about what language to use--or, at least, what language not to use. It should also be emphasized that Potter and other SDS radicals understood perfectly well what capitalism was. They were not naive liberals nor, as Potter insisted, were they opportunists. First and foremost, they did not want to fall into the trap of adopting the mechanical, outworn rhetoric of the Old Left; and it is true that the continual incantation of words like capitalism and imperialism was essentially identified with the liturgy of Marxism-Leninism. And yet, just what were they to call "the system"? The dilemma seems somewhat arcane and outdated in our own time when the use of words like capitalism and imperialism has greater currency and is no longer tied in our minds to the left-wing rhetoric of "the thirties." Potter's attempt to be scrupulous about language was, however, equated in the minds of some as an absence of radical consciousness and for the true believers this meant that the New Left needed Marxism in order to straighten out its "liberal" confusion. Marxists began increasingly to pose as the possessors of the true key to Potter's question about a name for the system, and with increasing determination they banged their historical materialist bibles to prove it.

The March on Washington marked an important watershed for SDS. Many efforts have been made to describe this change. Kirkpatrick Sale argues: "In the weeks after the April march, SDS continued to set itself on an inevitable path away from its old roots, its liberal heritage, its period of reformism." According to Sale, SDS's decision in May to move from its New York office to Chicago was "deliberately symbolic of a departure from the past." There was even a humorous reference to Potter's call to "name the system" in a National Office mailing that ended with the exhortation, "Crush Imperialism--the life you save may be your own." Sale summarized the transformation by writing, "SDS had spent five years, three of them with all the energy at its disposal, trying in the old Quaker phrase, to speak truth to power; but power did not listen, power did not change."[9]

However, SDS itself did change. Not overnight. But a definite transformation took place over the next year. The terms that describe that change are, however, highly contestable and subject to interpretation. For instance, is Kirkpatrick Sale's choice of terms accurate when he describes the movement of SDS from "its old roots, its liberal heritage, its period of reformism"? And, if so, what did it become? A revolutionary organization? A movement for radical change? The answers to these questions are not easy to find--perhaps because SDS never really found them either.

Political labels in America are easily deceptive--especially on the "left" of the spectrum. In my own interpretation, I believe it necessary to resort to the labels most often missing in American political discourse--*social democratic* and *social democracy*--in order to clarify the debates. I understand social democracy to represent a reformed capitalism in which the state controls certain key economic mechanisms in order to attentuate the worst excesses of laissez-faire or classic liberalism through regulation. Additionally, the state sponsors certain programs of social amelioration like social security and housing, health and welfare programs that compensate for the lack of such necessities for the weak, the old, the poor, and the otherwise disadvantaged in the regulated but still basically profit-oriented capitalist marketplace where the "bottom line" is the primary economic consideration. Welfare state capitalism of the variety sponsored by New Deal liberalism is the American form of social democracy--however inadequately achieved. More developed forms are found in the Northern European social democracies. American social democrats call themselves liberals and European social democrats call themselves socialists. Because the term social democrat is avoided in American political culture, there is great confusion about the term liberalism, which originally described the free-trade, laissez-faire economics (and political economy) of the 18th and 19th century schools of classical capitalist theory and the political tradition starting with John Locke. By this standard, Reagan-Bush and team are posing as classical liberals while calling themselves conservatives. Their "liberal" opponents in the Democratic Party would be best understood as social democrats (however wishy-washy about it). Certainly, however, this confusion is not just semantic; it reflects the strength of rampant individualism in American culture and the weakness of social democratic thought.

In the broad historical context of modern political and social theory, the conflict about this terminology in American left-wing political life reflects the basic split between reformist and revolutionary interpretations of the Marxist tradition, between the theories of Edward Bernstein in Germany and the Leninist tradition in Russia.

For our purposes, it is important to recognize that social democrats or New Deal liberals are not radicals--for radicalism implies a basic restructuring of economy, society, and polity in a decidedly non-capitalist direction. If Kirkpatrick Sale meant to say that SDS broke with its *early social democratic tradition* (translated into American political terms as *liberalism*) and became a clearly radical organization, then he is generally accurate from this author's viewpoint. The interpretation of this work rests partially on the identification of certain of SDS's roots as social democratic--both its parental heritage in the LID and *some* of its early membership. But, there is an important qualification this writer would make about early SDS: that while a portion of the early SDS leadership is best understood as social democratic, there was from the beginning a strong strain of authentic democratic radicalism that was evident in Tom Hayden's open-ended conception of participatory democracy in the *Port Huron Statement* and that was alive in the grassroots communitarianism of the ERAP organizers. However, it was an *experimental democratic radicalism* in search of itself.

A frank discussion in 1965 about the differences between social democratic reformism and small "d" democratic radicalism might have clarified the political discussions in SDS and the larger New Left with which it was increasingly identified. It might have avoided the often murky and confusing debates that were engaged in using the terms liberalism and radicalism. Too often the labels liberal and radical became epithets to describe opponents --"liberal" becoming the ultimate put-down and "radical" the ultimate scare-word. There were, of course, reasons for *not* having an open debate on those terms. Social democrats in the New Left *never* wanted to be known by that name, partly for fear of being identified with right-wing anti-Communism. And, such a debate might have been truly acrimonious and split the organization. One must ask, however, whether such a split did not occur *de facto* when the Old Guard withdrew from SDS and attempted to form its own "adult" New Left with the name "Movement for a Democratic Society" in 1967. It might have been better if the "social democrats" and the "radicals" had made a clean break in 1965-66. Then, at least, they might have had a good chance to discover what they really disagreed about. It is interesting to note the way in which social democrats within and outside of SDS regrouped a decade later under the name Democratic Socialists of America (DSA). Still refusing the social democratic title, this merger in 1980 incorporated the New American Movement (NAM), consisting largely of remnants of the New Left, and the

Democratic Socialist Organizing Committee (DSOC), made up of the former anti-New Left chairman of the LID, Michael Harrington, and his followers. These groups turned out to have much in common.

The debate over language and analysis in the New Left was, however, engaged on somewhat different terms.

◆ *The Concept of Corporate Liberalism*

Seven months after Paul Potter's speech at the March on Washington, a new President of SDS gave another landmark address at yet another national demonstration. Carl Oglesby was a complex figure in SDS's history. A relative newcomer to SDS, Oglesby was elected in June 1965 at the National Convention at Kewadin, Michigan, as a candidate of the Old Guard who was not quite one of them. From a southern working-class background, he had attended his first national meeting after the April 1965 demonstration. Oglesby, who worked as a technical writer for Bendix corporation, was a playwright and aspiring novelist and came to his task of National President with a brilliant gift of oratory, the romanticism of a Beatnik, and relatively little political experience. However, because he worked for a giant corporation with multiple contracts from and ties to the federal government and especially the Pentagon, he had first-hand knowledge which together with a first-rate intellect, made him a top-notch scholar on the subject of American imperialism. And yet, there was on his part a tendency to avoid the use of both the words imperialism and capitalism.

When Oglesby spoke to the anti-war demonstration (sponsored by the very cautious and liberal group SANE) in Washington, D.C., on November 27, 1965, he took up Potter's challenge of the previous spring to "name the system that creates and sustains the war in Vietnam." "Today," he asserted, "I will try to name it--to suggest an analysis which, to be quite frank, may disturb some of you--and to suggest what changing it may require of us."[10]

Oglesby went on to say that in opposing the war "we acquire the habit of thinking that it must be caused by very bad men." In so doing, he argued, "we only conceal reality." The "menacing

coalition of industrial and military power," the "blitzkrieg" against
Vietnam, and "the ominous signs . . . that heresy may soon no
longer be permitted" are the actions of "a Government that since
1932 has considered itself to be fundamentally liberal."

He illustrated this point by naming the major actors in
Vietnam policy-making.

> The original commitment in Vietnam was made by President
> Truman, a mainstream liberal. It was seconded by President Eisen-
> hower, a moderate liberal. It was intensified by the late President
> Kennedy, a flaming liberal. Think of the men who now engineer that
> war--those who study the maps, give the commands, push the buttons,
> and tally the dead: Bundy, McNamara, Rusk, Lodge, Goldberg, and
> the President himself.
> They are not moral monsters.
> They are all honorable men.
> They are all liberals.

Oglesby then added: "To understand the war, then it seems
necessary to take a closer look at this American liberalism." "Not
long ago," he confessed, "I considered myself a liberal" and if
asked what he meant by that term would "perhaps have quoted
Thomas Jefferson or Thomas Paine, who first made plain our
nation's unprovisional commitment to human rights." Oglesby
reminded his listeners that this tradition of American liberalism
was born of our own anti-colonial revolution and that the United
States was intervening against a revolutionary war being fought by
the Vietnamese--"a complex and vicious war" but "also a
revolution, as honest a revolution as you can find anywhere in
history."

That is not, however, of consequence to "our leaders" whose
"aim in Vietnam is . . . to safeguard what they take to be
American interests around the world against revolution or
revolutionary change, which they call Communism." Oglesby
identified this interest in Vietnam as "first, the principle that
revolution shall not be tolerated anywhere, and second, that South
Vietnam shall never sell its rice to China--or even to North
Vietnam."

He went on to outline in detail U.S. anti-revolutionary
interventions, most frequently organized by the CIA, among the
"two-thirds of the world's people [for whom] the 20th Century

might as well be the Stone Age"--in Iran, Guatemala, Cuba, British Guiana, Brazil, and the Dominican Republic. He laid out the intricate relationship between American investments and these CIA directed policies aimed at maintaining U.S. economic control around the world. In short, he described the operation of American imperialism without using the name. Instead he pointed out that "the Western democracies, in the heyday of their colonial expansion" justified their "system" by calling it "free enterprise, and its partner was an *illiberal liberalism* that said to the poor and dispossessed: What we acquire of your resources we repay in civilization. The white man's burden." According to Oglesby's account, the crisis of liberalism following "the collapse of the European Empires" required a new rationale "to hold together our twin need for richness and righteousness," which was found in "the ideology of anti-Communism." The anti-revolutionary crusade which this "anti-Communist ideology" justifies is the result of the system that Oglesby finally names, or seems to name:

> This is the action of *corporate liberalism*. It performs for the corporate state a function quite like what the Church once performed for the feudal state. It seeks to justify its burdens and protect it from change. As the Church exaggerated this office in the Inquisition, so with liberalism in the McCarthy time--which, if it was a reactionary phenomenon, was still made possible by our anti-Communist corporate liberalism.

If Oglesby's intention was to name "the system" *corporate liberalism*, then he certainly did so in a confusing manner. For one thing, in his analogy between corporate liberalism and the medieval Church, he gives the impression that he is talking about an ideology or an institution for the enforcement of ideological conformity rather than about a political-social-economic system. When corporate liberalism is said to "perform" a "function" for "the corporate state," it is unclear just what is being talked about--an ideology, a politics, or a system. Once again a prominent SDS spokesperson had avoided the use of the terms "capitalism" and "imperialism."

Some years later Oglesby justified his avoidance by arguing that his speech was

> an attempt to describe imperialism without giving it that name, and to

attribute imperialist policy to the structure of monopoly capitalism
without pronouncing that term either. . . . Imperialism and monopoly
capitalism were conceptions proper and necessary to the thorough
critique of US policy, but they had been effectively drained of meaning
by decades of strong pervasive and subtle Cold War propaganda. . . .
For most of the growing student movement in those days, these were
still out-of-bounds terms.[11]

The problem with this avoidance of those two words was that
it gave the impression that SDS favored democratic radicalism but
had no social, economic, or political analysis that described "the
system." And what was worse, this avoidance led easily to the
impression that SDS had fallen prey to the position commonly
espoused by "liberals" who argued that American industrial
development in the 20th century had gone beyond capitalism--that
the United States was somehow no longer a capitalist society
based on a capitalist economy. As a former Berkeley New Leftist,
R. Jeffrey Lustig, later wrote, "The bulk of mid-century writings
denied that the corporation was still a capitalist institution."[12] The
attempt to propagandize this supposedly "post-capitalist" and
"post-industrialist" transcendence had begun in earnest in the
1930s with the appearance of *The Modern Corporation and
Private Property* by Adolph A. Berle and Gardner Means. This
effort turned out to be a gigantic exercise in obscurantism,
whether consciously motivated or the result of liberal academic
blindness. It is unclear to what extent such thinking may have
influenced some members of early SDS. This "liberal pluralist,"
"post-capitalist," ideology became in any case, the major target of
radical analysis.

If Oglesby failed to clarify the use of the term corporate
liberalism for the New Left and the anti-war movement, he
certainly did manage to popularize it. Corporate liberalism came
to be a commonly used phrase in the New Left and, unfortunately,
it seemed to add further confusion rather than increased lucidity
to the political vocabulary of the Movement.

Although it was Oglesby's speech that gave the phrase
corporate liberalism its first widespread public exposure, Oglesby
was not the originator of the term. In an article in an early New
Left journal, *Studies on the Left*, Martin Sklar, a graduate student
in history at the University of Wisconsin, had published an article

in 1960 in which he first used the phrase as part of a larger reinterpretation of the development of 20th century United States liberalism and imperialism.[13] His was a critique of the standard interpretation of President Woodrow Wilson as a figure split between his "moralistic" and his "commercialistic" halves. Sklar endeavored to show that Wilsonian liberalism was of a single cloth before, during and after World War I in its support of the economic successes of giant corporations and of aggressive foreign expansionism. Wilson's attack on monopolies or "trusts" was not an attack on "big business" nor an effort to regulate the conditions of corporate growth. And, his "New Freedom" did not differ substantially from Theodore Roosevelt's "New National-ism." Sklar had been explicit in naming the system in a way Oglesby was not. Sklar contended, for instance, that "Wilson emerged as a foremost ideological and political leader of a social movement affirming *industrial corporate capitalism.*" [Emphasis added.]

Further on, Sklar wrote that

> Wilson's position was not that of a representative of the "little man," or "middle class," against "big business"; but that of one who, affirming the large *corporate industrial capitalist system,* was concerned with establishing the legal and institutional environment most conducive to the system's stability and growth, while at the same time preserving some place within the system for the "little man." . . . As such, *the Wilsonian and Rooseveltian variants of Progressivism signified, if not the birth then the coming of age, of twentieth century United States liberalism, whose present-day fundamentals, converging upon large-scale corporate capitalism at home and economic expansion abroad remain genetically true to the components of Wilson's world-view, their immediate parental source.*[14] [Emphasis added.]

Sklar had thus made clear that he thought that "corporate capitalism" was the appropriate name for "the system" in the United States in the 20th century and, furthermore, that the politics and political ideology of "twentieth century United States liberalism . . . may be accurately referred to as corporate liberalism. . . ." Sklar was also unequivocal in stating that "modern United States liberalism [is] the bourgeois Yankee cousin of modern European and English social-democracy."[15]

The concepts that Sklar employed were essential to debates in the New Left. I, personally, first encountered the arguments concerning the rough equivalence of European social democracy and modern American liberalism not through Sklar's writings but in discussions with my fellow left-wing graduate students in European history at Cornell University in 1959-61. These discussions, a true political and social theory symposium which nurtured several New Left activists, were focused, interestingly, on the identification of the American Socialist Party-Michael Harrington nexus in New York as "social democratic."[16]

It would be hard to exaggerate the effect of the New Left on political thought in the United States. It is evident that the intellectual and activist thrust of the New Left and the anti-war movement in response to United States involvement in Vietnam blew the ideological consensus of "corporate liberalism" wide open. And it is of fundamental significance that it was a war of aggression against the Vietnamese that exposed the ugly imperialist and militarist face of United States corporate capitalism. Built into the ideology of American capitalist expansion had been a carefully concealed hypocrisy--an hypocrisy that American corporate liberals had concealed even from themselves. As Martin Sklar had pointed out:

> It no more occurred to such liberals as Wilson than it did to the so-called Dollar Diplomatists before him, or than it does today to the "internationalist" liberals, that investment in, and ownership of, other nations' resources, railroads, and industry by United States capitalists, constituted imperialism or exploitation. Imperialism to them meant British and European-style colonialism or exclusive spheres of interest. . . . it meant 'free trade.'[17]

The New Left was unmasking the hypocricies and contradictions concealed behind the masks of American liberal democratic ideology. However incomplete his presentation in October 1965, Carl Oglesby had laid out the fundamental guide-lines for distinguishing between a radical and a liberal analysis of United States history and the social-economic-political system it represented at home and abroad. The politics of "corporate liberalism" was the politics of corporate capitalist domination and imperialist expansion. The New Left had found a target--*liberals, corporate liberals.*

The terms "corporate capitalist society" or "corporate liberalism" describe, however, only one aspect of modern American life, and the exclusive reliance on these categories obscures dynamics other than capital accumulation and production for profit in determining the world that New Leftists faced. The modern world is not only the product of capitalist dynamics, it is also the result of technological, military, and bureaucratic imperatives. The term "corporate capitalist society" obscures these other aspects of the operation of *power* in modern society. Our society is an advanced technological society, a militaristic society, and a "disciplinary society," controlled by a highly bureaucratized state, as well as being corporate capitalist and imperialist. The narrow-minded insistence of some radicals (mostly Marxists) on naming only the corporate capitalist and imperialist faces of the United States to the exclusion of these others aspects and dynamics of power is one of the reasons the left was unable to speak more clearly to the life experience and needs of broader sectors of the American people. The inclusion of the category of "consumerism" in this debate broadened its terms somewhat by explaining the need for expanded internal markets and the resultant consumerist culture. However, even this focus still restricted the debate to economic dynamics and made cultural alienation and cultural demands simply a function of those economic imperatives.

The New Left needed social, political, and economic analyses that gave coherence to the technological, economic, military, and bureaucratic elements in the operation of power in the society and that reflected its spiritual values and democratic idealism. Marxist economic reductionism did not serve the New Left well and fed its narrowing and rigidification.

If the unaddressed philosophical question facing the New Left was how to justify its intuitive democratic idealism, then the theoretical question was how to describe the functioning of power in modern societies that are driven by bureaucratic, technological, corporate capitalist, and other dynamics. The narrowing of theoretical discourse in the New Left to the economic and class dimensions of society was in part a reaction to liberal obfuscation of those features of social life and also a direct response to the overwhelming sense of political urgency created by the Vietnam war and the pressing need to understand the nature of American military and economic imperialism. Instead of developing such a multi-faceted analysis, the New Left tended in the latter half of the 1960s to fall into the traditional left-wing dichotomy that emphasized either the primary role of capital or the primary role of the state while ignoring other factors like technology. In so doing, the New Left set the stage for reenacting the century-old drama which pitted Marxism against anarchism.[18]

Wini Breines, a New Left activist and scholar (and one of the later participants in those political discussions at Cornell of which I had been a part) has emphasized the curious fact that young people in the New Left were radicalized with increasing frequency by the issues of imperialism and "foreign" military involvement rather than by the traditional "domestic" issues of capitalist exploitation and poverty which had been the basis of the Old Left and the labor movement.[19] The process of political radicalization in America was being turned upside down. And with that came an inversion of the total framework in which activists perceived America, the national vision, and the proclaimed ideals of American democracy. This transformation through disillusionment revealed an "American dream" built in part on a cruel nightmare of dominion through expansion, and it led young people to reject allegiance to an America enmeshed in hypocrisy and lies. Some chose to rename their country "Amerika."

This process of disillusionment rapidly became central to the politicization, radicalization, and alienation of a generation of young Americans from their own culture and country. It was in Southeast Asia that the hidden history of a nation built on the genocide of Native American peoples began to unfold as nightly television broadcasts brought the slaughter of Vietnamese peasants and American youths into our living rooms--exposing in Asia what had remained largely concealed from view during two centuries of carnage along the U.S. frontier. The myths of American democracy and American manhood toppled one by one as the "heroes" that Hollywood had incarnated in the John Wayne image fell with blood and napalm on their hands. Manifest Destiny gave way to the manifest horror that Americans had been waging against innocent peoples since the founding of the Thirteen Colonies.

Few Americans had truly appreciated the brutality inherent in the imperialist side of American corporate capitalism until the Vietnam War held up a mirror to America in which the shock of self-recognition far exceeded even its encounter with the vicious face of racism and apartheid in the American South. When young

Americans saw the horror, they reacted with outrage and shame and a profound sense of guilt that they were hard-pressed to exorcise. Having uncovered the falsehoods of corporate liberalism, they took a new look at American history and uncovered the diary of an imperialist adventure which cloaked a "Trail of Tears" in democratic platitudes. Unfortunately, in this process, "Amerika" became in their minds not something to be challenged and changed according to its professed democratic ideals as the framers of the *Port Huron Statement* had determined to do, but something to be destroyed. From 1965 onwards, the struggle within the New Left for a politics of hope was increasingly challenged by a politics of hate and an unwritten question was raised, whether the democratic, nonviolent, and loving spirit of "the Movement" could be kept alive. The "politics of compassion" needed a new determination if it was to survive.

◆ From Protest to Resistance

If there was one area that joined the issues of individual responsibility, spiritual values, and political activism, it was draft resistance. It was the arena in which personal choice and political conviction were forced into an intimate encounter. It was also the issue that brought the New Left into direct confrontation with the state. As usual in the New Left, activism outran theory, and the confidence that draft resistance was morally correct preceded any analysis of the role of the state. This was also the issue that raised the "anarchist" question of the very legitimacy and necessity of the state in the governance of human society. The draft resistance movement strengthened the decentralist and libertarian tendencies within the New Left at the same time that authoritarian Marxism was beginning to offer a serious challenge.

SDS was by no means the first organization to adopt a draft resistance resolution. In New York, the May 2nd Movement (an anti-imperialist youth group founded and controlled by the Progressive Labor Party) published the first "We Won't Go" statement in May 1964. PL-M2M did not, however, oppose all conscription even though it took an anti-imperialist position. Its statement read: "We understand our obligations to defend our country and serve in the armed forces." In the words of draft resistance activists and historians Michael Ferber and Staughton Lynd:

> Progressive Labor forfeited whatever chance it might have had to unify the draft resistance movement when, in the fall of 1965, it decided to stop supporting induction refusal. Thereafter its members made use of the draft issue in anti-war propaganda on campus and played a prominent role in discussion of the draft within SDS, but for practical purposes the Party followed the Leninist policy of entering the army and agitating among the troops. This was also the orientation of the Trotskyist Young Socialist Alliance. In the summer of 1966 members of two other tiny Marxist groups, Youth Against War and Fascism, and the American Liberation League, formed the New York Anti-Draft Union. . . . It accomplished little and does not seem to have survived past October.[20]

Ferber and Lynd go on to argue: "Neither pacifism nor Marxism could organize the thousands of white students who were ready by mid-1966 to say publicly that they would never fight in Vietnam. Most of these students were moral without being pacifist and political without being Marxist."

One group did fit the bill. End The Draft (ETD) had been organized in 1962-63 by David Mitchell, a drop-out from Brown University who became involved in founding the new group after becoming disillusioned with pacifist approaches to conscription and symbolic resistance. Mitchell was a political radical with an anti-imperialist perspective; he had a highly moral political stance without being a pacifist. However, the attempts of ETD to create a unified draft resistance movement failed, and it later turned to SDS for leadership that organization proved reluctant to provide.[21]

SNCC, the other major organization regarded as "New Left" in its politics, did in fact support draft resistance without initially organizing it. In McComb, Mississippi, local blacks, who had been originally organized in SNCC's voter registration drive, issued a call for draft resistance in July 1965. It was largely in response to this local initiative that the Executive Committee of SNCC issued its statement of "sympathy" for draft resisters in December 1965. SNCC was the first organization outside the traditional peace movement to do so, although SNCC organizers generally were unwilling to resist the draft directly and risk imprisonment; they were more likely to encourage draft evasion and were reluctant to pursue a course that might put all their organizers in jail for long terms. However, after the beginning of the "Black Power" agitational campaign in the summer of 1966, SNCC launched the slogan "Hell no, we won't go!" and became directly involved in demonstrations at the Atlanta induction center and suffered arrests as a result. The organizers were placed in solitary confinement.[22]

SDS continued to waffle on the question of the draft as it did on the question of leadership in the anti-war movement as a whole. But the draft presented an increasingly urgent issue for SDS because male members were faced with very personal decisions about their lives. SDS had the same reservations about the draft resistance movement that it had about the growing anti-war movement. It was first, as Ferber and Lynd put it,

> the conviction of many members, that the single-issue movement to end the war must become a multi-issue "movement to change America." According to this argument, radicals should forego the hope of influencing the Vietnam war directly, and instead build new constituencies around domestic issues which would have power to do something effective about future wars. This came to be known in SDS as the argument for "stopping the seventh war from now."[23]

The second reason was the "fear of repression." At the June 1965 National Convention in Kewadin, Michigan, where SDS failed to develop a program on the question of its relationship to the anti-war movement, it also failed to take a clear position on draft resistance. At that meeting, former President Todd Gitlin argued against making the Vietnam war the central issue for the organization while the outgoing National Secretary, Clark Kissinger proposed that SDS issue an appeal to American soldiers to desert and use the resulting criminal indictments as a forum for anti-war organizing. The "Kissinger Kamikaze Plan" failed to win support. That was largely a victory for the Old Guard who were still able to control the national convention but were increasingly out of touch with the rapidly growing majority of the organization from west of the Hudson River. The presence of large numbers of these new recruits at Kewadin troubled "old-timers" who came mostly from eastern backgrounds and schools, often from Old Left families, and were frequently Jewish. The new SDSers were more typically from the Midwest and the West and from state colleges

or universities rather than elite institutions. Jeff Shero from
Austin SDS, elected the new Vice-President, was typical of the
new mentality. He summarized the difference this way:

> We were by instinct much more radical, much more willing to take
> risks, in a way because to become a part of something like SDS meant
> a tremendous number of breaks. If you were a New York student and
> became a member of SDS, it was essentially joining a political
> organization, which was a common experience. In Texas to join SDS
> meant breaking with your family, it meant being cut off--it was like in
> early Rome joining a Christian sect--and the break was so much more
> total, getting involved with something like SDS you had to be much
> more highly committed, and you were in a sense freed, 'cause you'd
> get written off. If you were from Texas, in SDS, you were a bad
> motherfucker, you couldn't go home for Christmas. Your mother
> didn't say "Oh, isn't that nice, you're involved. We supported the
> republicans in the Spanish Civil War, and now you're in SDS and I'm
> glad to see you're socially concerned." In most of those places it
> meant, "*You Goddamn Communist.*" There was absolutely no
> reinforcing sympathy. . . . So we were strong, the commitment in those
> regions was stronger than it was in the East.[24]

It was not, I think, a difference in the strength of
commitment. It was that the new generation of SDS, who were
generally not from leftist backgrounds, had broken with authority
in joining SDS and had taken a stand that made the question of
outright opposition to the state, like that implied in draft
resistance, a more natural part of their overall political commitment. In addition, many like Shero, had strong convictions about
the "anarchist," left-libertarian tradition and had *fundamental*
political differences with the social-democratic-liberal politics of
many early SDSers. They were also more likely to regard Marxism
as just another brand of authoritarianism. Clearly the question of
draft resistance became one of the issues--*perhaps the most
important*--which distinguished the politics of these new radicals
from the Old Guard. It was another year and a half before that
difference became more clearly defined in national SDS. The
interim can best be described as a period of "hesitation and
ambivalence."

Because SDS was a predominantly student organization, it
found itself faced with the ambiguity created by Selective Service
regulations granting student deferments under the 2-S classifica-
tion. 2-S delayed military service for male college students who

maintained passing grades and remained enrolled. Since the effective cut-off age for induction was twenty-six, this meant that continuation of studies in graduate or professional schools effectively exempted many students from the draft. How should an organization like SDS address what was perceived as "student (middle-class) privilege"? How could students accept deferments while white working-class and minority youth fought a war in their stead?

SDS dealt with the moral dilemmas it faced by first passing a fairly mild program of support for conscientious objection. CO status was presented as a "legal" form of resistance to the war. However, this attempt to evade the issue of illegality and confrontation with the state did little good. The "International Days of Protest" on October 15 and 16, 1965, were called by the Berkeley Vietnam Day Committee and the National Coordinating Committee to End the War in Vietnam. And yet, SDS was attacked by the Senate Internal Security Subcommittee and the press as instigators of the protests and claims were made that SDS was linked to "subversives" and "communist" organizations. The program supporting conscientious objection was portrayed as a conspiracy to undermine the draft and SDS was denounced as the mastermind of the supposed conspiracy.

The growing gulf between SDS's hesitant leadership and its radical membership was highlighted by the response of National Secretary Paul Booth and President Carl Oglesby who drew up a statement urging "alternative service" for "democracy" as an answer to conscription. "Build, Not Burn," as the strategy came to be known, was regarded as a liberal cop-out by significant sectors of the organization and was unquestionably a colossal political blunder on the part of Paul Booth who read the statement before the National Press Club in Washington. The mistake was compounded by the fact that Booth had set policy for SDS without regard for democratic procedures in the organization. Radicals in the organization did not take the misdeeds lightly and Booth's reputation suffered disastrously. No matter what he attempted as penance to prove his radicalism, he was henceforth regarded with suspicion and sometimes treated with contempt. In important ways, Booth had sounded the death knell for the leadership of the Old Guard and guaranteed that the issue of the draft would be a crucial and definitive dividing line between the generations of SDS. The notion of "alternative national service" became synonymous with "collaboration" in the minds of the new radicals, and *collaborator* had unequivocal connotations for activists increasingly dedicated to the idea of *resistance*. The Booth strategy was quickly lampooned by SDS wags who touted a counter-slogan, "Build Not, Burn."

This issue was intensified when the Selective Service System decided to increase pressure by "ranking" students academically through special examinations and thus dividing them amongst themselves vis-a-vis the draft. These proposed nationwide tests provided SDS with the opportunity to protest "the rank" by distributing an alternative examination at testing sites on campuses. The SDS counter-examination was that organization's most important program on the draft up to that time. SDS printed and distributed 100,000 copies of the counter-exam in May, 1966. But the hesitancy of the organization to endorse draft resistance continued to prevail over the numerous proposals that came from the growing radical constituency at the grassroots.

This failure of SDS in the winter of 1965-66 to adopt a vigorous draft resistance program led to two parallel developments. On the one hand, increasing pressure developed within the organization to displace the Old Guard and support draft resistance. At the same time, New Left radicals, both members and non-members of SDS, began to organize draft resistance outside of that organization.

Individuals like Jeff Shero, Tom Bell, and Bill Hartzog were pushing for a resistance program within SDS and at the same time joined with men like Mendy Samstein and Staughton Lynd who were beginning to organize independently. Samstein (my best friend in graduate school and a participant in the Cornell political discussions of which I was a part) had left his graduate studies in European history to teach and organize for the black civil rights movement in the South where he became a full-time worker for SNCC. When SNCC initiated its version of black nationalist politics under the slogan of "Black Power" in 1966, whites like Samstein were gradually excluded from the organization. Samstein returned north with a determination to make draft resistance happen. He envisioned a northern version of SNCC composed of dedicated resisters and resistance organizers. With the help of Staughton Lynd, a radical historian and activist at Yale, Samstein organized an initial meeting in New Haven in July 1966. According to Ferber and Lynd, his goal was "finding a means where whites could commit themselves as strongly against the war as blacks had against racism."[25] The New Haven meeting produced a commitment on the part of eight men to resist conscription by returning their draft cards. Furthermore, they pledged to carry their message to others and organize a national meeting in Des Moines, Iowa, on August 25 and 26 just before the SDS National Convention at Clear Lake, Iowa. Four or five of the organizers fanned out around the country. Samstein traveled all the way to the west coast, stopping in Chicago to meet with myself, by then working full-time as Assistant National Secretary of SDS and editor of *New Left Notes*, and my companion Jane Adams, interim National Secretary.

Like many others in the second generation of SDS leadership, I was impatient with SDS's failure to take a strong stand favoring draft resistance and pledged to give my close friend all the help I could. The intensity of these encounters was deeply moving for the participants. As a self-acknowledged gay male with a bisexual history, I was particularly aware of the psychological ramifications of the intimate sharing that characterized draft resistance organizing--especially as pursued by a man of Samstein's warmth, sincerity, and compassion. He must also have been aware of the psycho-sexual implications of his method of work. He had been a student of Herbert Marcuse at Brandeis University before coming to Cornell in 1960 and was the person who first introduced me to Marcuse's writings, especially *Eros and Civilization* which became particularly important to discussions of sexual politics and sexual liberation in the New Left. While reading me passages from that text in the spring of 1961, Samstein once said to me: "You know Marcuse believes that after the revolution we'll all be bisexual." Mendy Samstein's being communicated in every word and gesture the possibility of love and brotherhood amongst men--whether sexualized or not--and the effect was intensely liberating.

Much has been said by the feminist movement in criticism of draft resistance organizing. The broadest accusations came in Sara Evans book, *Personal Politics: The Roots of Women's Liberation in the Civil Rights Movement and the New Left*,[26] where draft resistance organizing is portrayed as sexist and exclusivist. This argument misrepresents the movement. In fact, it was Mendy

Samstein's style of intimate, heart-felt and soul-searching encounters as the basis of organizing--a style which had been nourished in the "Freedom High" wing of SNCC--that gave "personal politics" its first exposure on the national scene.

The confrontation with conscription involved reexamining the traditional male role of warrior and the traditional definition of masculinity. The possibilities opened up by this encounter were enormous in terms of the exploration of gender roles and sexuality in a political context. Draft resistance was not the origin of the idea that "the personal is political": that understanding had been implicit in Beat Generation cultural politics, and it had emerged in the confrontation with racism, which provoked its own reappraisal of sexual repression and sexual stereotypes in America. The brand of draft resistance organizing initiated by Mendy Samstein in 1966 pushed personal and cultural politics into another arena--manhood and male liberation. Collective, rather than simply individual, draft resistance organizing offered young men the chance to support each other in opposition to militaristic values, to learn to care for each other as they exposed their fears and vulnerabilities in draft resistance "soul sessions." These experiences stood in sharp contrast to ordinary experiences of male competition such as sports, business, or combat against a common male "enemy."

At the same time, draft resistance organizing stimulated rather than inhibited discussions of women's liberation and the necessity for women's self-organization was recognized from the beginning. When the travelers returned to New Haven to share experiences before the Des Moines conference, they recognized the "vast potential for organizing young women" where there was "such a vacuum organizationally and programatically," and, furthermore, they "felt it would be up to women themselves to develop corollary programs to our draft resistance." Ferber and Lynd point out that there "were in fact women's workshops at the subsequent Des Moines meeting and at the We Won't Go Conference in Chicago the following December."[27]

The Des Moines meeting on August 25-26 drew between forty and fifty draft resisters from around the country including Paul Booth and Jeff Shero, outgoing national officers of SDS and frequent political opponents. The participants were impressed by the seriousness of discussions and the mutual respect granted each other. The decision was made to promote the formation of local, community-based draft resistance unions, which would be decentralized and only loosely linked, and which would set their own timetables for action rather than engage in one national "big bang" event. No proposals were developed for the SDS National Convention the following week. Although the SDS meeting at Clear Lake, Iowa, shifted leadership from the Old Guard to a new generation of SDSers represented by Carl Davidson, the new Vice-President, and myself, the new National Secretary, no draft program had been prepared. Although the new President, Nick Egleson, from an elite Eastern background, was something of an anomaly, the Clear Lake convention represented a decisive victory for the party of student syndicalism and draft resistance. It was only a matter of a few months before SDS adopted a broad and militant draft resistance program.

Typical of the way in which SDSers acted in the wake of the Des Moines and Clear Lake gatherings was the role that Tom Bell played at Cornell. An SDS activist for barely a year, Bell undertook the organization of a draft resistance union at Cornell on his return from Iowa. Although closely identified with SDS, he found it more effective to avoid political disputes and organize an independent group of resisters. Together with Bruce Dancis, Manny Goodman (Paul Goodman's son), Burton Weiss, and others, Bell helped build one of the most effective draft resistance groups in the country. The strategy of slow "organic growth" prevailed in the first months of work and was then given a dramatic boost when Bruce Dancis decided to resist the draft publicly and tear up his draft card on December 14.

The increase in group militancy was next evident in a decision to engage in mass civil disobedience. On March 2, a call was issued by five resisters from the Cornell group proposing that a mass draft card burning be held at the time of the Spring Mobilization on April 15. The call resulted in a demonstration in Sheep's Meadow in New York's Central Park where between one hundred fifty and two hundred draft resisters burned their cards.

In the meantime, national SDS had finally swung into the resistance camp.

✦ *Conscription and the State*

The adoption of SDS's draft resistance resolution at the National Council meeting at UC Berkeley in December 1966 was a momentous decision for the New Left. Without a serious debate within the organization about its deepest political implications, but with a sure instinct for expressing the mood of a growing majority of its members, the National Council voted to cross a line on the other side of which lay *illegality and opposition to the state*. At that point, SDS had moved quite clearly from a tradition of social democratic reformism to a radicalism that defied the power of the state in a way associated historically with the anarchist movement. It was, in fact, Carl Davidson, the articulate spokesman of an anarcho-syndicalist position in SDS, who presented the draft resolution with its decidedly anti-statist stance.

In its final form, the SDS resolution read:

1. SDS reaffirms its opposition to the United States Government's immoral, illegal, and genocidal war against the Vietnamese people in their struggle for self-determination.
2. SDS reaffirms its opposition to conscription in any form. We maintain that all conscription is coercive and anti-democratic, and that it is used by the United States Government to oppress people in the United States and around the world.
3. SDS recognizes that the draft is intimately connected with the requirements of the economic system and the foreign policy of the United States.
4. SDS opposes and will organize against any attempt to legitimize the Selective Service System by reforms. The proposals for a lottery or for compulsory national service would not change the essential purpose of the draft--to abduct young men to fight in aggressive wars.
5. SDS believes that a sense of urgency must be developed that will move people to leave the campus and organize a movement of resistance to the draft and the war, with its base in poor, and working class, and middle class communities.
6. SDS therefore encourages all young men to resist the draft.[28]

Although SDS was not the first organization to support draft resistance, the sheer size of SDS with more than 450 chapters, and its representativeness of the student and anti-war movements, gave its adoption of resistance to conscription a central importance that marked the development of the New Left as a whole. Not since the American Socialist Party and the IWW in World War I had a truly mass political organization adopted a position opposing the draft.

It was characteristic of the New Left that the ramifications of this decision were conceived more in moral and existential terms rather than in lengthy debates about the nature of the modern state. We had made a moral-existential choice and understood that to represent the very best of our politics. As National Secretary I wrote a short report in *New Left Notes*, the title of which, "From Protest to Resistance," soon became the predominant slogan of the anti-war movement. Of the resistance program I said, in part:

> That program does not talk about politics or the taking of power. It does not talk about the new society or the democratization of decision-making. It talks about "resistance." And finally, behind its rhetoric and its programmatic details, it talks about the only thing that has given life and creativity to "the movement." It talks about the kind of struggle which has been most meaningful to the new left--the revolutionary struggle which engages and claims the lives of those involved despite the seeming impossibility of revolutionary social change--the struggle which has the power to transform, to revolutionize human lives whether or not it can revolutionize the societal conditions of human existence. It is the struggle which has offered imprisonment and even death as a way of being free--which says that "this is what a human being must do, no matter what the consequences, because this is what it means to be a human being."[29]

CHAPTER 7

CONSCIOUSNESS AND IDENTITY:

Students and the New Working Class

The denial of the class nature of our society is a central part of the ideology of American corporate liberalism. In the mid-20th century, this viewpoint had been elaborated *ad nauseam* by the "pluralist" ideologues of "political science" and sociology. Pluralist arguments maintained that "power" was distributed among various "interest groups" in the society and that the concept of a capitalist, class-structured social order that also conditioned the forms and direction of political life was naive, ideologically hide-bound, and out-of-date.

It was predominantly against this liberal pluralist viewpoint that radicals of the New Left were forced to argue both in universities and in living rooms. It was the viewpoint of the overwhelming majority of their professors and of their "middle-class" parents. The concept of the "middle class" was also part and parcel of this ideological mystique, which promoted the idea that notions of hierarchical social stratification--such as "upper class" or "ruling class" and particularly "working class"--were merely remnants of the antiquated rhetorical baggage of the Marxist Old Left.

Most Americans--including my father who labored most of his working life for wages in a lumber mill and had been an activist in his labor union--believed that this mythical social obfuscation represented reality. Radicals who understood that American corporate capitalism concentrated wealth and power in the hands of a small segment of the population had largely been driven out of universities in the McCarthy era and their opinions were exiled from all but a tiny handful of obscure publications. There was one left-wing weekly newspaper, *The National Guardian*, which arrived concealed in a brown-paper wrapper at the office of the Old Left sympathizers with whom I happened to get a job in Springfield, Oregon, while attending the university in Eugene from 1955 to 1959. The paper presented a fairly uncritical orthodox Marxist line in its attempt to hold together the remnants of the Progressive Party movement of 1948, the Old Left's last effort at "popular front" politics. I was fortunate that this was not my only source of radical information while in college. The University of Oregon had the courage to hire a former Socialist Party member and labor historian, Val R. Lorwin, who had the great honor (at least in my eyes) of having been denounced as a "Communist" on the floor of the U.S. Senate by Joseph McCarthy himself. That Lorwin had worked during World War II for the OSS (Office of Strategic Services, the predecessor of the CIA) made little difference to me in the heyday of anti-Communist paranoia. He was eventually cleared of the charges and his arrival at the University of Oregon gave me the almost unique opportunity to learn some economic history from a true social democrat of revisionist persuasion who was proud of his politics. (He was a member of SDS's parent organization, the LID, and had grown up in the New York Jewish left.) Unless one had access to such privileged sources as mine, the fact that America had a capitalist economy based on the exploitation of labor and a far-flung military and economic empire was probably one of the best kept secrets in the history of human affairs during the politically barren years of the late 1950s.

The most coherent critique of the liberalist obfuscation of the capitalist dynamics of economy and society was, of course, that developed by Karl Marx and Friedrich Engels in the mid-to-late 19th century. At the heart of what had become *Marxist doctrine* was the belief that the industrial working class (and it alone), situated at the point of production and the only authentic producer of that surplus value which is appropriated by capitalists through exploitation of its labor, could "make the revolution." Lenin's rather drastic modifications of this thesis for "backward" Russia had not fundamentally altered the argument as regards developed industrial capitalist societies. The culture of "middle-classness" in American society represented the development of "false consciousness" among the workers. The task of good Marxists was to organize themselves to lead the workers when they awoke from this social and political dream-world.

The New Left, with its notions of participatory democracy and democratic radicalism, arose in the political wilderness between liberal obfuscation and Marxist dogma. And it grew most rapidly in the multiversity, the very institution that was transforming the character of the American work force more than any other since the introduction of the factory system itself. The major intellectual task facing the New Left was to develop an analysis and understanding of this transformation and to comprehend its relationship to prior radical analyses--especially Marxism. This challenge to New Left thought led to the development of the concept of "the new working class."

✦ *The Autobiography of an Analysis*

In June of 1966, I attended my first meeting of SDS's National Council (a quarterly gathering of chapter representatives and individual members). I had recently left my faculty position teaching history at Iowa State University in Ames, where I had helped to organize an SDS chapter and initiate an alternative political newspaper, *The Iowa Liberator.* I was actively involved with young radical ministers in the campus church foundations, helped organize civil rights and anti-war demonstrations, did a lot of public speaking, took students to visit the SDS ERAP project in Chicago, and generally became a focus of that university's campus radicalism.

My intensive involvement in the work of the campus ministries was particularly important for my general political and philosophical development. It was there that I was immersed in the milieu of religious existentialism which pervaded the thought-world of emerging Christian radicalism. Christian existentialism was to the 1960s what liberation theology became to the 1980s.

Although my family was not religious, I had been taught the fundamentalist version of Christianity in a Sunday school that I attended by my own free choice from the age of eight to twelve, and I became a believer in Jesus' gospel of love and forgiveness although the idea of "God" never seems to have become important to me. I did not belong to a church and my real house of worship was in the hills, streams, and mountains of the Pacific Northwest, which began ten minutes from my home and where I spent my every free moment and nourished a nature-centered spirituality that has remained at the heart of my true sense of devotion. During my adolescence I made systematic visitations of most of the Christian denominations in my home town, and I later joined the Disciples of Christ church as a senior in high school. It was there that I had my first real experience of organized religion and my first homosexual experiences as a young adult. Spirituality and unorthodox sexuality became intimately linked in my deepest being and I planned for a time to become a minister.

A disastrous sexual experience and a liberal college education ended my brief membership in the Christian church. I decided I was not a theist and became interested in Quakerism while at the University of Oregon through the influence of my freshman physics professor Francis Dart. Dart's class, the very first I attended in college, was the most brilliant demolition of the limits of scientific rationalism and materialism I have ever encountered. This mild-mannered Quaker mystic ranks among the half-dozen most important teachers in my life. When asked about Quakerism during a special social gathering of my class at his home, Dart once said that Quakers "had no theology." This idea struck me as terribly important and I began to translate this notion of *non-theological religion* into *non-theistic spirituality.* I was aided in my quest by three sources. First, I began to read *The Humanist,* a journal I discovered in the university library and where I explored the notion of humanistic spirituality or spiritual humanism. Secondly, an older friend of mine, Roger Weaver, who was a poet[1] and later became a Quaker, challenged me to read a compendium on Eastern spiritual traditions, *The Wisdom of China and India,*[2] where I began to discover the non-theistic spiritual paths of Buddhism and Taoism and first learned something of Hinduism. The third influence was my first living contact with the Buddhist tradition in the person of Mitzi Asai. The third daughter of a Japanese-American from a Zen Buddhist background, Mitzi was a teacher, pacifist, and (for a period of her life) a member of the Disciples of Christ church. She had spent part of her youth during World War II as a deportee in a U.S. concentration camp for Japanese-Americans. When her family was finally released from the camp and returned to Hood River, Oregon, the names of her two brothers who had served in the U.S. armed forces had been stricken from the American Legion's public Honor Roll. Her story, her past suffering, her good humor, and the idea of her Buddhist background, made a deep impression on me.

It was because of the influence of Francis Dart that I became an occasional participant at Quaker meetings, which seemed to me to convey the same sense of spiritual peace and wonderment I had known in my boyhood mountain ramblings. Moreover, Francis Dart gave me my first lessons in political nonviolence. He himself had refused an offer to work on the development of the atomic bomb in the Manhattan project. With his encouragement I began to make myself unpopular in the compulsory ROTC classes, which I thereby failed twice and was forced to repeat.

As a freshman I read Louis Fischer's *The Life of Mahatma Gandhi*[3] and was so deeply moved that I took it home and tried to talk to my father about it. I showed him the photograph on the back cover of the few simple belongings which were all Gandhi left behind at his death. "*That*," I said, "is how I want to live my life."

After finishing my B. A. in History at Oregon, two years of graduate study in European and American History at Cornell, four years of marriage, and a divorce, I spent twenty-six months in France. There I met and lived in a relationship with a young Frenchman, Jean Deveau, whose mother, a Catholic mystic, had a great influence on me. Jean Deveau was an activist in the *Parti Socialiste Unifié* (PSU), a "New Left" political party attempting to realign the French left from under the domination of the Stalinist Communist Party and the social democratic S.F.I.O. (*Section Française de l'Internationale Ouvrière*). With my companion, I was active in demonstrations against the Algerian War and learned of the work of *Jeune Résistance* (Young Resistance), a group of French draft resisters. I returned to the States in September 1963, took my comprehensive exams for my doctorate at Cornell, and was offered the job teaching History of Western Civilization at Iowa State a few days later. I planned to earn enough money to return to my new home in France. Unfortunately, my relationship came apart and I stayed at Iowa State for two-and-a-half years.

My work with the Christian student groups in Iowa came at a time when I was trying to reconcile the political radicalism developed as a student in the U.S. and France with both my sexual libertarianism and my increasingly unorthodox spiritual quest. It was during my years as a college teacher that a former student from Cornell, Jim Mitchell, introduced me to Vedanta Hinduism. A follower of Swami Bashananda, he lived part-time in the Vedanta Center in Chicago. I had begun to read about Buddhism, and E. A. Burtt's compendium, *The Teachings of the Compassionate Buddha*,[4] had become my personal spiritual guidebook. Encouraged by some campus ministers, I attended three seminars on Christian theology at the Ecumenical Institute in Chicago where a mix of Christian existentialism, intentional community, Maoism, and authoritarianism were combined under the rather dogmatic leadership of Joseph Matthews, the former mentor of Sandra (Casey) Hayden at the Austin, Texas, Faith and Life Community. My deep doubts about the Ecumenical Institute's attempt to rescue Christian theology from the historical dustbin were perhaps best expressed when I was asked to deliver a sermon during a visit by Matthews and his staff to Iowa State to conduct one of their seminars. I chose as my text a Buddhist teaching story, "The Parable of the Mustard Seed" (not to be confused with the New Testament parable of the same name.) I was becoming more at home with the Buddhist, non-theistic spiritual path though I occasionally attended the Ames Quaker Meeting. I should add, however, that I owe two debts to the Ecumenical Institute. I learned from them a great deal about modern Christian theology (including the work of Paul Tillich) and about the dangers of ideologically-centered, authoritarian, and sexually repressive organizations.

My first attempt to raise the question of gay liberation as a public political issue as well as a question of cultural change was in the winter of 1965-66. I helped organize a workshop on sexual liberation under the sponsorship of the United Campus Ministry and invited my closest gay American friend, Bob Buckle, to lead an encounter group. Buckle was a non-combatant conscientious objector serving as a psychiatric social worker in the U.S. Army at the time. He smuggled himself out of the military for a weekend and flew to Iowa at my behest. In preparation for the workshop, our underground newspaper, *The Iowa Liberator*, re-published an important statement on sexual freedom (including homosexual freedom) written by a group of British Quakers that first appeared in this country in *Liberation* magazine.[5]

It was also at Iowa State that I took my first public stands on the question of draft resistance. Among other activities, I arranged for the regional director of the Quaker-based American Friends Service Committee to speak in favor of opposition to the war and about draft resistance options in a public forum at the University. I also wrote the first political article I ever published in *The Iowa Liberator*. It was an editorial in response to Norman Morrison's act of self-immolation as a protest of the war on November 2, 1965.[6] I had been deeply moved and was very disturbed by Morrison's act as I had been by the self-immolation of Buddhist monks in Vietnam. I seriously wondered at the time whether such acts of self-sacrifice were the only way to resist the war. In my article, I defended Morrison's decision against those who would "psychologize" away its importance.

After two-and-a-half years at Iowa State, I thought it was time to move on and I tried to get a teaching job in Chicago which would have allowed me also to apply for the vacant position of editor of *New Left Notes*. I did not get the teaching job in Chicago and turned down another in upstate New York in favor of finishing my dissertation for Cornell. Because of my complex bisexual history, I did not want to become a national political figure. It had been painful enough living in a fish bowl as a radical teacher and organizer in Ames, Iowa. I did, however, like the idea of working full-time in the National Office of SDS in a relatively inconspicuous position.

My need to work in a more fully-committed role in the Movement was due in part to my feeling that I should be running the same risks as my students whom I was counseling to resist the draft. I found it morally indefensible to ask young men to risk prison while I held a cushy college teaching job. My companion,

Jane Adams, was also a powerful role model. She was a remarkable organizer who had spent two years working in the southern civil rights movement and had left to work for SDS, first in the National Office (NO) and later as regional organizer for the Upper Mid-West Region of SDS, which included Iowa. One of the early outspoken feminists in the New Left, she did not want to return to the fractious NO, which was notoriously male chauvinist. I convinced her to attend the National Council (NC) meeting in Ann Arbor in June 1966.

There we met two representatives of New York SDS, John Fuerst and Bob Gottlieb. Both were Marxists of an unorthodox persuasion and regarded me as somewhat of an anomaly, because I was not Jewish or from New York but knew something about Marxism and a lot of economic history. It was in a conversation with John Fuerst that I expressed my personal (though hardly original) political assessment of Marx's theories in relation to the New Left. I said I thought it was important to use certain "Marxian concepts," particularly categories of radical political economy, but that Marxism as an ideology should not be adopted by the New Left. My attitude was formed largely by my experience of living for two years in Paris with Jean Deveau, who regarded Marxists as *croyants* (true believers) and whose friends, Roland Barthes and Michel Foucault, were acute critics of Marxism. My explicit use of the term "Marxian" rather than "Marxist" was intended to convey my political distance from the ideological mainstream of Marxist dogmatism. I also argued with Fuerst that we should continue to use the terms "brother" and "sister" as forms of address, rather than the Marxist formulation, "comrade," because of the Quakerish roots of the American New Left.

Bob Gottlieb was from a Jewish Old Left background, but had become a kind of "neo-Marxist," having spent a year as a student at the University of Strasbourg in France where he had been involved in the Situationist International (*Internationale situationiste*), an action-oriented radical group focusing in particular on cultural criticism and the role of the media in consumerist society.[7] Gottlieb was familiar with the work of French neo-Marxists like André Gorz and Serge Mallet about whom I knew nothing.

Our major political activity at the Ann Arbor NC concentrated on convincing Jane Adams to run for the job of National

Secretary, which she eventually consented to do, probably against her better judgment. Her experience of working in the NO under its male chauvinist leadership had been devastating, and her commitment to feminist ideals was fueled in part by her experiences of a male-dominated New Left both in the South and in the North. She was elected National Secretary on an "interim" basis because neither she nor anyone else wanted to make a year-long commitment at that point to an overwhelming job that involved grueling work and promethean responsibilities at a salary of $15 per week.

I accompanied Jane Adams to Chicago and eventually went to work for her in the NO as Assistant National Secretary (office manager) and later as editor of *New Left Notes.* Jane Adams was adamant in her refusal to serve in her position past the end of the summer, and (turnabout being fair play) she and some other activists worked to elect me National Secretary at the Clear Lake National Council meeting immediately following the National Convention in late August-early September 1966. I accepted the job against my better judgment. I was too tired to resist.

Clear Lake was a watershed for SDS and the New Left as a whole. The election of Carl Davidson whose anarcho-syndicalist views were presented in his position paper, "Towards a Student Syndicalist Movement,"[8] marked the victory of the new "decentralist" tendency in the organization. My own radical roots were planted in the tradition of the IWW, of which my Finnish grandparents had been members and the principles of which I had studied and admired. Neither Davidson nor I were Marxists but we were both fairly well acquainted with Marx's ideas. We worked closely together for more than two years and many of the ideas associated with the "middle years" of SDS, between the Old Guard of 1960-66 and the factionalization of SDS in 1968-69, are associated with our names and were nurtured in long conversations we had together. Carl Davidson traveled, spoke, and wrote extensively. I was largely occupied with the tasks of coordination and administration in the National Office until, after the passage of the Draft Resistance Resolution in December 1966, I also began to travel and speak publicly. I had little time in those years of workdays often lasting sixteen or eighteen hours to write lengthy articles. The task of writing was more generally Carl Davidson's province.

How two young activists who were so closely attuned in their political outlook could have ended up later in such different camps has always been a major question in my mind. While I moved in the direction of a deeper commitment to the democratic, decentralist, and libertarian values that had been for me the most important aspect of the New Left's "participatory democracy" and that I identified with the IWW tradition in America, my friend who had embraced anarcho-syndicalism and became one of the most articulate spokesmen for the ideas associated with "new working class theory," eventually embraced a style of Old Left blue-collar "workerism" and Marxism-Leninism. In the radical divergence of our political paths lies some of the intimate history of the factionalization of the New Left.

♦ Manpower Channeling and The New Working Class

In the fall of 1966, new faces appeared in the new offices that SDS had occupied on Chicago's West Side. Among them was a young woman who had recently graduated from Swarthmore College and been working for the Congressional peace campaign of Bob Kastenmeier in Wisconsin. Cathy Wilkerson was an earnest, self-sacrificing person with a wry wit and a tenacious devotion to the New Left and the principles of human freedom and justice. She came from an upwardly-mobile middle-class background in Stamford, Connecticut, and her family had no ties to the Old Left. She describes her mother as a "very humane" woman who "attempted to deal with life on a very just basis" and who became a Quaker.[9] As a young person, Cathy had attended an innovative Quaker summer camp in Vermont called "Farm and Wilderness." She also attended a prestigious Quaker college, Swarthmore. She had resented the male intellectualist chauvinism of some of the leadership in her campus SDS chapter at Swarthmore and found the atmosphere in the National Office with its "Prairie Power" decentralist politics and its non-sexist libertarian style to be a breath of fresh air in the Movement.

She later said of her experience in the National Office that the

crowd of people there were . . . completely different than the Swarthmore male leadership. I felt I would be respected for my work,

not ignored because I was a woman. They were much more interested
in organizing and in reaching out. They were intellectually much freer.
They were willing to ask a lot of questions and did not ridicule people
for dissenting opinions. In a lot of ways, stylistically, I was much closer
to them. They were not so arrogant and competitive, and snooty, and
they had a sense of humor.[10]

Late that winter of 1966-67 Wilkerson began working on a
paper with Peter Henig from the Ann Arbor Radical Education
Project (REP). Their concern was with the specific issue of how
the Selective Service System used both conscription *and* deferments from military service to satisfy the labor power needs of an
advanced technological industrial society. Their paper (which
unfortunately bore only Henig's name) was entitled "On the
Manpower Channelers." Based on interviews with Selective
Service personnel and documents published by the System,
Wilkerson and Henig assembled pieces of data and analysis which
blew the minds of SDSers so thoroughly that their impact
amounted to the beginning of a revolution in mind-set, a true
gestalt switch in the way SDSers like myself approached questions
of political and social theorizing in the United States. This was
analysis born not of Marxist dogma nor of liberal cant but derived
from very clear-eyed questioning of a particular mechanism of the
state by two young New Leftists whose minds were critically
informed but not bound by ideological rigidity and whose use of
language was clear and free of jargon.

In a passage that laid the groundwork for subsequent thinking
about the "new working class," their paper quoted a Selective
Service memorandum to local draft boards on "Channeling" which
read:

> The line dividing the primary function of armed forces manpower
> procurement from the process of channeling manpower into civilian
> support is often finely drawn. The process of channeling by not taking
> men from certain activities who are otherwise liable for service, or by
> giving deferment to men in certain occupations, is actual procurement
> by inducement of manpower for civilian activities which are manifestly
> in the national interest.
>
> While the best known purpose of Selective Service is to procure
> manpower for the armed forces, a variety of related processes take
> place outside of delivery of manpower to the active armed forces.
> Many of these may be put under the heading of "channeling
> manpower." Many young men would not have pursued a higher

education if there had not been a program of student deferment. Many young scientists, engineers, tool and die makers, and other possessors of scarce skills would not remain in their jobs in the defense effort if it were not for a program of occupational deferments. Even though the salary of a teacher has historically been meager, many young men remain in that job, seeking the reward of a deferment.

The memorandum spoke of the effectiveness of "the club of induction" and "pressurized guidance" and exposed the totalitarian face of American militarism in two sentences that were repeated over and over in New Left speeches on the war and the draft:

> The psychology of granting wide choice under pressure to take action is the American or indirect way of achieving what is done by direction in foreign countries where choice is not permitted. Here, choice is limited but not denied, and it is fundamental that an individual generally applies himself better to do something he has decided to do rather than something he has been told to do.[11]

♦ Naming a "Class"

Bob Gottlieb of New York SDS (whom I had met at the June 1966 NC in Ann Arbor) had teamed up with David Gilbert and Gerry Tenney to write a long position paper for SDS which came to be known humorously as "The Port Authority Statement." This lengthy document drew heavily on the work of the French neo-Marxists, André Gorz and Serge Mallet. Gorz, actually of Austrian origin, had been a long-time associate of Jean-Paul Sartre and served on the editorial board of *Les Temps Modernes*, the leading existentialist journal. Gorz's *Strategy for Labor*[12] and Mallet's *La Nouvelle Classe Ouvrière*[13] were the most important neo-Marxist attempts to update the Marxian framework to account for the radical change in the composition of the labor force. It was from Gorz and Mallet that Gottlieb, Gilbert, and Tenney borrowed the phrase "new working class."

The three authors of "The Port Authority Statement" were active in a political education effort in the New York Region of SDS. This New York regional Radical Education Project planned a conference to present the general framework of ideas about the "new working class." It would be held in Princeton, New Jersey, in

February.

Since this was to be a conference of predominantly New York Jewish left-wing intellectuals, the probability that it would end in sectarian mayhem was regarded as very high. That is most likely why I was invited to speak. During my sophomore year at the University of Oregon, I had lived as a gentile guest in the only Jewish fraternity on campus. Since I was intimately acquainted with Jewish culture, had always had many Jewish friends, and knew a lot of Jewish in-jokes about gentiles and a few choice bits of Yiddish, I was a perfect moderator between the New Yorkers and the outlanders. I also knew something about Marxism, the *lingua franca* of the New York crowd, and that made me intellectually acceptable even if my IWW ancestry was highly suspect. In reality, I was somewhat intimidated by the hyper-intellectualism of the New York Jewish intelligentsia who were as likely to use Marxian concepts to control political debates as for any clarification of arguments. Political debates in these circles always seemed to me "Talmudic" in their spirit of contentious disputation and I had begun to think of Marxism as a kind of secularized, materialist Judaism.

This unusual ethnic-political situation reminded me of the problems of the IWW in the Pacific Northwest where that organization had been overwhelmingly identified with the Finnish community of which I was a part as a child. So much had this been the case that Finn Halls and IWW Halls were almost synonymous, and the ensuing ethnic narrowness had been something of an obstacle to the outreach of the organization in that region.

Clearly one of the obstacles to open, honest communication in the New Left was the taboo on discussions of the role of Jews in the Movement and in the history of the American left. This prohibition was born of very real sensitivity to the immense tragedy of the Nazi extermination program and the fear of being labeled "anti-semitic." A truly frank discussion of these questions still remains to be held. The only New Left writer to have touched on the subject is Daniel Cohn-Bendit, the French anarchist of partially Jewish background, in his book *Le grand bazar.*[14]

I had met with Gottlieb and Gilbert on perhaps three occasions between the passage of the SDS Draft Resistance Resolution at Berkeley and the proposed Princeton Conference on February 17-19. We were becoming friends. I also became acquainted with others who were part of the group calling themselves the New York Radical Education Project (in contradistinction to the Radical Education Project in Ann Arbor). New York REP members were deeply committed to the idea of developing radical theory for the New Left. I shared their concern for the general lack of effective political education in SDS and agreed to support their pet project: a radical theory supplement to *New Left Notes* that would provide a forum for serious debate on theoretical issues. The National Administration Committee (NAC) which oversaw the workings of the National Office approved this project "on an experimental basis" with the proviso that it would be overseen by an editorial board based in New York. The board was made up of volunteers living in New York and included the three authors of "The Port Authority Statement"--Gottlieb, Gilbert, and Tenney--plus John Fuerst, Steve Halliwell, Laurie Mamet, and Beth Gottlieb. The supplement was named *Praxis* and the lead article of the first edition was entitled "Praxis and the New Left,"[15] which was described as "the first part of a new paper called The Port Authority Statement." Gottlieb, Gilbert, and Tenney went on to say that their paper was "a joint effort to try to inject further development of radical socialist theory for the New Left." Their use of the term "radical socialist" instead of simply "radical," the use of "praxis" as their key concept, and the regular reference to Marx and Marxist texts placed them clearly within the Marxist tradition. The following paragraph leaves little doubt about their orientation and commitment to the framework of Marxist discourse.

> Praxis can first be defined as the development of consciousness through men's relations to production. Through that process, theories of society, of class, and of man's relation to man and nature gradually develop and then reflect back on men's human practical activity. Knowledge comes from activity and in turn affects and shapes that activity. This knowledge becomes political consciousness when it develops out of the class relations of production. Therefore, class consciousness is the highest form of political consciousness. Class-in-itself (in terms of its relation to the means of production) becomes class-for-itself (consciousness of its political and historical role).

It was sophisticated. It was incomprehensible to most SDSers.

It presented a classic Marxist "materialist" view of the question of consciousness. And it was the open lid of Pandora's Box.

Back at the National Office after several weeks of extensive traveling related to draft resistance organizing (and frustrating efforts at fund-raising), I barely had time to read the *Praxis* supplement. Furthermore, I was appalled to find I could not understand the lead article. Like most Marxist theorizing, it seemed turgid, abstruse, abstract, and stultifying. Above all it contained a specifically "materialist" formulation of the question of consciousness that I had never been able to absorb in all my years of exposure to those ideas. Something deep inside me rebelled at the shallowness and narrowness of this view of consciousness. Its reductionism made no intuitive sense to me.

Rather than *grounding* consciousness in real life activity (activity of the hand, the heart, and the spirit), this Marxist formulation turned consciousness into a narrow question of intellect as a mirror of the so-called "material world" and reduced consciousness development to a sociological issue. It was a "materialism" that in the guise of concreteness actually promoted intellectual abstraction. Rather than helping New Leftists clarify their experience, it downgraded experience, feelings, and intuition and promoted a cult of intellectual elitism which lorded it over those who could not master the intricacies of the language. The use of Marxist jargon rather than ordinary English in itself was sufficient to promote the creation of an elitist cult in which a few "theorists" would interpret the "meaning" of the sacred canon. For the New Left in particular, which drew its creativity and its originality from its openness and experimental sensibilities, this movement away from experiential groundedness to "grand," intellectually abstract theory was a disaster. While claiming to reunite consciousness with the "material conditions" of human life, Marxism reduced consciousness to the mechanical reflection of sociological processes and denied those dimensions of human experience that relate to spiritual, emotional, moral, and aesthetic consciousness. All the latter, *plus politics*, must finally be reducible to "men's relations to production" in order for the entire system to work.

I believe it is safe to say that the Marxist concept of consciousness and its development bore little relation to what most New Left radicals believed about consciousness--whether or not they adhered to any theory or philosophical school. By tying the important insights about the multiversity and their key idea--the "new working class"--to the Marxist materialist notion of consciousness, the "Port Authority" writers doomed what might have been an elucidating sociological concept to the arena of abstruse sectarian debate.

My years of spiritual seeking and my sense of human life told me that there was something fundamentally wrong with what I read in *Praxis*. But I did not know how to articulate all that in terms that I felt I could defend publicly. I was intimidated by my own apparent inability to comprehend what these people--these new friends of mine--were saying. And yet I was invited to speak at *their* conference.

✦ *Resigning From the Draft*

There were other things pressing on my mind with a greater sense of urgency than how to define *praxis*. I had recently made a decision I thought would send me to jail.

Draft resistance was the most important priority for SDS organizing in the winter of 1967 for me and most of my close associates. My personal situation vis-a-vis conscription had long been troubling me. Since I was twenty-nine, I was three years beyond eligible draft age. And yet, the same moral imperative that had operated in my decision to leave college teaching for full-time work in the Movement also affected my thinking as National Secretary. How could I continue to organize young men to resist the draft and risk imprisonment while I myself remained exempt from jeopardy? Actually, organizing draft resistance was itself punishable by a $10,000 fine and/or five years in jail. But that did not satisfy my conscience. I wanted to become a total non-cooperator and do it in a way which would promote SDS's draft resistance program.

Fortuitously, the connivance of the United States government provided me with the perfect opportunity. SDS had been invited to attend a conference in Washington, D.C., organized for the purpose of co-opting the draft resistance movement, and thus undercutting opposition to the war by promoting support for a

"voluntary army" and a program of "voluntary national service."
The NAC agreed to send me to the conference with the goal of
organizing a radical caucus in opposition to this blatant attempt at
liberal co-optation of the student movement. It was also agreed
that I would use this occasion, if possible, to read a personal letter
of resignation from the Selective Service System that would place
me in the status of non-cooperator. This was designed both to
fulfill the needs of my own conscience and to promote SDS's draft
resistance program. It was felt that the imprisonment of the
National Secretary for non-cooperation would not only provide a
good example to individual SDSers but perhaps stir chapters to
collective action. I did exactly what had been decided by the NAC.

In an article written for *New Left Notes* after the conference,
entitled "The Moderation of Cooptation,"[16] I outlined the
meeting, which had been held under the sponsorship of *Moderator* magazine, apparently a government front the exact ties of
which remained unclear. I had challenged the conference in the
name of "the most militantly democratic organization in the
country." I explained to the assembled delegates of the 17 other
national student organizations that SDS had "a democratically
arrived at position of draft resistance." The key speaker for the
Moderator (i.e., *government*) position was a Mr. Bob Greenway
who just happened to be the Deputy Director for Institutional
Relations of the United States Peace Corps, which I characterized
in my article as "the Salvation Army of American Imperialism."
Mr. Greenway first invoked Norman Vincent Peale's *power of
positive* (read "positivist") *thinking.* He then quoted "a classical
Greek politician" who allegedly said, "What we need is a good
war!" to boost his argument that what America "needs is a good
definition of 'commitment' in terms of 'voluntarism.'" I characterized Greenway's presentation as "double-think" which, combined
with the insistence on narrowing the discussion to the draft while
refusing to discuss the war in Vietnam and its relation to
American corporate capitalism, expansionism, and imperialism,
represented "the voice of cooptative corporate liberal society." I
spent most of my time at the conference caucusing with the
dissenting radical participants from the University Christian
Movement, the American Friends Service Committee, and the
Federation of Newman Clubs, who managed to limit the final
statement of the conference to two points: "united opposition to

the draft and a common concern for involvement in relevant social action." Beyond the radical minority, there was in my eyes

> a frightening blindness to the relatedness of issues, to the links between any military establishment in America and its use in implementing America's imperialist foreign policy, between student alienation and social concern and the need for radical social change in America, between opposition to coercion at home and American coercion abroad.

At a press conference following the *Moderator* meeting (which included both the U.S. Student Press Association and the professional Washington press corps), I read a radical minority statement which called not only for the abolition of conscription and stated that "aggressive American policies towards underdeveloped countries should be changed," but also advocated draft refusal and non-cooperation with the Selective Service System. I then read my statement of non-cooperation to the assembled press in the form of a letter of resignation to my local draft board.

When I had finished, the press applauded. Then, much to my dismay, Sherman Chickering, Editor of *Moderator* magazine, "pulled out of his pocket a telegram which he read to the press, from 'Paul Booth, past president of SDS'":

> Regret unable to attend. Believe Left can work with voluntarist position on service. Urge you call, with cooperation of appropriate groups, nationwide open student convocation for Spring to adopt resolution on draft and related questions.

There it was again: "Build, Not Burn!" It was what was called in the National Office of SDS "the Booth-MacNamara Proposal." In that moment was contained for me the true political substance of the profound difference between the politics of the social-democratic "Old Guard" of SDS and the new generation of radical libertarian and decentralist democrats.

After the appearance of my article describing these events, a leading spokesperson of the Old Guard called me at the National Office and accused me of having "the politics of Timothy Leary and Prince Kropotkin." At the time I knew nothing about the rather opportunistic Dr. Leary. I had experienced one LSD session with the guidance of a friend (a part-time Vedanta monk who shared my spiritual interests), and I am ashamed to admit that I had never read a single word from the writings of the Russian anarchist, Prince Peter Kropotkin. Like most New Leftists of a decentralist persuasion, I was woefully deficient in my knowledge of the writers of the anarchist tradition. My only real knowledge of the historical roots of the decentralist alternatives to Marxist centralism was my understanding of the American IWW.

The same week that the *Praxis* supplement appeared along with my article on the *Moderator* conference, I wrote another short article before leaving for the Princeton REP Conference that, I feel, says more about my politics than the criticisms that were hurled at me at the time and since. The article was entitled "Democratic Decentralism,"[17] a phrase I coined to describe what I felt was the substance of *both the politics and the organizational form* of SDS and the New Left more broadly conceived. It was a direct reaction against the authoritarian Leninist doctrine of cadre organization called, misleadingly, "democratic centralism." In addition, it was a reaction to "sectarian anarchism" of the rigid, dogmatic type that mirrored the sectarianism of the Marxist-Leninists. I chose to use this term because it identified more substantively for me the content of the New Left's politics than did the phrase "participatory democracy," which I felt relied too much on the rather vague, and cooptable notion of "participation," without designating clearly enough the radical *structural* grassroots vision of a decentralist approach. It was, after all, possible for both liberals and Marxist-Leninists to argue that they, too, favored "democratic participation." This notion of "democratic decentralism" was an attempt on my part to find a political vocabulary that would break the stranglehold in which the century-old battle between Marxists and Anarchists had ensnared the left.

Unfortunately, SDS never learned the important lesson that structures and responsibility are absolutely necessary ingredients of any democratic political formation--be it a primitive village or a national movement--and that these two questions are intimately intertwined. Unhappily, once the Marxist-Leninist invasion of SDS began in earnest, it was too late to learn how a large, democratic organization could be structured to realize decentralist principles. In the disarray caused by increasing numbers of Marxist-Leninists within SDS, "participatory democracy" risked becoming empty rhetoric in the name of which all manner of manipulation took place.

♦ *The Crisis of Black Power and the Maoist Invasion*

There were concerns that I brought to the Princeton REP Conference other than the problem of reconciling the insights of neo-Marxist New Yorkers with Prairie Power decentralism. The rise of the Black Power movement, launched by SNCC and propagated nation-wide by that organization's new Chairman, Stokely Carmichael, was creating a crisis of major proportions in the ranks of white radicals. Carmichael's election had displaced the five-year tenure of John Lewis, whose Christian pacifism no longer suited the mood of organizers grown impatient with Gandhian non-violence and the whole notion of racial integration as a program and goal. The self-suffering that in Gandhian terms was supposed to create spiritual-political power, was increasingly perceived as only creating more suffering.

Black Power was a version of the politics of revolutionary black separatism that had been preached by Malcolm X. It was diametrically opposed to the politics of Martin Luther King, Jr., and marked the end of the spirit of "black and white together" that had been absolutely essential to the unity and survival of the Movement. The adoption of black nationalism and the attendant racialist separatism by SNCC was marked by the exclusion of white organizers from its ranks. Mendy Samstein was one of the first whites to challenge this policy in the SNCC Atlanta Project where black separatism first emerged in the winter of 1965-66,[18] and his later work in organizing draft resistance was spurred by the need to find a white corollary to the new brand of SNCC militancy. Samstein's effort was reflective of the crisis among white radicals. How could they respond to the challenge that SNCC posed and still maintain their integrity? How not simply to be placed in the role of an auxiliary to the black movement? If Black Power was an assertion of black selfhood, then it was also a challenge to the selfhood of white radicals.

The second difficulty that preoccupied me in the period before the Princeton Conference involved the invasion of SDS by the Maoist Progressive Labor Party. PL was the product of a handful of Marxist-Leninist diehards from the American Communist Party who had refused to accept de-Stalinization and Kruschev's new Soviet party-line of peaceful coexistence.[19] In their break from the CP, they adopted the ideological stance of the Chinese Communist Party and became the major organizational expression of Maoism in the United States.

They would most probably have remained an obscure Stalinist sect had they not decided to invade SDS and treat it as a front organization to be manipulated and from which to recruit new cadres at the very point where SNCC's Black Power stance demanded a response from white radicals. It was probably the most disastrous decision of SDS's history not to exclude them. A proposal was made in 1966 in response to their appearance at the Clear Lake Convention (still in small numbers) to exclude members of outside Leninist organizations, but it failed out of naive loyalty to the old "non-exclusion" principle that had been adopted by SDS as a way to fight the anti-Communist hysteria left over from the McCarthy era. I regret to admit that I was one of the naive opponents of exclusion at Clear Lake and, like many others, came to realize too late that we had opened the door to the destruction of SDS.

PL was not only an organizational threat. It was also a bearer of the whole issue of Third Worldism and peasant-based, Marxist-Leninist-led revolutionary guerrilla warfare like that being waged in Vietnam, while at the same time espousing a particular brand of blue-collar workerism. In addition, there were two other challenges embodied in part in the PL invasion, but also represented by other small sects operating on the fringes of SDS. These may be named the challenge of "ideological Marxism" and the challenge of "Leninist organizational authoritarianism." There was increasing pressure on the New Left, especially after SNCC's adoption of the Black Power stance, to adopt a rigid ideological formula and an equally rigid organizational structure. Orthodox Marxism and the military command structure of Lenin's so-called "democratic centralism" (in reality a political version of a military general staff plus an army with certain discussion privileges) were the leading contenders for those roles.

Another, and perhaps the most decisive, issue being raised by the Marxist-Leninist challenge, reached to the very heart of the question of the identity and the authenticity of the student movement and the New Left. This question was made all the more urgent by the fact that SNCC had cast the identity question in racial terms. What response could white student radicals give to the new assertion of *black revolutionary identity*? The traditional Leninist formulation that categorized students as a privileged sector of middle-class intellectuals or, to use the European terminology, as "the petite bourgeoise intelligentsia," offered a safe, decisive, time-honored definition that played into the hands of the various Communist sects. It was, I believe, this question of identity that determined the emerging crisis of the New Left and its subsequent devolution.

All these developments--Black Power, Maoist Third World-ism, guerrilla warfare, Marxist ideology, and Leninist organization--offered direct challenges to white radicals. My oft-reprinted speech was an attempt to address these challenges. It can perhaps best be understood as an existentialist version of "Not By Bread Alone."

◆ The Princeton Speech

Thoughts on these questions had been stirring in my mind and were current in conversations among my close associates in SDS. I was, however, still in a state of intellectual turmoil when I arrived at the Princeton Conference. The first, rather chaotic evening of the gathering was marked by a decisive event. After David Gilbert had presented a rambling summary of "The Port Authority Statement," Max Gordon, a former editor of the Communist Party's *Daily Worker* rose to denounce the new analysis. In terms worthy of the pompous arrogance and not so subtle elitism of the Stalinist Old Left, Gordon railed against the "idealistic values" and cultural criticisms of the New Left, arguing in the most condescending tones that *the workers don't care about your values or ideals or cultural sensitivity--what they care about is bread--you students are the middle-class intelligentsia who must stop talking about their values and start talking about the material things workers want, bread and wages.*[20]

Gordon's speech was both offensive and enormously stimulat-ing in its negativity. Every piece of a complex puzzle began to fall in place in my mind and the elements of a new theoretical framework began to assemble themselves. Whoever Marx Gordon, the orthodox Marxist-Leninist, believed us to be, we certainly were not *that*. In reaction to his obviously fallacious portrait of our identity and of the values that motivated us, I painted a new picture. That night, with David Gilbert sleeping on the floor beside me, I furiously scribbled the notes for the morrow's speech.

It began with a story told in the spiritual-existentialist-psychotherapeutic style that had come to mark my brand of political presentation:

> Let me begin by telling you a story which I recently heard. It is a story about the guerrilla forces in Guatemala and about how they work. I do not know what image you might have in your head about the operation of the Guatemalan guerrillas--I am not certain about the accuracy of this story. But in any case it makes sense to me and it speaks to me about who we are--the new radicals.
>
> It is said that when the Guatemalan guerrillas enter a new village, they do not talk about the "anti-imperialist struggle" nor do they give lessons on dialectical materialism--neither do they distribute copies of the "Communist Manifesto" or of Chairman Mao's *On Contradiction*. What they do is gather together the people of the village in the center of the village and then, one by one, the guerrillas rise and talk to the villagers about their lives; about how they see themselves and how they came to be who they are, about their deepest longings and the things they've striven for and hoped for, about the way in which their deepest longings were frustrated by the society in which they lived.
>
> Then the guerrillas encourage the villagers to talk about their lives. And then a marvelous thing begins to happen. People who thought that their deepest problems and frustrations were their individual problems discover that their problems and longings are all the same--that no one man is any different than the others. That, in Sartre's phrase, "In each man there is all of man." And, finally, that out of the discovery of their common humanity comes the decision that men must unite together in the struggle to destroy the conditions of their common oppression.
>
> That, it seems to me, is what we are about.[21]

There seem to have been several motives in my recounting of this perhaps mythical story in this way. First and foremost, I was reacting against the materialist reductionism and the elitism of Max Gordon's speech the prior evening. The notion that some human beings (the workers) live for bread alone was both vulgar Marxist rubbish and horribly elitist in my eyes. As a young man from a blue-collar working-class background, I was deeply offended by this brand of New York Bolshevik snobbery. Secondly, my exposure to existentialism, both religious and secular, had provided me with a vocabulary for talking about spiritual concerns without resorting to traditional Christian or Judaic categories (thus the reference to Sartre). Thirdly, I intended to undercut the romanticism that was developing around the growing cult of Che Guevara and guerrilla warfare, a development that was clearly both dangerous and captivating. The Guatemalan guerrilla story was not intended to romanticize guerrilla warfare but to offer a humanistic interpretation of that movement as a specific mode of *political organizing* in which human solidarity is built not through armed conflict but through self-revelation and through the most sensitive attention to the bonds that are created by the honest exposure of self. Finally, I intended to reaffirm a mode of organizing through self-revelation that had developed in my encounters with men like Mendy Samstein--a method of personal politics that affirmed the healing, or psychotherapeutic, benefits of openness and honesty. It was the method of the "soul session," which had developed spontaneously in the "freedom high" wing of SNCC and which was being threatened by the new style of militant machismo spawned by the Stokely Carmichael wing of SNCC. It was the method that argued for putting our deepest selves, as well as our bodies, on the line and that had begun to be the key dynamic in draft resistance organizing.

I went on to draw a picture of the development of values and consciousness that emphasized libertarian ideals of freedom and the necessary union of personal liberation and political radicalism. It was the contrary of the objectified materialist approach of Max Gordon or other Marxist-Leninists for whom the very idea of self-revelation as an integral part of organizing was "subjectivism" and "decadent bourgeois self-indulgence" at its worst. I also intended to clarify the deep psychological and existential dynamics that divided New Left radicals from reformist liberals. I said:

> Contrary to what was suggested here last evening, revolutionary mass movements are not built out of a drive for the acquisition of more material goods. That is a perversion and vulgarization of revolutionary thought and a misreading of history. Revolutionary movements are freedom struggles born out of the perception of the contradictions between human potentiality and oppressive actuality.

I offered an operational definition of the word "freedom" used in a political context and of "revolutionary consciousness":

> Revolutionary consciousness interprets those social, economic and political structures which maintain the existing gap between potentiality and actuality as the objective conditions of oppression which must be transformed. Revolutionary consciousness sees the transformation of those oppressive conditions as the act of liberation and sees the realization of the previously frustrated human potentiality as the achievement of freedom. The bonds of oppression are broken and the new reality is constructed.

These concepts of "freedom" and "human potentiality" are the imprint of existentialist thinking on my mind, not the product of the study of Marx or economic history. They are more the product of my study of existentialism and of my work with campus religious groups at Iowa State University than of any association with organized leftists. Finally, they are the product of my own spiritual journey that had led me, as early as my freshman year in college, to identify with the "inner light" tradition of the Quakers, the pantheism of St. Francis, Vedanta Hinduism, and later with the spiritual humanism of the Buddhist tradition. It is more accurate to portray me as an existentialist and champion of "prefigurative politics," as Wini Breines later did,[22] than as a "near Marxist" as others have done. But it is also true that I owed a great debt to the study of economic history which was, of course, influenced by Marx's contributions. And I believed very strongly that it was necessary to incorporate insights on political economy and social class into the thinking of the New Left if it was to stand up to orthodox Marxism. Additionally, I had read the translations of Marx's so-called "humanist" writings, "The Economic and Philosophical Manuscripts of 1844," and was aware of the attempt in the late 1950s and early 1960s to portray a Marxist humanism in contradistinction to the later "scientific" Marx. I had even delivered a sermon on "Marxism and Existentialism" at the Unitarian Fellowship in Ames, Iowa, in 1965.

I was not, however, a philosophical materialist (dialectical or otherwise) and both my spiritual roots and existentialism were decisive in shaping my moral and political outlook. Why, it has been asked, did I not express myself directly in religious or spiritual language? I can only say that in the New Left as I experienced it, the taboo on talking about spirituality was as great if not greater than the taboo on homosexuality. The existentialist vocabulary enabled me to talk about spiritual values just as the work of Herbert Marcuse allowed me to talk about forbidden topics of sexual politics. Neither approach was entirely adequate to the task of dealing honestly with sexuality and spirituality. However, in 1967, there was little else available to New Leftists struggling to bridge the chasm between political theory and their personal experience.

"There is only one impulse," I argued at Princeton, "that can create and sustain an authentic revolutionary movement. The revolutionary struggle is always and always must be a struggle for freedom. No individual, no group, no class is genuinely engaged in a revolutionary movement unless their struggle is a struggle for their own liberation."

These fairly heady phrases were born of the conviction that New Left radicalism grew out of a fundamentally different psychological dynamic than liberal reformism, Social Democracy, or the Old Left. I was convinced that our movement grew out of the deepest longings for human freedom and that the struggle for this freedom--the struggle for the birth of a new selfhood--was the heart and soul, the very core of what we were about and that was what we meant by "liberation."

My target was a threat larger than Marxism-Leninism or Black Power separatism; it was the monster that would eventually consume the New Left, *the politics of guilt and self-hatred.* It was the politics I associated with liberal reformism. I argued that:

> The point which is important to understand is clearly illustrated by the difference between radical or revolutionary consciousness and "liberal" consciousness. The profound gap which separates a liberal reform movement from a revolutionary freedom movement is revealed in the dynamics of the participants.
>
> Liberal reformists (including revisionist social democrats inside and outside the CP) react out of guilt motivation. . . .
>
> The liberal reformist is always engaged in "fighting someone else's battles.". . .
>
> The liberal does not speak comfortably of "freedom" or "liberation" but rather of justice and social amelioration. . . .
>
> Liberal consciousness is conscience translated into action for others.

The image of guilt-ridden liberals fighting other people's battles and unaware of their own unfreedom was drawn from real-life experiences of work in the American New Left. Its language--e.g., "action for others"--was most probably an unconscious reference to Sartre's notion of "being-for-others," a state of existential unfreedom.

My argument was not that we should act only in our selfish interests and ignore the needs of others, but that we needed to be in touch with our own unfreedom if we were to act authentically in concert with others. In my mind, this is what distinguished liberal reformism from genuine radicalism. It was the translation of the Guatemalan guerrilla myth into American political realities. I said that:

> Radical or revolutionary consciousness perceives contradiction in a totally different fashion [from liberal reformist consciousness]. The gap is not between oneself, what one is, and the under-privileged but is the gap between "what one could be" and the existing conditions for self-realization. It is the perception of oneself as unfree, as oppressed--and finally it is the discovery of oneself as *one of the oppressed* who must unite to transform the objective conditions of their existence in order to resolve the contradiction between potentiality and actuality.

♦ *The Question of Class*

At that point I took a step which I have regretted many times. In order to deal with the theoretical challenges facing us, I had to face *the question of class.* In so doing I did not dismiss Marx's contribution but I attempted to use some Marxian ideas while updating the whole question of "class analysis" and thereby to outrun orthodox Marxism. My first move was to appropriate the concept of "false consciousness" and secondly to adopt the category of "the new working class" being developed by the authors of "The Port Authority Statement." I accomplished the first by essentially equating "false consciousness" with the existentialist notion of "inauthenticity" and thereby linked the "gut-level alienation" of New Leftists to the social ideology of "middle classness" in America. In my mind, the greatest obstacles to the healthy radicalization of the student movement were the "myth of the middle class" and the belief that the only *real* form of oppression was material deprivation. Here American ideology and Marxist materialism joined hands in obfuscating the reality of the New Left as an authentic political force. I believed that the social and political consciousness of most students was the result of pervasive ideological conditioning designed to convince them that the vast majority of Americans were members of the "middle class." The strongest argument for this belief was the relatively high level of material consumption and the relative marginality of poverty.

The revolt against consumerist materialism was already part of the sensibility of the New Left and had been nourished by the writers of the Beat Generation in their artistic and cultural revolt. It remained to demonstrate just how an advanced capitalist economy needed to promote consumerism in order to maintain a large and growing domestic market to absorb increased production and avoid crises of overproduction. This exposure of the true nature of affluence was combined with the theory of multiversities and the new working class to expose the undemocratic nature of the society and the economy. It raised the issue of *control* as the primary political, social, and economic issue in America and as such, extended the framework of *participatory democracy*.

I chose the Marxian category of "false consciousness" to describe the hold that the myth of the middle class had on the American mind. It was to my mind the clearest conceptual tool for understanding how vast numbers of human beings could remain blind to the class nature of their society and to their real interests. In fact, I had little idea what Marx had said on this subject. False consciousness was a category I had most probably gleaned from political discussions over many years and it seemed quite appropriate to me, especially given the ideological blindness so apparent in the United States.

In the years since the demise of the New Left, the concept of false consciousness has been repeatedly scrutinized and attacked. It would be possible to substitute another, non-Marxian phrase (for instance *social and political blindness*) but the fact remains that without some critical category to explain this important social reality, one is left with a totally non-critical *positivism*. This is, after all, the real issue of radical political and social thought: not Marxism versus anti-Marxism but *radical critical theory versus liberal positivism*. It was precisely this issue that had motivated Herbert Marcuse to write *Reason and Revolution: Hegel and the*

Rise of Social Theory.[23] And although Marcuse later denied that
his effort was designed to revive Marxism, such was, in fact, the
side effect of much of his work. Coming from the Frankfurt
School in Germany, Marcuse represented a tradition of sophisticated analysis regarding Marxist studies that had no counterpart in
the United States where a virtual ban on the teaching of Marx
created a general naivete which, instead of "inoculating" intellectuals against what the conservatives regarded as a "political virus,"
in fact predisposed rebellious youth not only to eat of the
forbidden fruit but to swallow it whole.

✦ *The New Working Class*

I want to make clear that the idea of the new working class
did not develop *for me* out of reading French neo-Marxists but
out of trying to understand the multiversity and the concept of
"manpower channeling" as developed by Peter Henig and Cathy
Wilkerson. I had never read Serge Mallet or André Gorz nor had
I been involved in discussions of their work. The phrase "new
working class" did, however, enter my vocabulary from conversations with Bob Gottlieb and David Gilbert, authors (together with
Gerry Tenney) of "The Port Authority Statement." My own
interpretation of what the phrase meant was worked out without
reading their work or that of their sources. I had a fairly loose
definition of "the working class." As a young man from the
industrial blue-collar working class, I defined the working class as
anybody who had to work for somebody else for wages or salary.
The major distinction in my mind as I grew up was the difference
between the boring, stultifying work in the mills and less
oppressive jobs, be they soda jerking in drugstores or the work of
school teachers. By the time I spoke at the Princeton Conference,
the working class meant for me anybody who did not own capital
or who did not (like professionals, farmers, and shopkeepers) have
an independent livelihood. Workers were people like my father
who had worked in a lumber mill or like me who had worked as a
college teacher.

The basic issue for me as a working-class New Leftist was
people's control over their lives. My point in adopting the term
"new working class" was not to create an elitist notion of

college-trained workers, but to convince all of these wonderful young people, like the ones I had taught at Iowa State, that they were not going to be part of a mythical "middle class" but part of new strata of the working class. My goal was to convince them that their real interests were the same as the interests of blue-collar workers with whom they should join, not as an elite of Marxist-Leninist cadres, but as fellow workers in a common struggle for freedom and democratic control of their lives. My definition of "workers" was in essence the same as that of the IWW of my Finnish grandparents, which had always been willing to welcome into its ranks all people who worked for a living except lawyers (whose work depended on the existence of the state).

The Marxist criterion of the production of surplus value and the attendant labor theory of value were not of particular concern to me. My concern was that of participatory democracy--people's control over their lives. I was deeply concerned that they maintain the values they had developed in the New Left, the values of radical democracy, anti-militarism, greater cultural and personal and sexual freedom, racial equality, nonviolence, and particularly the style of gender equality and liberation from oppressive models of femininity and masculinity. All these libertarian values were absolutely essential to my personal vision of liberation and my deepest hope was that as the New Left grew to include the vast majority of the American people, old working class and new, its values and vision would be nourished and grow. My deepest fear was that its finest sensibilities would be denied and destroyed by a reversion to the life-hating, authoritarian practices of the Stalinist Old Left.

I wanted to enlist certain Marxian concepts in the service of libertarian ideals. The effect was unfortunately the opposite.

◆ *Conversion to the Marxist Paradigm* [24]

The idea that the New Left could absorb certain Marxist concepts without becoming entangled in the whole ideological enterprise of Marxism *per se* was naive and poorly executed. Because of my close association with the French "New Left" where my best friends were well acquainted with the Marxist tradition and knew its problems and the pitfalls of dogmatism and sectarianism, I naively assumed that the American New Left would be able to absorb the lessons of radical political economy with equal discrimination. As I look back, I marvel at my own naivete and shudder at my mistakes. I had failed to understand just what Marxism is and how it functions.

"Marxism implies a closure," were the words of an SDS organizer as he and I argued his decision in the spring of 1968 to join one of the available Marxist organizations. Those words capture with great clarity a certain aspect of Marxism that is often noted in other terms (i.e. discussions of its narrowness and sectarianism), namely the engulfing of consciousness in a closed system that makes conversion to the Marxist paradigm resemble so closely conversion to a religious belief system.

I now believe that this conversion phenomenon is neither a truly religious nor a genuinely scientific experience, but represents a *conversion to a totalizing scientistic ideology* with elements of religiosity. That is to say it is neither an experience of ego-transcendent consciousness nor is it like "grasping" a scientific theory such as Einstein's theory of relativity. Rather it talks like science and feels like religion without being either. By "ideology" I mean a system of ideas designed to organize power. "Totalizing" refers to the claim to encompass the entirety of human experience. And "scientistic" refers to the assertion that human society can be understood by methods similar to the natural sciences in their rigor and verifiability. Marxism is a belief system that claims to explain the totality of human experience in a scientific manner. The resemblance to religion rests on the peculiar act of faith required to believe in the "science" since its ultimate verifiability rests on its ability to produce the classless society of socialism and, at a higher stage, communism. It bears a particular resemblance to the orthodox Judeo-Christian-Islamic traditions because of its reference to the "Book," holy writ that is read and interpreted and has authoritative status and the interpretation of which is the basis of legitimation of all the various schools, tendencies and sects.

It is a closed system although subject to strikingly different readings. It has its orthodox and heretical interpretations, its fundamental Gospels written by Marx and Engels and its pragmatic Paul to pull the church together in the person of Lenin. It even has (or had) an Eastern Orthodoxy (Maoism) that has split from its Vatican, and still other distant churches which have maintained some communion with Rome. And when it has not won its converts by persuasion it has been propagated by the sword. To become a Marxist means to decide "which side you are on." Although it does not promise salvation, it gives its adherents the self-righteous sense of being on the side of (proletarian) good in the struggle against (capitalist) evil. Whether its founder, Karl Marx, would recognize it as his own any more than Jesus of Nazareth would recognize in Christianity his message of love and forgiveness is irrelevant; the ideology works in either case to create and legitimate power in this world.

It is also true that the works of Marx and some of his followers contain many important insights--particularly in the application of radical political economy to the analysis of power in capitalist society. It is not, however, these insights that were fundamental to the process of conversion to Marxism in the sixties. The totalizing belief system and its apparent resolution of the identity crisis of the New Left, in combination with the organizational crisis within SDS, produced the massive and rapid shift from the discourse of participatory democracy to Marxist discourse in the period 1967-68.

◆ An Idealist Alternative: The Work of Staughton Lynd

The intellectual dilemma facing New Left activists was that although Marxist materialism bore little relation to the lived experience of their existential radicalism, there was no clear alternative that had equal credibility among political radicals. The crux of the problem was that only a theory of political consciousness grounded in philosophical idealism could provide an adequate framework for the New Left's intuitive politics, its instinctive sense that politics and morality must go hand in hand, and its struggle to give a political voice to spiritual convictions. However, philosophical idealism was generally regarded as bound up, both logically and historically, with political conservatism (as in Hegel) or liberalism (as in Kant) and therefore considered highly suspect by the traditional left.

There was one major effort to develop a framework in which New Left radicalism could find historical and philosophical roots in an idealist tradition. This effort was the work of the New Left activist, thinker, and writer Staughton Lynd. The son of the famous American sociologists Robert S. and Helen Merrell Lynd,[25] he became a radical American historian and a professor of United States history at Yale University. Lynd's career, however, was hardly that of a typical academic, and he might best be described as a *radical activist-scholar*.

Lynd had been educated from "pre-kindergarten through 12th grade" in "a private school system of the Ethical Culture Society" in New York that he describes as "a kind of reformed Reform Judaism." What struck him most were the words inscribed above the platform of its meeting hall: "The place where men meet to seek the highest is holy ground."

Lynd was "discharged from the Army as a subversive after completing non-combatant basic training to be a medic," and, shortly thereafter, moved to "a commune in the hills of northeast Georgia called the Macedonia Cooperative Community," where he lived and worked together with his wife Alice from 1954-57. "The persons already living there had been conscientious objectors in World War II." Formally unaffiliated, the Macedonia community contended "that there is a common religious experience that persons may express in very different words. . . . like the willingness to be 'vulnerable,' the need for 'total commitment,' and so on." Finally, the commune broke up and everyone in the community but Alice and Staughton Lynd "joined the Bruderhof [a communitarian Christian sect], and came to espouse an orthodox Christianity." He states that "the ending of the community was the most painful experience of my life" and adds that his "vision of the good life still presents itself to my imagination as high pastures in a bowl of hills where I still rise at 5 AM each day to milk the cows."

Lynd's spiritual-political path not only led him to conscientious objection and cooperative spiritual community but to civil rights activism and a commitment to work with poor people that was in part inspired by seeing a movie about the life of St. Vincent de Paul. Before teaching at Yale, he devoted himself to the civil rights struggle and was director of "Freedom Schools" for the Mississippi Summer Project in 1964 and closely identified with the work of SNCC. When SNCC adopted its Black Power stance in 1966, Lynd found himself as one of the "former civil rights activists seeking a home in the North" and, together with Mendy Samstein, Dennis Sweeney, and Dan Wood "sought through draft resistance a functional equivalent of the civil rights ambience." Simultaneously with the beginning of this organizing in the summer of 1966 (which led to the Des Moines Conference in August), Lynd worked full-time on the manuscript of a book about the origins of American radical thought.

In the same issue of the first *Praxis* supplement of *New Left Notes* (February 13, 1967) that contained the introduction to the neo-Marxist Port Authority Statement (entitled "Praxis and the New Left"), Staughton Lynd presented the introduction to his new book, originally to be called *Freedom Now: The American Revolutionary Tradition, 1760-1860.* Under the title "The Right of Revolution," this introductory essay made explicit his intentions:

> The thesis of this book is that the political philosophy of the Declaration of Independence derived not only from the bourgeois worldly wisdom of Locke and Harrington but from an essentially religious vision of the good society as a covenanted community under the law of God. Originating in the Radical Reformation, translated into eighteenth century terms by English Protestant Dissenters and American Quakers, this element in the ideology of the rights of man was developed by nineteenth-century abolitionists in the direction of civil disobedience and confiscation without compensation of private property; and by the early Marx in the direction of Communist revolution."[26]

In retrospect it seems rather amazing that this bold and apparently crucial paragraph was deleted from the introduction when Lynd's book finally appeared under the title *Intellectual Origins of American Radicalism.*[27] Lynd had been under pressure from his publisher to make this book more of a "social scientific" undertaking and suggests that there may have been "a change in tone between manuscript and book" which "might be described as a change from the proposition, 'The Movement is a religious enterprise,' to the proposition, 'The Movement uses a natural rights language that is religious in origin'."[28]

In the Preface to the published version of *Intellectual Origins,* Lynd did, however restate his intention of establishing the historical lineage of what he now called "existential radicalism" as opposed to "deterministic radicalism":

> But let me put the boldest face on my intention. In one sense the concern of the following chapters is ahistorical. I am less interested in eighteenth-century radicalism than in twentieth-century radicalism. . . . I want to show, simply, that we are not the first to have found an inherited deterministic radicalism inhibiting, nor is ours the first attempt to make an opportunity of that dilemma. The characteristic concepts of the existential radicalism of today have a long and honorable history.[29]

The shift from explicitly spiritual or religious language to the language of existentialism seems to be one more rather striking example of the difficulty New Leftists had in expressing their spiritual convictions openly. What they were facing seemed to have almost the power of a taboo.

Lynd's argument in his book was basically that the radicals of the 18th century American Revolution (as well as the radicals of the 19th century abolitionist movement) reacted against the deterministic and materialist theory of consciousness developed by John Locke (his "environmental psychology") and elaborated an intuitionist model of consciousness and moral truth based on spiritual convictions that became the real basis of American political radicalism as embodied in the famous "self-evident truths" of the Declaration of Independence.[30]

This attempt to legitimize the spiritual or religious intuitions and values of at least part of the New Left by returning to an historical examination of American radical thought was met by a particularly vicious attack from a leading Marxist historian, Eugene Genovese. In the *New York Review of Books* of September 26, 1968, Genovese reviewed two recent books by Lynd, *Class Conflict, Slavery, and the United States Constitution*, and *Intellectual Origins*. Of the first, Genovese wrote:

> His argument is finally no more than an indictment of the Founding Fathers for having failed to take a moral stand against slavery. He refuses to see the ideology of nascent American capitalism as a process that had not yet matured to the point of regarding slavery as morally and materially incompatible with its own assumptions and *insists on holding up to it moral stands abstracted from any time and place*. [My emphasis.]

Genovese characterized Lynd's viewpoint as "subjective and ahistorical" and dismissed his emphasis on transhistorical spiritual values as "moral absolutism," a charge which he brought against the second work as well. Genovese went even further in his critique of *Intellectual Origins* where he contended that "Lynd seeks to prove that the essence of radicalism is something akin to obscurantism." Furthermore, he excoriated "this moralistic version of radical doctrine" as an expression of New Left anti-intellectualism, a "glorification of the 'common man'," and a failure to recognize the importance of Marx's insistence that "an intelligentsia and a leadership" were "decisive if the movement was to develop."[31]

In looking back on this episode, Lynd has written:

> What I think this says is that, however I may have flattened or intellectualized my original thesis in anticipation of attack, it did not save me from a savage onslaught against my idealism, my lack of a fully Marxist perspective, and so on. This was a very difficult experience for me. . . . I became ashamed of the book as an amateurish production. Fifteen or twenty years later I learned for the first time that there were readers to whom the book had been helpful or inspiring.[32]

The Marxist "onslaught" on Lynd's work does not, in retrospect, seem surprising. The question of consciousness is the weakest link in the Marxist attempt to create a total (or "totalizing") ideological framework. Its materialism--however much "dialectics" is summoned to the rescue--relies on a model of the human psyche that differs little from the "bourgeois" theory of consciousness propounded by John Locke (the human mind as a "*tabula rasa*") and that reappears in the work of Lenin as the mechanical determinism of the "reflectionist" model of human consciousness.[33]

In failing to develop a theoretical framework for its radical democratic idealism, the New Left was without an adequate philosophical ground on which it could stand and was therefore unable to defend its intuitive value-centered politics against the attacks of Marxist materialists determined to reduce the question of "consciousness development" to the deterministic categories of the sociology of knowledge. Had the New Left been better read, it might have heeded the warning of the French radical thinker and activist Simone Weil whose spiritual convictions combined with a careful study of Marx's writings pointed her to the heart of the problem when she wrote that *"one has but to examine closely the Marxist formula: social existence determines consciousness. There are more contradictions in it than words."*[34] [My emphasis.]

CHAPTER 8

CONFRONTATION AND THE STATE:

 The People at the Pentagon

The summer and fall of 1967 marked a crisis and a turning point for the New Left, which ended in disorientation and disarray. In retrospect, it is easy to say with Yeats that "the center" did not "hold." I believe it is more realistic to recognize that the "center" failed to constitute itself in the first place and that this was the case because the elements necessary for its composition were lacking. Those elements would have been a minimum of three. First, a continued commitment to interracial unity strong enough to transcend the need for the development of separatist identity. Secondly, an adult New Left organization beyond the campus with a strategy and commitment to long-range political organizing for the achievement of radical change in the United States--a strategy and commitment that would go beyond the issues of ending the Vietnam War and achieving civil rights for black people. And, thirdly, an unswerving commitment to both the principles of nonviolence and the kind of non-ideological, democratic and decentralist radicalism which had been implied in

the notion of "participatory democracy." Looking back, it is
difficult to see how the first of these elements--interracial
unity--could have been achieved in 1967, given the rise of the
SNCC-initiated Black Power movement.

✦ Unity, Faith, and Race

At a meeting on Chicago's South Side in the summer of 1966,
the Reverend James Bevel of SCLC (a former staff member of
SNCC) met informally with representatives of the staff of the
National Office of SDS, including myself and the National
Secretary, Jane Adams. The overriding concern of the discussion
was SNCC's newly initiated Black Power campaign.

The SDSers present were generally sympathetic to SNCC's
demand that blacks control the black movement. SDS had just
passed a statement of support for SNCC at its June National
Council meeting in Ann Arbor. James Bevel, the only black leader
present at the Chicago meeting, spoke with a voice of radical
caution regarding the stance of black separatism. He argued that
the conjunction of the words "black" and "power" in the
Movement would lead to political disaster, and then, pointing to
the problem of *identity* which he perceived as central to the
SNCC Black Power campaign, he said: "The trouble with some
leaders of the Black Power campaign is that they grew up in New
York and didn't know they were black until they were twenty years
old. I grew up in Alabama and I *always* knew I was black." I
recognized that James Bevel was presenting insights that represented a level of political, spiritual, and psychological clarity
uncommon in that tumultuous era and absolutely vital if the
Movement was to maintain its bearings and survive. They were
insights on which the unity of the Movement depended.

Just what was that unity and how had it been achieved?

In an America founded on European colonization, based on
the destruction of Native American peoples and the theft of their
land, resting on a heritage of black slavery and industrialized with
immigrant labor, the political and spiritual achievement of some
measure of black and white unity in the Movement across the
chasm of racial hatred and injustice had been an awesome
achievement. It had been the product of painstaking efforts on the

part of both black and white activists and it required the difficult endeavor of building trust between individuals and groups who had a great deal to fear and much to lose. It required a fundamental faith in the healing power of openness and self-revelation--a faith that despite all apparent barriers human beings could overcome the walls of separation and discover their basic unity and equality as humans. It required a willingness to engage in self-exposure that was painful and demanded deep spiritual conviction if it was to be sustained. It was postulated on faith in a process of redemption through encounter that was both political and therapeutic--a process in which severe spiritual and psychological wounds could be exposed and healed. It was a process that had only one guarantee, *faith*--faith in the basic goodness of humanity. Whether it was called the "inner light," our Christ-like selves, our Buddhanature, or just "basic human goodness," this faith was a *spiritual* conviction. It could rest on humanistic or theistic suppositions but was and remains a spiritual issue. The adoption of a "materialist" framework for the politics of the New Left was certain to obscure the foundation on which the unity of the Movement had been built. The very notion of *human equality* rested on spiritual--not materialist--arguments and convictions.

It is no accident that the rise of Black Power in SNCC had been concurrent with the increasing influence of Marxist ideology in that organization. The election of Stokely Carmichael as Chairman in April 1966 displaced the Christian pacifist leadership of John Lewis[1] and marked a break with the spiritual tradition that had been integral to SNCC's development. Although Carmichael was not a Marxist, his program of racial separatism or black nationalism was secular in inspiration and rejected the whole body of principles and convictions surrounding the idea of unity and integration. Running through this entire development was the fact that Christian theism did not represent the beliefs of an important part of SNCC's staff and that there was no other spiritual framework that offered a viable alternative. This crisis of belief was complicated by the fact that the form of Gandhian nonviolence preached by Martin Luther King, Jr., and SCLC was associated with "liberal" politics. Thus the adoption of a secular or materialist outlook in SNCC in its move to Black Power was associated in the minds of SNCC activists with an increasingly "radical," and finally "revolutionary" stance.

This shift in SNCC away from spiritually-grounded nonviolence to secular, materialist Black Power also marked a move from southern, often rural-based organizing to a new focus on northern urban ghettoes. Black Power had originally been adopted as a slogan by Willie Ricks, a SNCC organizer and self-described "black nationalist" who proved the effectiveness of this new rallying cry during a march in Mississippi organized to protest the shooting of James Meredith in June 1966. According to black historian Clayborne Carson, black nationalism "implied acceptance of armed self-defense by blacks and a generalized antipathy toward whites."[2] Black Power was never a political organizing strategy as much as it was a national agitational campaign designed to capture leadership of urban black communities in the North which were seething with rage and ready to erupt in riots against police brutality, poverty, and exploitation. But it was also a quasi-ideology which implied the rejection of both nonviolence and integration.

The ghetto uprising in Watts, a black neighborhood of Los Angeles, in 1965 had dramatically highlighted the volatility of black communities across the country. Dr. King and SCLC attempted to address the issue of Northern ghetto unrest by launching a series of marches into Chicago's white working-class suburbs in the summer of 1966. These tactics of nonviolent confrontation underlined the truth that racism and *de facto* segregation were as much a northern problem as were Jim Crow laws in the South. However, both black and white radicals had serious questions about the political and psychological effectiveness of these marches, which brought white working-class racism to the surface and provoked sometimes violent reactions without providing mechanisms for redemptive interaction and reconciliation. Reactionary whites argued that the black ghettoized poor were being mobilized against white workers who had more material security but little actual political power of their own. It seemed too often that the stage was being set for a white political backlash like that which occurred under the leadership of Governor George Wallace's American Party in 1968.

As a participant in these northern marches, I was deeply troubled by the lack of mechanisms for redemptive dialogue between black people and working-class whites. I could only imagine the reaction to such demonstrations had they occurred in the white working-class community where I grew up. Instead of creating openings for white working-class people who were not racists to speak out, I felt the King marches only threw down a gauntlet which was inevitably picked up by the most vociferous racists in these communities.

The apparent failure of SCLC to target the real structures of power in corporate capitalist America seemed to further justify the charge of "liberalism" that was leveled by Movement radicals against King. Additionally, SCLC's northern campaign produced little or nothing in the way of grassroots organizing. The long-standing accusation of SNCC organizers in the South that SCLC's "campaigns" were in fact detrimental to building long-range organizations at the local level appeared to find further justification in the North. And yet, it was this same summer of 1966 that found SNCC under Carmichael's leadership turning its own energies away from grassroots organizing and towards its own national agitational campaign to raise black consciousness.

Within a year of launching its Black Power slogan, SNCC's grassroots work in the South was essentially dead and the leadership of the organization had passed into the hands of H. Rap Brown, whose message of increased militancy was directing its appeal almost exclusively to the underclass of the urban ghettoes. SNCC was no longer the messenger of "student nonviolence" but the articulator of black rage and ghetto rebellion. This mood was both an anticipation and a response to the riots that broke out in American cities in July of 1967. The heritage of black slavery shook America as it had not been shaken since the Civil War.

With increasing numbers of Americans marching in outraged opposition to their government's genocidal war against the Vietnamese people and ghettoes across the land burning from the flames of seeming rebellion, it truly appeared that America was moving not only "from protest to resistance" but beyond.

◆ The Rise of the Counter Culture

It is ironic that just as SNCC was abandoning nonviolence and SDS was becoming enmeshed in Marxist rhetoric, the alternative values of peace, love, racial equality, nonviolence, and community were spreading like wildflowers throughout America and revolutionizing the consciousness of literally millions of young people. The counter culture[3] was coming of age and its symbolic adornments of beads and flowers were omnipresent at such political events as the Spring 1967 Mobilization in New York City, the largest anti-war demonstration yet.

The explicitly political New Left and the counter culture were never entirely the same but for a time they overlapped easily. It seemed that their merger was taking place organically and that the New Left would be an integral part of this generalized cultural revolt which had its roots in the Beat Generation. If the New Left had a culture in the late 1960s, it was certainly to be found in the Human Be-Ins, rock concerts, rallies, and demonstrations, which were partially expressions of political protest and partially celebrations of youthful community and a new sense of personal freedom. It was in these diverse expressions of the counter culture that the sense of spiritual rebirth, the creation of a new consciousness, and the development of new kinds of human relationships were most concretely experienced.

The point at which New Left analysis and the counter-cultural revolt coincided most clearly was in their mutual critique of consumerism and artificially managed scarcity. Advanced industrial capitalism needs an expanding internal market as well as foreign outlets for goods and investment in order to maintain the upward spiral of production and profit. The culture and economy of *scarcity* necessary for the process of capital accumulation during earlier periods of capitalist economic development had been displaced (at least by the 1930s) by a new set of imperatives which necessitated the development of consumerism and/or accelerated spending by the state in order to absorb surplus production.

The perception of *consumerism as oppression* rather than the official ideology which touted *affluence as freedom* had been a theme that the writers of "The Port Authority Statement" had been developing and that was first presented in a position paper for the summer 1967 National Convention of SDS entitled "Towards a Theory of Social Change in America."[4]

By demonstrating the similarity between the economic imperatives that created consumerism at home and imperialism abroad, these writers linked the opposition to the Vietnam War and the anti-materialistic aspects of the counter culture together in a comprehensible whole. Theirs was one of the most creative attempts to integrate cultural, political, and economic analysis in a coherent fashion that offered the possibility of genuine dialogue between culturally alienated youth. However, this analysis was crafted in Marxist discourse that did not communicate its insights in language easily understandable by people uninitiated into the whole rhetorical system. It appeared esoteric at best, and sectarian at worst; and it was generally dismissed as the sort of thing Marxist graduate students engage in.

In fact, the work done by people like Bob Gottlieb, David Gilbert, Gerry Tenney, and later Susan Suttheim provided some of the political-economic foundation for a uniquely New Left form of visionary utopianism that emerged in the notion of "post-scarcity society."

◆ Post-Scarcity

The exact origin of the phrase "post-scarcity society" is unclear.[5] It was first used in an SDS document by the "Port Authority" writers in May of 1967 and was current around the New York Regional Office of SDS in the fall of 1967. It might be regarded as a response to the common-sense question, "Why don't hippies want to work?" or as a neo-Marxist attempt to deal with the problem of the meaninglessness of work that Paul Goodman had presented in *Growing Up Absurd*.[6]

The slogan--"Make Love, Not War!"--was clear on its face. It represented a sensual alternative to senseless slaughter. But the question of work in traditionally Puritan America, with its "work ethic," demanded a more probing response. The answer which the New Left was evolving was that most work in advanced technological society was worthless and useless just as most production was increasingly "waste production." If war, consumerism, and waste were eliminated, most people would be required to work very little. Machines--through cybernation--could do most of the necessary work of production. Life could be given over to creative leisure.

However, the "Port Authority" writers were careful to point out that post-scarcity was a potentiality not an actuality and that the capitalist system could not realize this potential because of its built-in dynamics. Capitalism must maintain artificially managed scarcity in order to produce profits. Capitalism is incompatible with the ethic of "enough is enough." It must produce "more and more" even if it has to blow up the "more" in war or dump it on garbage heaps.

The intuitive perception of the possibility of "post-scarcity" and the ethic of "enough is enough" had become commonplace among a broad cross-section of young Americans by the latter half of the 1960s. The "baby-boom generation," having grown up with a measure of material security, was able to grasp the meaninglessness of consumerism and its materialistic conception of life. This perception was one of the most powerful sources of an alternative set of values. However, those values needed for their articulation a non-materialist philosophical framework and that is precisely what Marxism could not provide. The realization of a post-scarcity society is not possible, it seems to me, on the basis of a materialist philosophy.[7] Only a world-view that elevates spiritual above material concerns will put the economic realm in its proper perspective. Furthermore, the true value of human labor is not measured in the amount of material goods produced but in the level of creativity expressed, the degree of human fulfillment, and the overall extent of both spiritual and material satisfaction that is achieved.

An alternative framework for the presentation of these ideas was suggested by such leaders of the counter culture as the Beat Generation poet, Gary Snyder, whose "Buddhist Anarchism"[8] was slightly revised and reprinted as "Buddhism and the Coming Revolution" in *Earth House Hold* in 1969.[9] If it had been possible for the New Left to bridge the gap between the neo-Marxist writers from New York SDS and the "Buddhist anarchism" of Gary Snyder in San Francisco, a new and creative cultural-political dialogue might have emerged. In fact, there was all too little exchange between these two wings of the sixties Movement.

In a conversation in February 1967 at a restaurant on New York's Lower East Side, Allen Ginsberg explained his perception of this problem to David Dellinger, myself, and Peter Orlovsky, Ginsberg's lover. He argued patiently that hippies would not attend rallies because they could not stand to listen to Marxist speeches since, having once taken LSD, it was impossible for them to tune into mechanical, ego-driven materialist rhetoric. That is why he later proposed a separate but simultaneous counter culture event, "The Levitation of the Pentagon," for that fall's major anti-war demonstration. Whatever the role of psychedelic drugs, it is clear that Marxist rhetoric was creating an increasingly unbridgeable rift in the Movement and that the hippie movement and the New Left were beginning to diverge.

◆ Psychedelics and the Movement

Healing and spirituality have always been common themes in human culture, at least until the emergence of the so-called "modern world" based on scientific materialist rationalism and capitalist industrialism. In the spiritually vacant culture of advanced technological society, in the "Great White Marshmallow" of American consumerism, there was little toward which young people could turn for spiritual guidance and growth in the midst of their political rebellion and cultural revolt. Morally bankrupt and spiritually dead churches and synagogues hardly filled their needs--nor commanded the smallest modicum of intellectual respect. They turned instead to ancient tribal methods of mind-altering drugs and new forms of rhythm and song, and tried to create their own world of liveliness and healing and hope. Whoever dares to disparage their effort forgets their pain and their decent longing for a new culture. They did not forge a new spiritual tradition--but they did have the audacity to seek new spiritual possibilities out of a strange melange of the ancient and the modern. They touched the water's edges between things as tangible as the remnants of American Indian culture and as remote as Tantric Buddhism.

The role of psychedelic drugs in the counter culture and the New Left is difficult to discuss without provoking hysteria and denunciations.[10] Drugs of all kinds have become a major social problem in this country and elsewhere and have provided a political weapon for the forces of the New Right, which is much concerned with "moral decay" and "law and order" while foreclosing intelligent discussion.

There is overwhelming evidence of the usefulness of LSD and other psychedelic drugs in the treatment of psychological pro-

blems, in the development of human growth and awareness, and in
the investigation of human spirituality. Psychedelic substances like
psilocybin mushrooms and peyote cactus buttons have been used
in individual and collective spiritual-healing rituals by shamanistic
cultures for many thousands of years. These substances are not
addictive in the sense of the physical addictions produced by
alcohol, nicotine, heroin, and cocaine. Like any other mind-
altering substances, psychedelics may be abused destructively even
though they are not physically addictive. To classify them as
"narcotics" along with heroin and cocaine as the U.S. government
does is fraudulent and socially misguided since it confuses rather
than clarifies the question of "drug abuse."

    The use of psychedelics in the counter culture and the New
Left was neither formal psychotherapy nor pure spiritual ritual,
but it did have elements of both and the results were mixed. Some
people learned a lot about themselves and others. Many had
experiences of peace, love, joy, sensuality, unity, and spiritual truth
which they may have previously only heard or read about in books
on Eastern religions. The false hope of "paradise in a pill" is
perhaps the greatest pitfall associated with the use of LSD or
other psychedelics and can lead to dead-ended, repetitive use for
"getting high."
    However, a very different lesson may be drawn from the use of
psychedelics--the lesson drawn by countless shamanistic cultures
and by many experimenters in contemporary societies--namely,
that psychedelics can be useful for opening individuals to
potentials for spiritual growth which they may have only vaguely
sensed before. In the 1960s, spiritual experiences that Western
civilization had long isolated as "mystical" and believed to be the
exclusive domain of reclusive monks or disciplined yogis suddenly
become available to young Americans in modern technological
society. Thousands of people used psychedelics in the 1960s and
afterwards, and either embarked upon or renewed their commitment to spiritual journeys which have led them to the serious
practice of meditation and other spiritual disciplines. Others have
become members of a sub-culture of drug abuse. The direction
taken by a person who experiences psychedelics depends on a wide
range of personal and environmental factors.
    On the political and cultural levels, psychedelics tend to

reinforce the spiritual-psychological viewpoint that humans are, in their basic being, endowed with immense capacities for love, compassion, intelligence, and community, and to nurture a radical spiritual-communitarian politics. Neither the liberal-capitalist view of politics as the necessary regulation of an otherwise ruthlessly egotistical human race, nor the Marxist view of revolutionary politics as relentless class struggle fits with the general experience of psychedelic usage.

The emerging split in the Movement may, in fact, have been accentuated by the use of psychedelics in that, as Allen Ginsberg was suggesting, flower-power hippies and dogmatic Marxists came to operate on very different vibrational wavelengths. One thing seems certain: U.S. government drug policy that lumped LSD, marijuana, and heroin into one category of banned "narcotic" substances (while allowing the legal sale of highly addictive alcohol), had the effect of "criminalizing" large sectors of the Movement. The same government which was forcing young men to choose between their conscience and the law by waging war in Southeast Asia was also telling them that, if they wanted to experience altered states of consciousness, it must be with a psycho-depressant (alcohol) or a poison (tobacco) and not with innocuous plants or LSD. This forced criminalization not only fostered an anti-state mentality on the part of young people and made the police their automatic enemy, but promoted a kind of apolitical "anarchism" and an unfortunate identification with criminality in general. Furthermore, these tendencies led to a blurring of the lines between criminality and radical political action in defiance of the state and to the growth of a "street politics" that was alien to the radical movement's attempt to restore morality to its rightful place at the center of political life. This "politics of the street" was the inspiration for some of the most self-destructive developments in the 1960s.

◆ Draft Resistance and the Underground

In the summer of 1967, my term as National Secretary of SDS came to an end and I was looking forward to a long period of R&R on a New Left commune in the hills of Western Massachusetts. I was suffering from severe emotional and physical exhaustion. Immediately after the National SDS Convention in June, Dee Jacobson, outgoing Assistant National Secretary, informed me that I was needed for a task vital to draft resistance work.

Up to that time, I was only vaguely aware of the details of activities associated with clandestine support of draft resisters who chose to go underground or deserters who were being given sanctuary in Europe. Most activity of the "underground railroad" type occurred between the United States and Canada although cases of GIs deserting and being given asylum in Sweden were appearing in the press. As an elected national officer of SDS, it would have been highly inappropriate for me to engage in such activities. I was too visible in addition to the fact that I was ill-suited psychologically for such a task. The style of openness that I preached and tried to practice was not readily adaptable to the secretiveness needed for clandestine work.

I did, however, have a deep emotional attachment to the whole question of an "underground" because one of the people in SDS whom I cared for most had gone underground in Canada. Bill Hartzog was an SDS organizer whose qualities of warmth, sincerity, and spiritual radiance made him deeply beloved by those who were closest to him. He had worked closely with campus religious groups in civil rights activities, had been an activist in the South, and, like Mendy Samstein, felt that militant draft resistance organizing was the best answer white radicals could give to SNCC's challenge of Black Power. He shared Mendy's vision of a "white SNCC," a cadre organization of organizers in the North.

Bill Hartzog was from a blue-collar working-class background in Pennsylvania. He had been the candidate of the decentralist, "Prairie Power" caucus at the 1966 Clear Lake Convention for the office of President of SDS. A nervous and rather clumsy speech cost him the office, but he was elected to the National Interim Committee and remained a close associate of Carl Davidson and myself and eventually became a full-time draft resistance organizer for SDS. When he came to trial for non-cooperation with the draft in March of 1967, he made the courtroom a forum for opposition to the war.

After he had been found guilty but before his sentencing, Bill Hartzog chose to go underground in Canada. (I flew to Ohio to dissuade him, but arrived a few hours after he had fled.) This irreversible decision had far-reaching consequences. Apart from of my personal sense of bereftness, Hartzog was sorely missed by many others among his close friends and fellow organizers. Many wondered what this portended for their own lives. By this point, nearly all the male staff of draft age (plus myself) in the National Office were draft resisters and might face prosecution. Everyone on staff was involved daily in the illegal activity of aiding and abetting draft resisters across the country simply by helping in the implementation of SDS's national program. For several weeks after Hartzog's disappearance, a small box in *New Left Notes* read "Hartzog Lives!"[11] From that time on I lived with a sense of pain and a deep anxiety about his welfare. It was the primary reason that I even thought about the issue of clandestinity and the question of an "underground." As nearly as I am able to determine, draft resistance was the first instance of SDS's involvement in the notion of clandestinity, and decisions about an "underground" had nothing to do with the Leninist theory of party organization when SDSers were initially drawn into support for resisters and deserters. We were involved in the question of how to deal with the survival of friends like Bill Hartzog, and it was because of this concern that I accepted the task with which Dee Jacobson presented me.

It seemed to people like Jacobson (involved in providing support to draft resisters who were choosing clandestinity rather than going to prison) that more knowledge about how to organize such services was needed. New Leftists were hardly the sort of people skilled in such work. SDS had been approached by a representative of a clandestine training organization in France, which offered to teach the necessary skills. Dee Jacobson felt I was the only person qualified because of my fluency in the French language and my first-hand knowledge of the French left. I tried to beg off because of my deteriorating health and because I did not want to expose my personal life to more scrutiny. I had dealt with enough Marxist homophobia to last a lifetime. Additionally, I had been the target of a scurrilous press attack by the *New York Times* which left me feeling very vulnerable to criticism.

Dee Jacobson persisted and I reluctantly agreed. I regard my compliance with his request as one of the gravest errors of my life. For four weeks I received sporadic training in Paris in some of the basics of how to carry out clandestine activity. Most of this could

have been figured out by ordinary people working in the way
ordinary Americans had while supporting fugitive slaves before
the Civil War. I also listened to several long talks on Lenin's
theories from an aged and respected leader of the group, who had
been imprisoned during the Algerian War for providing aid to
young French draft resisters and deserters and direct aid to the
Algerian National Liberation Front. The people in this group had
far more in mind than providing us with a few technical skills.
They foresaw us forming a "base" of activity external to the
United States and using that as the springboard for the formation
of a new revolutionary Leninist-style organization. The model on
which they based their strategy was that of their work during the
Algerian War. Their misperceptions regarding the United States
were glaring. My training did not go well and I was very confused.
Finally, one of their number said something that made sense to
me: "You certainly don't need a clandestine organization. You
just need some minor clandestine services." He was known as
"Pascal" and I owe him a debt of gratitude. It was his formulation
that stuck with me.

I returned to the United States and tried to impart what little
I had learned to others. My involvement accomplished little other
than to divert my energies from more important tasks. Most of the
clandestinity turned out to be inept and farcical. What support
was needed for draft resisters and deserters could be best provided
by good friends with good sense--not by pseudo-professionals
playing cloak-and-dagger games. I finally stopped my involvement
altogether as it became clear that this type of activity was feeding
some of the worst romantic revolutionary fantasies in the
Movement.

◆ The Need for MDS

The New Left did not need a revolutionary underground but
an adult off-campus version of SDS that could develop a
long-range organizing strategy beyond the issue of the Vietnam
War and begin to build a radical democratic movement among
that constituency that was its natural base in the larger society,
namely, "the new working class," which could then ally with other
social strata. The whole analysis of university-trained workers was

designed to provide the New Left with a vision of how its belief in participatory democracy could be communicated to the majority of the American people. Without an adult organizational ally to balance the momentum and sense of urgency generated by the Vietnam War, SDS ran the risk of following the path of adventurism.

The name "Movement for a Democratic Society" (MDS) was commonly regarded as the designation such an organization would take. MDS should have been formed long before 1967. The Old Guard should have acted on the obvious need for a home for graduating SDSers early in its history. The creation of the ERAP projects in 1963-64, the lingering ties to the League for Industrial Democracy (LID), and the fact that the Old Guard operated largely as a friendship circle, probably had the effect of obscuring the need for an MDS. Such a need was apparent to anyone who was active in SDS and not part of the traditional in-group. Thus Jeff Shero, elected National Vice-President in 1965 and a native Texan from the "anarchist" Austin chapter, presented a proposal at the Kewadin Convention for organizing MDS on a decentralist basis.[12]

This and other attempts to form the adult organization failed largely because the tight-knit Old Guard leadership did not act on the issue until it had been decisively displaced at Clear Lake in 1966. Then they began to consider seriously the formation of MDS, but by that time it may already have been too late because of the suspicion with which the decentralist wing of SDS now regarded them. Their attempt to form MDS in the late spring of 1967 was doomed by their confirmation of the worst of the new leadership's misgivings. Instead of coming openly to SDS with a proposal to form MDS, they organized a large meeting called "Back-to-the-Drawing-Boards" in June of 1967,[13] without even consulting SDS and attempted to form an organization under the name of MDS that they would be able to dominate. This manipulative maneuver was opposed by the new leadership of SDS and the Old Guard's initiative failed. Had this vital question been approached in an atmosphere of openness and pursued in a democratic spirit, the whole history of the New Left might have been radically different. Had MDS been created in a fashion acceptable to SDS, it might have developed the balance and moorings that would have given it the perspective necessary to

grow and outlive the war. This failure, together with the
abandonment of leadership in the anti-war movement, were
probably the two greatest blunders of the Old Guard. They were
crucial to the long-range failure of the New Left.

◆ *Ghetto Rebellions and the Rise of Adventurism*

When I returned to the United States in August of 1967 after
my European trip, I encountered an outlook among my fellow
activists that was dramatically different from that of only four
weeks before. It was like returning to a different movement in a
different country. While I was being exposed to the rudiments of
clandestinity in Europe in July, the black ghettoes of Newark,
Detroit and 57 other American cities had exploded in an outburst
of frustration, rage, and fire. Suddenly, white New Leftists were no
longer looking, as Mendy Samstein had done in the summer of
1966, for a way to meet the challenge of SNCC's Black Power
militancy with an equally militant white draft resistance movement. Now young activists were asking how they could respond to
the insurrectionary violence of the smouldering black ghettoes
that SNCC leaders were characterizing as political rebellions. The
effect of this on the Movement was potentially disastrous.

I had received a painful lesson about the potential volatility of
this issue several months before and was still ultra-sensitive to the
problem. In April, while still National Secretary, I had been
approved by the National Administrative Committee to give a rare
interview to the press. Dee Jacobson had received a request from
Look magazine asking to interview me. The organization was still
very cautious about having the National Secretary speak with the
press because of the irresponsible use of the media by the Booth
administration. When I arrived for the interview, I was in a very
guarded mood. To my surprise and annoyance, no reporter
appeared from *Look* and I prepared to leave the office. While I
was discussing the annoyance with Dee Jacobson, a man arrived in
our offices who identified himself as Paul Hofmann and said he
was a writer from the *New York Times* who had been traveling
around the country preparing a story on the New Left and the
student movement.

With my guard now down because of the failure of the expected Look interview to materialize, I allowed myself to be engaged in conversation with Mr. Hofmann who did not request an interview, nor did he take out pen and paper. Because he was of European background, I was easily drawn into a discussion about European left-wing movements. We also talked some about Cuba and Che and Yugoslavia, about which I knew very little. Then, as we stood by the office window overlooking Chicago's West Side ghetto, the conversation turned to the possibilities of ghetto violence in the coming summer. Like everyone else who lived as we did in an urban ghetto in America, I fully expected major rioting in the next few months. Special plainclothes patrols had already been added to the Chicago Police forces, which in the best of times resembled nothing so much as an army of occupation in a Third World colony. I emphasized in speaking to Hofmann that the real tragedy of the inevitable riots was that they had little conscious political content and no political organization. I argued that the only hope for real change would come if black ghetto dwellers could somehow turn their anger and frustration into grassroots organizing for control of their lives and neighborhoods. Without such a political vision and without that kind of organization, ghetto uprisings would remain a fruitless outburst of despair. My remarks were little more than a rehash of dozens of conversations I had had or heard with SDS ERAP community organizers.

One month later, the Sunday edition of the *New York Times* carried a front page article under the headline, "The New Left Turns to Mood of Violence in Place of Protest," proclaiming me a leading exponent of "urban guerrilla warfare" in the United States.[14] It appeared alongside an article about the National Rifle Association entitled, "Rifle Club Sees Guns as Riot Curb." We had been set up and *had* by America's leading "liberal" newspaper. My opponents seized the opportunity to denounce me. Nick Egleson, National President of SDS, wrote a letter to the *Times*, which they refused to print, rebutting the article. In an article in *New Left Notes* of May 22, 1967, I explained how the incident had occurred and laid out my personal political convictions on the question of radicalism and violence:

Radical implies "getting to the roots of the problem." I believe that

killing is wrong as strongly as does Che Guevara, who wrote: 'Killing is
evil. . . . All countries are different and progress should be achieved by
peaceful means whenever possible.' I also live in what is rapidly
becoming the most violent society in the history of mankind. Though I
oppose and will continue to oppose with my whole weight the use of
repressive force, while it is used to maintain men in bondage, I also
support the right of men to fight for their own liberation. That is not
because I believe in or advocate violence, but because I believe that
men should be free to determine the course of their own lives and that
they must struggle together to eliminate the bases of the violence
which oppresses them.[15]

I also made my position clear on two other points. When
Hofmann asked "whether I could be called a 'Guevaraite,' I said
'No'. . . ." In addition, I emphasized "the decentralist and radically
democratic faith of the New Left" to which Hofmann had replied:
". . . you sound like my Spanish anarchist friends, always insisting
on workers control. . . ."

I was completely sincere in what I wrote. At that time, the
spring of 1967, I was not yet convinced that nonviolence could be
made to work in America to achieve fundamental change in the
corporate capitalist system. I most certainly, however, did not
advocate or take part in violence. I was not a Christian pacifist
and although I was deeply convinced of the truths of Quakerism
and Buddhism, many religious pacifists I had known exuded an air
of sanctimonious self-righteousness that I found offensive and
with which I could not identify. Most were also liberals and not
political radicals. It was only in the following period of time that I
came to know advocates of *radical nonviolence* personally. These
persons were to have a profound effect on my person and being.
My personal disposition towards nonviolence was very deeply
ingrained in my character. I had been the victim of violence both
as a child and as a gay man. What I needed was a concrete
demonstration that the power of nonviolence could match the
power of the state. That evidence came to me at the Pentagon
demonstration in October of 1967.

The hatchet job that the *New York Times* had done on me
convinced me of several things. First, we were obviously becoming
a serious enough threat to the liberal establishment that we were
worth discrediting. Secondly, the accusation of violence was the
easiest and most effective way of discrediting us and isolating us

politically. Thirdly, revolutionary romanticism about the use of violence was one of the biggest dangers within the Movement and could destroy the New Left from within. "Violence divides." That is, I must admit one of the few truly valuable things I learned from my European instructors in clandestinity. I had, however, already learned that lesson when I termed the strategy of the *New York Times*, "Divide and Rule."[16]

With these few practical insights, I faced my friends in the early fall of 1967, and for the first time I found myself having to make decisions that were not about building momentum for the further radicalization of SDS, but involved often very painful and increasingly unpopular decisions designed to curb the excesses now threatening to lead the Movement down the path of adventurism and self-destruction.

While in Europe that summer I had read a recently released book by a young French leftist, Régis Debray, called *Revolution in the Revolution?*[17] This enthusiastic tract was a celebration of the "*foco* theory" of Che Guevara and a simultaneous denunciation of the stodgy, even "counter-revolutionary" role of Soviet-led Communist parties. *If we dare to act, we can make the revolution happen*, was the basic message of Debray's version of Guevaraism. Nothing could have appealed more to the action-oriented instincts of young New Leftists horrified by the escalation of the war in Vietnam, desperately frustrated by their inability to affect their government's genocidal policy, and now challenged by the outburst of ghetto uprisings. The book appeared in English translation in the United States during my European sojourn (the same month as the ghetto riots), and I returned to find some of my closest friends, both women and men, practicing karate and rehearsing for street confrontations. Debray seemed to have the perfect answer to the life-hating politics of the Progressive Labor Party, which had developed a new Maoist version of the old Stalinist line of blue-collar workerism. The seeds of the final factionalization of SDS were all planted by the end of that fateful summer. In reaction to the ghetto riots and the increasing menace from PL, activists in SDS began to adopt either that peculiarly American form of Guevaraism, which became the Weather Underground, or their own form of workerism, which formed the basis of the Stalinism of the Revolutionary Youth Movement II (RYM II).[18]

Faced with these fast-moving developments, I was confused and uncertain where to look for help.

✦ *Reaching for Allies*

Given the unsatisfactory outcome of the attempt to form MDS, I was desperate to find allies for SDS by the end of the summer of 1967. That fall I was offered the opportunity to work for the New York Regional SDS office, and I soon found myself responsible for being the SDS liaison person to the New Mobilization Committee to End the War in Vietnam (known as "the Mobe") whose Chairmanship passed to David Dellinger with the death of A. J. Muste on February 10, 1967.[19] Since SDS had no formal relationship with the Mobe, I was in a delicate position.

Had the Mobe been a grassroots democratic organization, it might have been able to become the adult wing of the New Left. Unfortunately, despite the best democratic intentions, the Mobe functioned as a top-down executive committee with representation from affiliated organizations and little democratic structure. It is ironic that the radical pacifist leadership of the Mobe made crucial decisions in 1967-68 that led in the direction of adventurism and street confrontations with the police. This was due in part to the undemocratic structure of the Mobe, which often simply brought new members onto its executive committee by co-optation (the same method used by Leninists in their exercise of so-called "democratic centralism".) Since the Mobe was not a democratic membership organization, but rather a coalition of groups and individuals, there were severe limits to its representative capabilities. Groups adhering to the Mobe could, of course, have their own mechanisms for choosing delegates to the Mobe's executive committee. In practice, however, few if any of these organizations had any process of internal democracy and many were in fact liberal versions of cadre organizations.

Beyond these groups were the *individuals* on the Mobe executive committee who were often notables in the peace or (later) civil rights movements or ex-officers of other organizations. The basis for selection of these participants in Mobe policy-making was dependent on the assessment of a few persons of whom David Dellinger, as Co-Chairman and Editor of *Liberation* magazine, was the most important. However great the wisdom and good will of Dellinger and his community of radical pacifists, they had no democratic structures at the grassroots and were prone to many of the problems endemic to a centralist structure no matter how firmly they believed in decentralist principles. In brief, although the leadership of the Mobe may have sincerely shared many of the principles of the New Left, they failed inevitably in the practice of participatory democracy. There were radical pacifists who were aware of these rather glaring contradictions and who spoke up.

Staughton Lynd was one of the early participants in the *Liberation* magazine circle of radical pacifist leaders. Lynd was a courageous activist, a prolific writer, and an invaluable scholar in the New Left. He had been a close associate of Dave Dellinger and one of the first group of American antiwar activists to visit North Vietnam (with Tom Hayden and Herbert Aptheker). His own experience of participation in the leadership of what became the Mobe led him to question the organizational principles of this rapidly growing, loosely structured coalition. Lynd had raised serious questions about liberal-coalition politics in the summer of 1965 in an article in *Liberation* magazine entitled "Coalition Politics or Nonviolent Revolution,"[20] which argued that the Movement should not fall into the trap of politics built around coalitions of leaders but insist instead on organizing grassroots democratic radicalism. Staughton Lynd was one of the leaders (together with A. J. Muste, Dave Dellinger, and Bob Moses) of the Assembly of Unrepresented People which, in the wake of SDS's withdrawal from antiwar leadership, organized a march on the Capitol to protest the Vietnam War on August 9, 1965.[21] After this event and his trip to North Vietnam, Lynd decided to leave this leadership position which was now embodied in the National Mobilization Committee to End the War in Vietnam, partly because of what he felt was its elitist and undemocratic structure.

♦ Preparing for the Pentagon

I knew little about the internal politics of the Mobe, but I felt an instant connection with Dave Dellinger, whom I first met in

January 1967, shortly before A. J. Muste's death. SDS had passed
its comprehensive draft resistance resolution the month before
and I was invited to to a Mobe strategy meeting chaired by Muste
on Chicago's South Side. I was enormously impressed by Muste's
ability to handle a meeting in which representatives of the
sectarian left who had fought bitterly for years were actually able,
because of the power of Muste's spiritual presence, to communicate honestly rather than denouncing each other. My first personal
conversation with Dellinger was about fears among young New
Leftists of going to prison. Since I was about to declare
non-cooperation with the draft, his words of encouragement,
based on his own years of prison experience, were extremely
valuable in bolstering my morale. While I worked for the New
York SDS office as liaison to the Mobe the following fall, we
became close friends.

Looming on the Mobe's political agenda for October 21, 1967,
was a mass demonstration at the Pentagon and I became
convinced that the best antidote for the emerging problems of
Marxist-Leninist sectarianism in SDS was participation in the
anti-war movement on the national level. Such participation
would mean a reversal of the policy against national mobilizations
which had been SDS's position since the summer of 1965 (after
the first successful March on Washington)--a position that I felt
had been understandable but short-sighted.

In distancing itself from the Mobe on democratic principle,
national SDS, under the leadership of the Old Guard, had lost an
important opportunity for reaching a rapidly growing constituency
with its radical democratic message. In so doing, it appeared
stand-offish and purist. In addition, this policy failed to take
account of the fact that much of the rapid growth in SDS from
1965 onwards was due to the anti-war issue and that the majority
of new members wanted to join in national anti-war demonstrations whether or not the national leadership thought they
measured up to the principles of grassroots democratic participation. Certainly in the fall of 1967 a significant percentage of the
local membership of SDS intended to support the October actions
at the Pentagon. And it was, after all, an SDS slogan, "From
Protest to Resistance," which had been adopted by the Mobe for
the Pentagon action.

The real question for most SDS activists was how to make

that slogan meaningful so that the anti-war movement could indeed progress from liberal protest to radical resistance. It was precisely at this juncture that the New Left faced its most serious decision to date: How was it possible to pursue a *strategy* of radical resistance without falling into the trap of *tactical adventurism*?

Many SDSers (and other radical activists) found the pacifist tactics of getting arrested in nonviolent demonstrations that employed civil disobedience both psychologically too passive and politically ineffective. How could they engage in public demonstrations that were both sufficiently active and politically effective? The easiest answer to this dilemma was to develop more militant tactics and to forget about the question of strategy. Unfortunately, this is precisely the solution that began to capture the imagination of some of the most creative and adventuresome activists in SDS. Given the strategic impasse of the anti-war movement, which was all too evident in its apparent failure to retard President Johnson's policy of continued escalation, it is perfectly understandable why frustrated, idealistic young people would want to do whatever they could to achieve some kind of effectiveness. If passive nonviolence was not producing results, then perhaps militant disruption would. It was the only effective route that seemed open to many young radicals who realized that their government had no intention of listening to moral protest.

In my judgment, the emergence of tactical adventurism in October of 1967 marked the beginning of the end of the New Left. It was the primary development led to a new Debrayist pseudo-politics of action without adequate theory or strategy or moral principles for guidance and to a rapid devolution into street violence and angry confrontations with the police. It was a path that, once taken, led to the bloodbath at the Chicago Democratic Convention in 1968, to the formation of the Weather Underground and the Days of Rage in 1969, and to the impulse towards terrorism which punctuated the end of the New Left in the townhouse bomb-factory explosion in 1970.

◆ *"The Resistance"*

There was one important attempt in 1967 to develop a

non-Marxist radical organization that would adhere to the principles of nonviolence and avoid the ideological and tactical traps into which SDS was falling, and Staughton Lynd eventually became a part of it. In the same period that SDS was experiencing the strains of its commitment to the December 1966 draft resistance program and the search for a theoretical response to both the Black Power campaign of SNCC and the Marxist-Leninist challenge of PL, this new organizational response to the Vietnam War unfortunately brought additional division within the Movement just at the point when the New Left needed desperately to find unity.

The group of young draft resisters who came to call themselves "The Resistance" grew out of a friendship circle at Stanford University around the person of David Harris. In the words of a key organizer of the New England Resistance, "if anyone deserves the title of Founder of the Resistance it is David Harris."[22] He had been briefly involved in civil rights work in Mississippi and had participated in anti-war organizing. Unexpectedly, his unorthodox campaign for student body president at Stanford was successful in the spring of 1966, and Harris and a group of his friends established the "Palo Alto Commune" as a center of their lives and work during the following summer.

Seen from a slightly different perspective than David Harris's campaign, the founding of the Resistance was a culmination of Mendy Samstein's organizing efforts in the summer of 1966 and a partial realization of his vision of creating a "white SNCC" in the North that would use the draft resistance issue and the massive turn-in of draft cards as its initial organizing strategy. There had been a meeting in New Haven, Connecticut in July of 1966 at which Mendy Samstein, Staughton Lynd, Jeff Shero, Dan Wood, and four other men signed a joint pledge to refuse cooperation with the draft and to turn in their draft cards on November 16. During this meeting, the participants

> talked about the moderation and hesitation of SDS, and the dedication and aggressiveness of SNCC. One of those who had worked with SNCC [Mendy Samstein] stressed *the urgency of finding a means whereby whites could commit themselves as strongly against the war as blacks had against racism.*[23] [My emphasis.]

In addition, they called for the Des Moines draft resistance conference to be held on August 25 and 26.

While traveling across the country organizing support for this conference, Mendy Samstein met with his former SNCC co-worker Dennis Sweeney, who was part of the Palo Alto network, and planted the seed of this idea, which he also discussed with David Harris and other members of "the commune." Although Samstein (a victim of exhaustion and "burn-out") dropped out of this organizing effort in the fall of 1966, a process was set in motion that eventually gave birth to the Resistance the following spring. On April 15, 1967, at the mass anti-war march in San Francisco, David Harris proclaimed the existence of the new organization and its intention to organize a massive turn-in of draft cards on October 16 in Washington, D.C., at the Selective Service System's headquarters.

The Resistance was formed as a separate organization despite the fact that SDS had adopted its comprehensive draft resistance resolution in December of 1966 and had launched its program of organizing draft resistance unions. The decision by Harris and his friends was not overtly hostile to SDS although Harris personally did not like the organization. The decision seems to have been made without regard to the question of the unity of the Movement and there was an air of moralistic self-righteousness in the Resistance that often seemed to verge on condescension--or so it seemed to some SDSers.

Above all, there was an important political issue that tended to divide SDSers and members of the Resistance. SDS organizers were acutely aware of the necessity of maintaining a multi-issue radical perspective in their political work and this had been central to the building of a New Left in America. The creation of a single-issue organization based on draft resistance seemed politically restrictive and contrary to the spirit of multi-issue radicalism even if the organizers of the Resistance intended otherwise. In addition, the single-minded insistence of the Resistance organizers on the moral stance of non-cooperation and the associated tactic of returning draft cards *en masse* promoted the sense of a "holier-than-thou" moralism, which SDSers found offensive, and which contrasted sharply with SDS's attempt to promote a broad range of forms of resistance to the draft and to build resistance strategies in institutions and communities that would extend the work of the New Left to broader constituencies than middle-class students.

Finally, there was an uneasiness about the style of the Palo Alto Resistance organizers and the tone of "Big Sur machismo" surrounding David Harris and his friends. Staughton Lynd and Michael Ferber had this to say of the Palo Alto Resistance: "Into the antidraft movement they injected a way of thinking and working that derives neither from religious pacifism nor from revolutionary political theory--nor even from the pragmatic style of the New Left--but from a unique California blend of cowboys, Nietzsche, drugs, Jung, motorcycles, and Gandhi."[24] This style energized scores of young men to consider non-cooperation, and groups across the country joined the Resistance (particularly CADRE in Chicago and the New England Resistance). However, it did not lead to the realization of Mendy Samstein's dream of a "white SNCC" nor did it help to build unity in the New Left. Most unfortunately of all, it did not develop a clear alternative to the encroaching Marxism-Leninism and adventurism in the Movement and it seems to have contributed to the divisive "identity crisis" which was an increasingly volatile force among radicals.

✦ Mobile Tactics and the Oakland Stop-The-Draft-Week

The dress rehearsal for tactical adventurism and its first full-scale performance did not take place spontaneously but occurred as part of a well-staged production managed partly by SDS activists in San Francisco's Bay Area and partly by members of the Resistance and more traditional pacifist groups like the War Resisters League. The original idea had been spawned by West Coast members of the Resistance as a way of supporting the massive turn-in of draft cards that organization had planned for October 16, five days before the Pentagon demonstration. The planning committee for Stop-the-Draft-Week (STDW), however, was never controlled by the Resistance and soon became an arena of contention between advocates of nonviolence and opponents of traditional pacifist moral protest and passive civil disobedience. SDS formed a radical wing of this uneasy coalition. The split that developed over the issue of nonviolent tactics reflected much broader developments in the Bay Area radical movement.

The Berkeley movement was directly affected by two important forces: intense media exposure and the rise of the Oakland-based Black Panther Party for Self-Defense. The Berkeley student movement had, since the eruption of the Free Speech Movement in September of 1964, become the most concentrated focus of media coverage of the 1960s student rebellion, and there was an unhappy tendency on the part of increasing numbers of Berkeley activists to understand the effectiveness of their political efforts not in terms of long-range grassroots organizing, but in terms of the amount of media attention they gained. This shifted the focus of political energy away from the issue of building organizations towards the question of how to create the largest, most dramatic street confrontations.

The influence of the Black Panther Party on the Berkeley movement was many-sided, but hardly ever did it promote healthy, democratic radicalization in the student movement. The Black Panthers had first gained major public attention not through their organizing efforts in the black community in Oakland, but by a carefully staged protest against a proposed gun control law, complete with guns and black berets, on the steps of the state Capitol in Sacramento. The actual political ideas involved in the founding of the Black Panther Party are not entirely clear. Black historian Clayborne Carson writes that

> the founders of the BPP, Huey Newton and Bobby Seale, later asserted that they were inspired by SNCC's accomplishments in the deep South, but their evolving attitudes about SNCC revealed little understanding of its history. After reading a pamphlet about 'how the people in Lowndes County had armed themselves,' Newton and Seale adopted the panther symbol of the LCFO [Lowndes County Freedom Organization] as the name of their organization in Oakland, California. The two formulated a ten-point program in the fall of 1966 and began to monitor police conduct with armed patrols.[25]

Their super-militant stance gained media attention and new recruits to their cadre-style organization. It did not organize a broad base of support in the black community. However, it did gain the immediate attention and loyalties of large numbers of Berkeley's radical student community who were, unfortunately, all too willing to listen to the macho rhetoric and "honky-baiting" that was rapidly becoming the style of the militant black movement and in particular of SNCC's new leadership under H. Rap Brown.

Certainly, there were white radicals who perceived the Black Panthers' program of "armed self-defense" as an almost suicidal strategy based more on the Panthers' ability to mobilize masses of guilty "middle-class" white students on the UC campus at Berkeley than on their ability to organize realistic armed self-defense next door in Oakland. But, the response of a significant portion of the Berkeley movement seems to have created an illusion of political support for the Panthers that reinforced an ultra-militant posture almost certain to end in disaster. At the same time, student radicals felt driven to respond to Black Panther militancy with increasingly militant tactics of their own in order to "prove" themselves. It was not difficult to discern a very unhealthy dynamic in which "manhood proving" (always a hidden issue in black-white relations) created a spiral of "upping the ante." Black militance was implicitly equated with black virility and black sexual potency--the inversion of a racist myth into a sick politics. (The appearance of Eldridge Cleaver's *Soul on Ice*[26] in 1968 did much to foster this dynamic.)

Black Power in SNCC had threatened to replace what trust and unity had been built between blacks and whites in the Movement with a sado-masochistic relationship between divided black and white movements. The machismo, sexism, and blatant homophobia of the Black Panthers added a new intensity to this dynamic. At the point where white radicals began to make tactical decisions in order to prove that they were not "sissies" or "queers," the political judgment of the Movement was seriously impaired.

The demonstrations against the Induction Center in Oakland during the five days from October 16-20 began with a nonviolent sit-in (and a simultaneous turn-in of 300 draft cards at the Federal Building in San Francisco) coinciding with the national draft card turn-in in Washington, D.C., on October 16. They culminated in mass hit-and-run skirmishes with the Oakland police on October 20. These were more than the actions of frustrated white radicals desperate to find effective tactics; they were also part of a process of proving themselves to black militants. It is a dynamic that had begun when white staff members of SNCC like Mendy Samstein, themselves advocates of nonviolence, who had been excluded from the southern civil rights movement by Black Power separatism, began organizing around the draft partially in order to demonstrate a political commitment equal to Black Power militants. At the Oakland Induction Center, mass civil disobedience and arrests were insufficient "proof" of this militance and manhood, and in the first days of the demonstration only seemed to confirm the impotence of nonviolence in the minds of many participants. It was only when white activists showed their willingness to fight with police, using the new "mobile tactics," that they seem to have "proved" their worth to themselves. However, like all forms of competitive ego-inflation, this dynamic was truly a "no-win situation." False ideas of "manhood" are never achievable since, rather than resting on balance and groundedness, they are based on false, neurotic strivings born of insecurities that can never be resolved by offering "proof." They only lead to endless, repetitive testing--over and over again until the participants are shocked back to their senses, back into reality. The events in Oakland in the fall of 1967 launched the white radical movement on a trajectory which did not stop until the Weather Underground bomb-factory explosion on March 6, 1970.

The Berkeley movement was not, however, the only place where this dynamic took hold. Events at the University of Wisconsin during the same week, where anti-war protests turned into a bloody battle between students and police, had led to similar developments.[27] Furthermore, the dynamic of proving one's militance by upping the tactical ante was by no means limited to men. The Oakland Stop-the-Draft-Week saw the emergence of a new image of the "street-fighting woman" as well as her male counterpart. This attitude was perhaps best expressed by Karen Wald who wrote an enthusiastic report to *New Left Notes*:

> The real success of the day lay in the de-mystification and de-sanctification of the middle-class hangups which had prevented us from functioning effectively until now. . . . Today we had tasted something different--we had taken and held downtown Oakland for the past four hours, *we had seen the cops back away from us, we had seen the dubious black community begin to overcome their original distrust of us and join in our action, and we no longer felt we had to prove ourselves by getting clubbed and busted.* . . . Not only the sanctity of property and the sanctity (invulnerability) of cops had been destroyed that day, we had begun to establish new goals, new criterion

[*sic*] for success in what were clearly the early battles of a long, long war.[28] [My emphasis.]

The events of October 16-20 in the Bay Area did not represent the appearance of "the first rationale in the New Left for the use of violence."[29] Staughton Lynd and Michael Ferber have described the attitude of some activists that nonviolent civil disobedience was ineffective in confronting the structures of power *and* that it was an expression of white "middle-class" timidity, which turned off black militants and alienated white working-class youth. This line of argument had been presented three weeks before Stop-the-Draft-Week by John Veneziale of the National Office of SDS (a self-proclaimed "anarchist" in the process of becoming a Marxist-Leninist) who had written in *New Left Notes* in September that

> I don't think the working-class people of this country will ever take the student struggle seriously until students become people again, and come off the campus, and be willing to kill and die for their freedom.[30]

Nonviolence was being condemned not only for its purported ineffectuality but also because it did not appear "tough enough" to appeal to supposed working-class values

◆ *The Pentagon*

Under the banner of "From Protest to Resistance," the Pentagon demonstration was scheduled for Saturday, October 21, 1967, the day after the end of the Oakland Stop-the-Draft-Week. I spent that week in non-stop meetings preparing for the largest, most militant demonstration against the war yet to take place. Plans for the demonstration included a rally at the Lincoln Memorial followed by a march across the Potomac to a second rally a short distance from the Pentagon and then a final march, by the most determined, right up to the Pentagon itself where civil disobedience was planned.

I was in a quandary about what to do. The new mood of militancy fed by the ghetto riots of the previous summer was creating the same dynamic on the East Coast that fueled the events in Oakland. I was approached by friends of several persuasions arguing that events in the black community demanded an equally militant response by white activists and specifically that the situation required that whites prove their ability and willingness to fight with the police in the street. The example of the Japanese Zengakuren's tactics of using bamboo poles in street confrontation with police was held up for Americans to emulate. In the Washington, D.C., office of the Mobe, Jerry Rubin, former Berkeley activist who had been brought onto the Mobe staff at the urging of Dave Dellinger to be a project coordinator for the Pentagon action, argued that after the initial rally marchers should sit down *en masse* on the Washington freeways and provoke the disruption of the entire Eastern Seaboard's transportation system. Several members of the "SDS house" in Washington, including Cathy Wilkerson and Tom Bell, wanted to organize a spray-painting spree targeting downtown buses. Students of former-Trotskyist-turned-anarchist Murray Bookchin who constituted the Up-Against-the-Wall-Motherfucker Lower Eastside of New York chapter of SDS wanted to trash downtown Washington in Zengakuren formations.

As I shuttled from New York to Washington, D.C., for Mobe meetings and negotiations with the GSA (the General Services Administration in charge of the capital's five police forces,) I had long talks with Dave Dellinger about the necessity of adhering to the principles of nonviolence if the Movement was to maintain its balance and humanity and not self-destruct in adventuristic violence. Dave Dellinger had become a beloved friend and perhaps my closest ally. In addition, he was a true teacher whose vision of revolutionary nonviolence[31] seemed increasingly to me to provide the only framework which could guide the Movement in a sane direction. Although I came to have serious differences with Dave Dellinger about strategic initiatives in the following year, he was one of the most important influences on my life and thinking and I credit him with having helped me maintain my political equilibrium at a crucial moment.

Another practitioner of nonviolence and Movement theorist, Barbara Deming of the CNVA (Committee for Non-Violent Action), also provided me with important guidance at this critical juncture. During a long conversation from New York to the GSA headquarters in Washington, Barbara Deming asked me more significant and provocative questions than I was accustomed to in a month. This brilliant and humane woman raised precisely the kinds of psychological and political issues that I was asking myself. I did not have a male friend in the Movement with whom I could freely share my convictions on psycho-sexual-political questions. As a result of her prodding, I began to conceive of the idea of a teach-in to the troops at the Pentagon. In retrospect, I have wondered if what I shared with Barbara Deming for that short period of time was a non-heterosexual perspective on the issues of masculinity and manhood-proving, which made us both question the wave of violence-prone machismo threatening to overwhelm the Movement. Barbara Deming later presented some of her insights in a brilliant article, "On Revolution and Equilibrium," which was the first major challenge in print to the politics of Black Power by a Movement radical. Her views were later elaborated in a book, *Revolution and Equilibrium*.[32] Dismayed by the force of sexism and machismo in the Movement, Barbara Deming later became a radical separatist feminist.

Bolstered by my contacts with these advocates of radical nonviolence, I faced my comrades at the SDS House in Washington on the day before the demonstration and announced that if they were going to rampage through downtown D.C., I was going to join Dave Dellinger at the Pentagon and get arrested performing civil disobedience. They were appalled.

When I made it clear that I was absolutely serious, I became an instant outcast, but I remained firm and knew where I stood. I fully expected to be arrested the next day. If I was not able to prove to my friends that this was the only sane option, at least I wanted to make clear that in a choice between adventurism and moral protest, I had come down squarely on the side of nonviolence. At that point, I did not have a clear notion of how nonviolent action in such a situation could be infused with radical content and I was resigned to being liberal-baited out of the New Left. (The gay-baiting was already making my life quite painful in any case.)

That evening (Friday, October 20) while Berkeley radicals were celebrating the "victory" of mobile tactics and street fighting, I sat down for dinner with Dave Dellinger to discuss the morrow's action. Also present was a man I had not known before, Arthur Kinoy, one of the brightest and most dynamic lawyers I ever met,[33] who worked as legal counsel for the Mobe. For two hours the three of us pondered the situation with agonized concern over the splits that were happening in the Movement and might get dramatically worse the following day. I explained the painful dilemma I was in and my decision to stand with Dave Dellinger on the question of nonviolence even if it meant the end of my career in SDS. Kinoy painted a picture that dispelled my gloom. He presented two interrelated and compelling arguments for the correctness of our decision to go to the Pentagon and demonstrate nonviolently. First, he justified the target by arguing that the U.S. government had itself drawn the line at the Pentagon by stationing troops inside and also by putting all U.S. military on alert from the East Coast to Colorado. Secondly, he argued that nonviolence was appropriate because it was the only way to maintain the "unity of the Movement." By the end of dinner, the three of us were elated. Arthur Kinoy and I went off to the SDS House where for two hours we argued the necessity of maintaining the unity of the Movement through nonviolence and the necessity of confronting the state at the Pentagon where it had chosen to demonstrate its military power.

We slowly won over the audience. Those who were not absolutely convinced by one or the other argument had been forced to think twice about the other alternatives. At no point did the argument degenerate into the false dichotomy between ineffective nonviolent moral protest and trashing (or other forms of violence or adventurism.) Militant, radical nonviolence seemed to have won out over the impulse toward tactical adventurism and fighting with the police. There were, however, rumblings of discontent. My female companion of the preceding six months, Karen Ashley (later of the Weather Underground), would not speak to me because, she said, I had betrayed the Movement. I sensed that what I had really betrayed was her dream of being the partner of a revolutionary hero.

◆ The Pentagon Paradox

On Saturday, October 21, perhaps 50,000 people gathered in front of the Lincoln Memorial to rally against the war. The crowd was restive. Just what did it mean to move "from protest to resistance"? For many it meant at least doing something more than easing their consciences by listening to speeches at rallies. The need "to put their bodies on the line," that act of determination in the New Left which had always expressed its sense of ultimate existential commitment, was a driving force for many as they filed out from the first rally and marched across the Potomac to a second site where yet more speeches were to be heard. The official plan of the Mobe was to make the second rally an opportunity for those who wanted to do civil disobedience at the Pentagon to participate one last time with the bulk of the demonstrators before separating and continuing on.

As soon as we had crossed the Potomac and long before reaching the second rally site, Tom Bell grabbed me by the arm and yelled: "Let's Go!" Almost before I knew it, I had become part of the new line of march which was half running towards the Pentagon. After about half a mile, we discovered that the GSA had carried out its threat to build a chain-link fence between the second rally site and the Pentagon in order to prevent demonstrators from reaching the building itself. The first canisters of tear gas were already being thrown by police. It was both exciting and somewhat frightening. When we reached the fence, Tom Bell, whose years as a full-back on the football team in high school and college had conditioned him well for physical confrontations, started to overwhelm the fence with sheer force. My many years as a farm boy had taught me much about both building and tearing down fences and I threw myself into the task.

With the fence now partially flattened, we ran straight for the Pentagon steps, avoiding the clouds of tear gas as best we could. Ahead of us was a group of adventuristic crazies, the "Revolutionary Contingent" from New York armed with long bamboo poles held upright and flying Viet Cong flags. We started up the Pentagon steps with hundreds of demonstrators now following behind us. The rank of marchers we now were part of included Marilyn Buck and Cathy Wilkerson.

When we emerged onto the great terrace between the top of the stairs and the actual doors of the Pentagon perhaps fifty yards away, we were facing a long line of federal marshals standing shoulder to shoulder with their billy clubs drawn. In front of us the Revolutionary Contingent was using its flag-topped bamboo poles to try to provoke a violent confrontation with the marshals. I was very afraid that the marshals would be provoked into firing tear gas into the crowd which, had it panicked and attempted to flee back down the steps, would almost certainly have trampled people in the surging mass that now poured up the stairs.

My instinctive reactions, formed by a childhood fraught with physical violence, were fear and the compelling need to get the situation under control in order to prevent bloodshed and violence. Tom Bell's reactions, conditioned by years on the football team, were to rally the team and urge them to head for the doors of the Pentagon. Some far-sighted SDSers had commandeered a set of bull-horns and Tom Bell grabbed one of them. Now standing on a balustrade, waving and yelling through the bullhorn for the crowd to charge ahead to the doors, he was suddenly faced with a federal marshal, baton in the air and ready to strike. With the grace and strength of a true athlete, he grasped the baton in mid-air and slowly twisted it out of the marshal's hand. The frightened cop slowly backed away and Tom Bell again began to urge the crowd to press ahead and break through the line. At the same time, the Revolutionary Contingent was still trying to provoke violence and a lone determined pacifist was trusting his throat against a cross-held billy club, taunting a marshal and trying to get arrested.

It was one of the tensest moments of my life. I was scared and I hated football, and Tom Bell appeared to me totally possessed by the heroic gridiron role he had played out for years. With fear in my guts and a certain sadness in my heart, I jumped up beside him, looked straight in his eyes, and told him with all the force I could summon to stop before someone got killed and to get down off the balustrade. "This is *not* a fucking football game," I yelled. He faltered, began to deflate, and slowly got down. I took the bullhorn and began urging the crowd to sit down. Paul Millman, another SDSer with a bullhorn, did the same from another balustrade a hundred feet away. Slowly what could have been a violent confrontation became a mass nonviolent sit-in and teach-in to the hundreds of troops who had suddenly appeared from the doors of the Pentagon and replaced the federal marshals with three ranks of young soldiers. The forces of the state had indeed been called to act by using the Army to defend the Citadel of American Imperialism. It was a serious error on their part.

Suddenly the anti-war movement was faced with the same young men it had been urging to resist the draft and not to fight in Vietnam. We were nose-to-nose with the very soldiers to whom we wanted to talk. Instead of provoking them to bloodshed we were able to exercise the most powerful tool a radical nonviolent movement has--the appeal to the human heart--and we communicated a very clear and compelling message: "You don't belong to the generals up there in their offices. You belong with us. This is their war, not yours or ours." And then with a tremendous shout that rang over and over through the afternoon and evening air we chanted the most beautiful mantra I have ever heard: "Join Us! Join Us! Join Us!."

A few did--throw down their arms and join us.

Later that night, after being forced to change its wavering contingents of youthful soldiers several times, the generals in the Pentagon ordered a squad of fresh troops to drive a wedge into the seated crowd and to beat and arrest all who resisted. Some speakers took the bullhorn and begged for mercy, asking that they be allowed to be arrested peacefully. That seemed to me a psychological disaster, which threatened to turn a radical victory into a liberal defeat. It seemed to me that a radical nonviolent movement needed to be able to claim its victory and then call for a retreat. It did not need to deliver itself into the hands of the state.

I climbed up on the balustrade once again and gave a speech claiming a victory in which I sincerely believed. I addressed myself to the troops with the same message of solidarity that had been embodied in the appeal to "Join Us!" Then I said we should retreat--until we returned one day as part of a larger movement of the majority of the American people who would come to dismantle the Pentagon together with the structures of power and empire for which it stood. Most of the crowd responded with relief and simply walked away. A small minority, largely pacifists, stayed and got arrested. Later that night Jerry Rubin denounced the "SDS sell-out" of the demonstration. Later still he met with a man named Abbie Hoffman and together they made plans to join forces in the Youth International Party (a media-oriented radical group.)

I left the Pentagon that night absolutely convinced radical nonviolence had worked and was the salvation of the Movement. Furthermore I was convinced that we had demonstrated that it was possible to confront the state nonviolently and effectively without falling into adventuristic tactics of street-fighting with police or trashing property. The event changed my life. It was another step in the completion of a new political gestalt that has guided me every since. Others experienced the event in very different ways and drew very different conclusions than I did. There is no doubt in my mind that this moment in the history of the New Left, not just at the Pentagon but in the weeks preceding and following it across the country, marked the Great Divide in the Movement of the 1960s. I have recounted the story in personal, experiential terms because I believe no account of abstract ideas can explain the fate of the New Left. Only the lived experience of its participants holds the key to understanding its power and its self-destruction.

Part of what happened to me at the Pentagon was the deepening of an understanding that I found most clearly expressed years later when I read an interview with Jean-Paul Sartre, who said quite simply: "The real revolution will happen when we can all tell the truth about ourselves."[34]

◆ Pentagon Postscript

The belief that abstract theorizing in the mode of the social scientistic pretense of value-free objectivity can lead to true knowledge of human affairs is one of the most powerful myths against which the New Left was struggling with its experiential and experimental politics informed by deep spiritual values. It temporarily lost the struggle for a new brand of political theorizing that is grounded in experience and that integrates values and spirituality, because it did not know how to articulate a new framework of understanding in a way that could compete with either the liberal or the Marxist versions of political and social theorizing, which have dissected and, I believe, distorted the history of the New Left. It is, of course, possible to distort history in the name of experiential groundedness as well as in the name of "science"--badly executed oral history intended to prove a biased viewpoint is quite capable of gross distortion.

I have looked back at the experience of the Pentagon demonstration and asked myself many times how one event could have been experienced so differently and interpreted so diversely by people I knew so well. Perhaps there is a special way in which only I can truly *know* my own experience and am left to *intuit* and *interpret* the experience of others. In any case, I want to pause and ask two questions: Who experienced what at the Pentagon, and why did their differing experiences of the same event lead them to such different conclusions and political decisions?

Marilyn Buck experienced the Pentagon demonstration as a new step in radical militancy that did not go far enough.

She later wrote:

> The peace movement as such was beaten, nearly to death. But in that defeat the resistance arose as a political force. The government seemed to be afraid, evidenced by its violation of the rules and boundaries which it had issued for their own benefit, not the Mobilization's. The resistance movement can and will feed itself on the fear and the consequent repression of its people. The people of the U.S. and the world will gain freedom only through struggle. The Cubans knew that. . . . The Vietnamese know that. . . . The Blacks in the U.S. know that and now we, the whites of America, are quickly acknowledging this fact. Imperialism can not be defeated by cardboard signs and flowers.[35]

She went on to become a key supporter of the Black Panther Party and, later, of the Black Liberation Army. She was convicted in 1988 and sentenced to 50 years for involvement in the Brinks armored car robbery of 1981 in Nanuet and Nyack in which a security guard and two police officers were killed.[36]

Cathy Wilkerson experienced the Pentagon as a missed opportunity "to fight," which was thwarted because of the lack of leadership. My move to stop Tom Bell from leading a charge through the line of federal marshals was for her an example of a leader unwilling or afraid "to fight." She organized large numbers of students in the Washington, D.C., area and later joined the Weather Underground. Her parents' home in Greenwich Village became the "bomb factory" which blew up killing three of her comrades on March 6, 1970.[37]

Tom Bell's experience of the Pentagon was to have his conditioned reflexes for physical confrontation thwarted by his friend, Greg Calvert. He realized, however, that he had almost crossed the line into tactical adventurism. He was grateful when I called for an orderly retreat. ("Thank God we can leave," he later reported saying to himself.) He went on to be one of those people who tried (quite successfully for a time) to organize a city-wide Movement for a Democratic Society (MDS) on a grassroots basis in Springfield, Massachusetts. His efforts crumbled as SDS tore itself apart at the national level in 1969-70.

I experienced the Pentagon as a victory and a confirmation of the power of radical nonviolence in a new framework that emphasized communication with those young men who had fallen prey to the blandishments of the state, rather than clinging to tactics of civil disobedience which would have delivered us into the hands of the state. I did not, however, believe that this meant more and more militant mass demonstrations. Those, I felt, would lead in the direction of a false sense of meaningful confrontation with the state in the form of street violence and fighting with police. What had been revealed to me on the terrace of the Pentagon that afternoon and evening was the vulnerability of the centralized and militarized modern state, the power of which rested finally on the allegiance of frightened young men like myself whose hearts were also open if we could speak to them with love and compassion and human solidarity. The vision I tried to communicate to the demonstrators and troops that night was that we should go home and organize until we had reached the majority of the American people who could then exercise their collective strength nonviolently and dismantle the Pentagon as one part of a democratic political and social transformation.

I went on to try to organize a city-wide MDS in Austin, Texas. But I also dedicated my efforts to organizing GIs against the war at Ft. Hood in Texas and then, after the decentralist MDS efforts had failed, Tom Bell recruited me to organize Air Force personnel in 1971-72 at Westover Air Force Base in Massachusetts. I also made several unsuccessful attempts to reformulate a decentralist democratic viewpoint for the disintegrating New Left.[38] I later became a lay psychotherapist and drug-abuse counselor and worked part-time with returned veterans suffering from delayed stress difficulties. When the political logic of the New Left had been broken, there still remained for me the spiritual and moral logic of reaching out that had been embodied in that chant, "Join Us!".

There were, I think, basically two images of the future that emerged from the "Pentagon Moment" in the New Left; both were based on perceptions of power and effectiveness. One was a vision of long-range organizing born of the New Left's traditions of decentralist democracy and the spiritual and moral values embodied in nonviolence, but coupled now with a new sense of the power of *active* nonviolence focussed on communication to new constituencies rather than simply on moral protest through civil disobedience. The other image projected direct confrontations and street disruptions as the way to break the impasse of the politics of protest, and increasingly abandoned the nonviolent tradition of the Movement in favor of a new brand of macho militancy; its adherents lost touch with the spiritual and moral values which were at the heart of nonviolence. The first viewed the police and military power of the state as vulnerable and saw police and troops as potential allies. The second viewed the state apparatus as the primary target of physical confrontations including the possibility of street fighting with police and "armed struggle." These two images, although never totally distinct but often blurred and overlapping, governed the future course of the Movement.

◆ The Underground

On March 6, 1970, the mid-day routine of Greenwich Village life was broken by the massive explosion of the Wilkerson townhouse on Manhattan's West 11th Street a few doors from the New School for Social Research. The blast killed three young former SDS organizers in the house, which had been turned into a Weatherman bomb factory. Two others, Kathy Boudin and Cathy Wilkerson, daughter of the wealthy owners of the townhouse and one of my closest friends in the Movement, escaped and went into hiding. The explosion also punctuated a fact which had been apparent to many activists for some time--that the New Left and "the Movement" of the 1960s were dead. That outpouring of human courage, anger, creativity, and hope that had once been marshalled under under the banner of "Black and White Together" and built the largest, most vital movement of democratic radicalism in America since 1919 now lay in ruins as irreparable as the once luxurious home of Cathy Wilkerson's parents. Boudin, Wilkerson and their dead companions were part of the recently formed Weather Underground, which captivated the imagination of young radicals over the next decade but left no legacy of radical democratic organizing--creating instead a legend of romantic clandestinity, senseless bombings, and brutal bank robberies. The mystique of the Weathermen paralyzed all initiatives to rebuild the New Left in the 1970s by filling the arena of radical political imagination with romantic revolutionary fantasies. The destruction of the Black Panther Party completed the mythology of an armed revolutionary movement destroyed solely by government repression, supplying a pantheon of black martyrs untouchable by any (especially white) political criticism.

Although the anti-war movement continued to grow and students held the largest demonstrations ever after the Kent State massacre of April 1970, there was no longer a credible national organization with a program of multi-issue democratic radicalism to coordinate or benefit from that spontaneous insurrection. SDS had been destroyed the year before by an invasion from the Maoist sect known as the Progressive Labor Party and by the factional infighting among the various other Marxist-Leninist groups that made up the sad remnants of the organization. Without SDS there was no political forum where the New Left could debate political issues and create political strategies. No matter how many feminist, gay and lesbian, anti-nuclear, anti-war, or environmental groups and movements flourished in the 1970s and beyond, the relative unity which had come from the heart and once been the living soul of *the Movement* was never recreated. As a result, multi-issue democratic radicalism failed to coalesce in the post-sixties era into a meaningful political force. Without spiritual and organizational unity there was no one to perform the vital task that had been the central contribution of SDS--the linkage of diverse issues and movements into a comprehensible radical critique of American society and the articulation of a coherent vision of a radical democratic alternative. Where did "the Movement" go?

It went "underground" in many different ways and there it has remained in search of itself ever since, although parts of it surface from time to time but fail largely to recognize their commonality with other members or the desirability of recreating a whole. What was once one body more or less in love has remained a disparate contentious coalition at best.

The faith of democratic radicals is based not only on a belief in the basic goodness of human beings but also on confidence in the integrity of human consciousness. As an anarchist psychiatrist friend of mine once said: "We are all whole persons whether we like it or not." It is this knowledge of the basic indestructibility of human wholeness which sustains the faith of radicals that a truly different kind of human world could be built in which this wholeness could be more fully realized and human lives lived in a more integrated fashion.

The strength of the New Left lay in its tenacious conviction that human beings could and must live integrated lives as fully as possible in the context of a political struggle which builds the new society "within the shell of the old." Day-by-day in the here-and-now the Movement called for human beings to respond from the depths of their hearts and with the totality of their persons to the call to be human in an inhumane world. This was an appeal for spiritual-political wholeness, but its language was not entirely clear and it succumbed to the seduction of 19th century materialist thinking and the appeal of adventurism in its moment of crisis.

It has been my perception since the summer of 1967 that the psychological appeal of clandestinity and the Underground had very little to do with Leninism or political strategy, but was basically symbolic and represented a need to explore the hidden issues of the Unconscious. This need to integrate the world of the human unconscious psychologically and spiritually had been inherent in the Movement from its beginnings and explicit at many points. The task of striving for that kind of integration in the midst of a political struggle involving such enormous issues as racism and the Vietnam War was always potentially overwhelming, frequently chaotic, and occasionally catastrophic. The integration of the political, the personal, the moral, and the spiritual created a burden that was often too difficult to bear psychologically. When the political crisis of the sixties Movement developed, one way of coping with the inability to resolve difficulties and to integrate experiences was to go "underground" either physically or psychologically.

The moment of truth came for me in the summer of 1967 when I met clandestinely with an underground draft resister of whom I had been enamoured for some time. Despite a valiant attempt to abide by the rules of clandestine contact, we were unable to resist our need to spend the night together and consummate our relationship. In the context of the New Left with its jittery homophobia, the Underground was the only place, physically and psychologically, where we were safe to explore our homosexuality. The experience had a profound effect on my outlook and the insight which I gained probably prevented me from acting out my psycho-sexual-spiritual needs by joining the (actual) Underground at the end of the 1960s. I realized that issues like homosexuality which were lurking in the Unconscious of the Movement needed to be brought above ground and worked through and integrated in the daylight of full awareness.

It is no accident that I and many other New Left activists became psychotherapists and spiritual seekers in the 1970s after the disintegration of the Movement. Our need for the integration of the psychological and spiritual levels of our being with our political convictions was made even more urgent by the demise of our "world"--the social milieu in which our lives had been developing. The implosion of the Movement left tens of thousands of activists without the social support system in which they could sustain their struggle for wholeness.

The retreat into the actual Underground on the part of some of my former companions was in part a desperate attempt to save a remnant of the world of the New Left in clandestine form. It is no surprise that stories of truly bizarre psycho-sexual behaviors have emerged from that experience. It is also no surprise that some of that experience was sadistic and brutal. Without the light of day of the real world, some of the worst impulses of the dark side of human nature undoubtedly found their home in the Underground.

The alternative solution to the end of the Movement was saner but also not entirely satisfactory--the above ground involve-ment in psychotherapy and spirituality without an integrated political and social context. That is the solution which has sustained many Movement activists and newcomers to the world of political activism in the two decades since the 1960s. There has been an uneasy dance that involves remaining active in causes and organizations which are politically unsatisfactory because not truly radical while involving oneself in psychotherapeutic or spiritual undertakings which are frequently apolitical, devoid of social conscience, and motivated by self-indulgent individualism. The search for wholeness that was central to the New Left at its best is imperfectly mirrored in the various psychotherapies which vaunt their "holistic" character while failing totally to engage the inner struggle of human consciousness with the outer world of political and social struggles.

On the other side of the coin, there persist a variety of Marxist-Leninist ideological sects which attempt to deny the reality of the inner world of human psychological and spiritual growth by externalizing or projecting all human issues onto a screen of stridently proclaimed "political struggle." Between the politics of projection and navel-gazing, it is difficult to find a balanced common ground of personal and political sanity. The need to live morally, spiritually, and politically integrated lives may have constituted the most authentic "revolutionary" demand of the New Left.

CONCLUSION:
THE LEGACY
OF DEMOCRATIC IDEALISM

 Along with the spiritual values of peace, justice, freedom and equality that moved the hearts of Movement activists of the 1960s, there was one overriding spiritual concern which perhaps inspired their commitment beyond all the others. It was the search for community. Community, as it was understood by New Leftists, was a spiritual-political experience--an experience of shared political actvism in open association with others who had similar ultimate concerns. Furthermore, it rested on a spiritually open, outgoing, and inclusive sense of belonging (Join Us!) rather than a closed, sectarian exclusivism. This quest was sustained by the lived idealism of the sixties generation and their forebearers in the radical pacifist movement and the Beat Generation. It was embodied in the day-to-day relationships built in political and cultural undertakings that frequently demanded a good deal of moral courage and the very best qualities of the participants.

This idealism and the community of "the Movement" that it sustained disintegrated quickly once the twin evils of sectarianism and materialist ideology captured the leadership of organizations like SDS. The process of disintegration was fueled first by Black Power separatism and then accelerated by a series of other separatisms--Chicano nationalism, the Native American Movement, women's liberation and the ideology of feminist separatism, and, finally, the development of gay liberation and its lesbian separatist wing. All of these movements brought new issues, new vitality, and a new sense of selfhood to "progressive" politics in America, but none of them brought "the Movement" back together again. The particular quality of personal risk-taking and self-exposure that had built bridges (however small) across the chasm of racial hatred in America and produced a movement which marched under the banner of "Black and White Together" was replaced by a series of independent movements which militantly asserted their separatist identities but lost sight of the whole. The spirit of unity and the psychodynamic of "reaching out" disappeared quickly and left a very different political landscape marked by the new "politics of identity."

The story of the factionalization and demise of the Movement of the 1960s is intertwined in a complex manner with the emergence of this spectrum of successor movements that have dominated the outlook of American radicalism in the ensuing decades. The exact relationship between these two processes of disintegration and emergence is difficult to untangle but their interrelationship is crucial to an understanding of the state of American political life in this generation.

Two radically differing interpretations have emerged regarding the final devolution of the Movement of the 1960s. The majority voice argues that the development of a spectrum of successor movements catalyzed around issues of identity has been a healthy, positive outcome of the 1960s era. Another, more pessimistic viewpoint argues that the separatist politics of identity that replaced the relative unity of the 1960s Movement has marked the demise of democratic radicalism as a force in U.S. politics. The development of a divided movement, this second interpretation contends, has meant not only the substitution of divisive agendas for a radical political program but also the absence of the kind of overall radical political critique that might challenge corporate liberalism in the way the New Left once did. Since the demise of SDS there has not even been a national political forum where the ideals of democratic radicalism could be debated on an ongoing basis.

An in-depth analysis of the rise of the politics of identity is beyond the scope of this work. It has, however, been my intention here to establish that the democratic idealism of the far-flung community which called itself "the Movement" rested on spiritual values and convictions. Furthermore, I have meant to suggest that any future deepening of the dialogue about democratic idealism and democratic decentralism must take into account the importance of those spiritual values.

♦ Spiritual Humanism and Democratic Decentralism

The debate in American radicalism about the role of spirituality and politics was a central, if muffled, theme of the 1960s. The opposition between the traditional theistic Judeo-Christian position of the SNCC "Founding Statement," the non-theistic Buddhism of Gary Snyder and the Beats, and the broad statement of humanistic spiritual values in the *Port Huron Statement* will certainly remain unresolved for a long time in the religiously pluralistic United States. The central issue in this debate remains the relationship between spirituality, political philosophy, ethics, and democracy.

In the period since the 1960s, the influx into this culture of Eastern religious practices and beliefs, which was integral to the Beat Generation and the Counter Culture, has been enormous. The result has by no means been a uniform adherence to democratic practices. While Gary Snyder and some of his friends have nurtured a model democratic Buddhist community (Ring of Bone Zendo) near Grass Valley, California, many others have followed the authoritarian leadership of Eastern gurus into a spiritual politics that fails above all else to "question authority" and that bears little resemblance to the spiritual-political activism of the 1960s. It is surprising to see the way in which hierarchical religious authority has gained the obedience of tens of thousands of Americans who seem to have left their quest for democracy at the doorstep of their meditation hall or temple.

In the absence of any social, economic, or political theory to explain historical and social reality, Eastern religions revert to the doctrine of *karma* to fill the void. The highly individualistic viewpoint that interprets human affairs as the working out of individual destinies through many lives unfortunately produces reactionary social and political theory. It was this void that Gary

Snyder described in his original manifesto on Buddhist anarchism. Matters are worse in many other of the strictly spiritual movements. The right-wing authoritarianism of the "Moonies" (followers of the Rev. Sun Yung Moon) and the fundamentalist Christian New Right (the "Moral Majority") might appear to be the most discouraging examples of political-spiritual involvements in the 1970s and 1980s. However, even in a non-theistic and presumably progressive movement like the American version of Theravada Buddhism (called "Vipassana"), the level of political awareness is frighteningly low.

In many ways, the current situation in this society has changed very little since the 1960s. There is an abundance of "religion" without social or political theory and a lot of social and political theory without any grasp of the importance of spirituality and spiritual values. As in so many other areas, American society in the 1980s was a replay of the Eisenhower era of the 1950s. Much of the interest in Eastern spiritual traditions has become a form of political and social escapism.

I have had to remind myself that there are democratic interpretations of both the Dharma based on the Buddha's *Kalama Sutra* (a remarkably libertarian discourse on tolerance), and of Christ's teachings understood as a Social Gospel. Neither Buddhism nor Christianity has any claim to a monopoly on democratic thought or organization. What Gary Snyder wrote of institutional Buddhism could probably be as easily said of institutional Christianity, namely, that it "has been conspicuously ready to accept or support the inequalities and tyrannies of whatever political system it found itself under." Snyder had further argued that "This is death to Buddhism, because it is death to compassion." (See Chapter 1 above.) Any sincere Christian who is socially and politically aware would argue the same for his or her own tradition.

One is forced to ask why some of the heirs of the New Left of the 1960s have failed so badly in maintaining their democratic principles while deepening their spiritual quest. Perhaps the destruction of the New Left--the shattering of their "Beloved Community," their spiritual-political home--was too much to bear. Faced with disarray and the total disruption of their lives, they were desperate for answers. Truly democratic models of spiritual-political communities were not readily available.

All is not grim, however, and the urge for spiritual-political integration persists in the land. The model of the democratic and decentralist Quaker meeting remains the most vital example in American society of a living tradition of spiritual communities organized on grassroots democratic principles and in direct opposition to the power of the centralized, militarized state. Quakers were a powerful example of spiritual-political community for many activists of the New Left and remain so for contemporary decentralist movements.

There are numerous other examples of spiritual-political communities that have survived the 1960s without falling into the pitfalls of guru-centered authoritarianism. Some of these are Eastern in inspiration, some are Jewish or Christian, some are eclectic. The basic Quaker model of a spiritual community with deep social and political involvements has yet to be successfully replaced. It is perhaps the balance of personal spiritual seeking with social and political activism--together with a commitment to internal democracy and decentralism--that has kept Quakerism alive. The one-sided focus on the attainment of Enlightenment so characteristic of some Eastern traditions tends to downgrade the importance of political involvement and to focus devotion on "Enlightened" teachers. This tends to make of Enlightenment an end product to be revered and objectified rather than a process of growth shared by all in a human community.

✦ Spirituality and Democracy

In many ways, the disaster of the break-up of the New Left destroyed much of the heritage of that unity of spiritual values and radical democratic politics that had animated the sixties Movement.

The triumph of Marxist-Leninist sectarianism and Guevaraist adventurism produced not only political disarray but foreclosed discussion of the relationship between radical democracy and spiritual values. Instead of deepening the spiritual-moral-political discourse of the Movement and exploring the implications of democratic idealism, much of the intellectual thrust of the post-sixties era in the American left has been the revival of sterile Marxist debates--especially in academia. Marxism, in the 1970s and 1980s, became an intellectual credential for young academics with or without activist backgrounds in the 1960s. There has been an outpouring of dissertations and books from the multiversities on sociology and social history, most written in a Marxian mode, but very little has been produced that has dared to raise the question of spirituality and politics in the 1960s. This almost tabooed subject has been largely driven out of the academy and has found its exponents and audience chiefly among activists in the various eco-political formations that fall under the general rubric of the Green movement (as distinct from any one green "party"). Spirituality and politics is an issue of lively debate among many Greens.

This divorce between the academic world and the most lively forms of political activism is hardly new or surprising. The Movement of the 1960s was not the product of academic debate in the universities but the work of committed political activists motivated by moral passion. Although students (and a few faculty) were perhaps the largest constituency of the Movement, it was never a narrowly "academic" phenomenon. Its activism was, in fact, partially a reaction against the "arm-chair socialism" of the universities of the 1950s.

While the discussion of spiritual values has been largely removed from political theory in the academic world, a similar but opposite development has occurred in another arena of the larger society. The widespread development of the "human potential movement" with its groups, workshops, and growth centers has eagerly taken up the issue of the centrality of spirituality in human growth but has largely ignored social and political issues. Except for an occasional weekend workshop (and a high-level exchange with the Soviet Union), the most prestigious growth center, Esalen Institute in Big Sur, California, largely avoids issues of political activism.

Neither democratic political consciousness nor moral wisdom and compassion can be fully cultivated in the silence of meditation retreats or in the therapeutic atmosphere of personal growth workshops. The development of the virtues of a democratic citizenry requires active involvement in building democratic political organizations and communities. People do not learn the importance of democratic peoples' power in a political vacuum. The greatest virtue of the New Left of the 1960s lay in its determination to build that sense of popular participation at every level of its work.

The same holds true of the virtues of moral wisdom and compassion. The Greeks argued that practical moral wisdom (*phronesis*), though it could be cultivated by contemplation, was dependent on the active involvement of citizens. Contemplation might indeed be the source of the highest human wisdom, but the morality of good citizens was refined in the active life of their community or city-state.

The ideal of a life of action was not necessarily superior to the contemplative life for Greek philsophers, and in many ways the differences between the idealization of action and contemplation said to characterize much of the distinction between Western and Eastern civilizations has been simplistically overdrawn. However, contemporary American culture seems to be experiencing a reaction to a generalized perception of those differing ideals and many young people of the post-1960s generation have opted for an escapist version of the Eastern, contemplative ideal. Perhaps, over time, a new balance will eventually be struck that blends a more contemplative style together with serious political involvement. The debate on this subject has only recently begun in earnest.

It may be that the most important contribution of Western civilization to the world community will not be the ambiguous legacy of its science and technology, but that ideal of active democratic citizenship as the school of morality which was bequeathed to us by the first distinctively *Western* people, the Greeks. For all their faults, they made Western civilization and the idea of democracy a close, if rarely achieved union.

The question of the relationship between political philosophy, nature, and spirituality that has begun to surface in the world of environmental activism and eco-philosophy is as old as the Western philosophical tradition itself. When the Greeks turned from myth and traditional religion to philosophy for answers in the 6th century B.C., they originally sought both solutions for human affairs and an understanding of physical phenomena in *physis*--in nature. In the 5th century, first the Sophists and then Socrates and his followers sought *humanistic* answers to *human* problems in the *human* realm. This turn towards humanism was, however, never divorced from spiritual issues in the minds of Socrates, Plato, or Aristotle. It was, in fact, the intent of Plato to find a human answer to the question of political affairs and yet link the issues intimately with the spiritual realm of *the Good*. Although Aristotle differed radically from Plato in his approach to political philosophy, he was unwavering in his insistence that the political was inseparable from the ethical.

The classical quest for an answer to the proper relationship between spiritual, ethical, and political life seems to have been revived in the 1960s with a particular twist that linked it to the radical wing of the Protestant Reformation. New Leftists of the 1960s sought an idealist political solution in a radical democratic framework and thus opened the door to a discussion of democratic idealism--an approach that both linked them to the classical tradition of political theory yet distinguished them from it. Rather than build a society ruled by philosopher-kings who would seek *the Good* through training in philosophy, New Leftists sought to build a democratic society that would rest on the full development of *the Good in all persons* through democratic institutions and practices. Perhaps in this way they were effectuating a reconciliation of the conflict between the democratic party and the idealist philosophers that had raged in classical Athens.

♦ The Heritage of Democratic Idealism

The price of the disunity and disarray that resulted from the splintering of the New Left has been high indeed. Although the once relatively unified Movement of the 1960s spawned a variety of separate social movements that flourished after the 1960s, the failure of these movements to coalesce as a unified political opposition in the United States has condemned the American left to relative impotence in the succeeding two decades since the splintering took place. Clearly the two greatest failures of the 1960s were the abandonment of the goal of racial integration in favor of racial separatism (or black nationalism) and the breakdown of attempts to form an adult, post-university, New Left organizational framework--some version of a Movement for a Democratic Society. The attempt to recreate the unity of the

Movement of the sixties through the Rainbow Coalition, organized to support the presidential campaigns of Jesse Jackson, has never recaptured the political-spiritual elan of the 1960s. Jackson's campaigns have suffered from the defects of movements organized around a charismatic leader and thus failed to incorporate the critique of SCLC developed by Ella Baker in her notion of "group-centered leadership" and the decentralist organizing style of the early SNCC whose formation she sponsored.

Furthermore, the Rainbow Coalition has failed to carry out the strategy of grassroots democratic organizing embodied in SDS's notion of participatory democracy and thus suffers from all the weaknesses of liberal electoral strategies which the New Left sought to counter with *both* the organizational *and* strategic direction I have called democratic decentralism, and which Wini Breines captured in the phrase "prefigurative politics." It was this attempt to recreate grassroots democracy from the bottom up by building democratic community on a decentralized basis that was at the heart of the New Left's most creative political activity whether in civil rights, community organizing among the poor, student organizing on campuses, or the myriad initiatives of the anti-war movement and resistance work. The attempt to carry this organizing to constituencies like university-trained workers (the "new working class") through Movement for a Democratic Society projects on a city-wide basis or along professional lines was truncated by the abrupt turn of a small segment of the New Left to adventurism, violence, and a romantic version of clandestinity. At the same time and in partial tandem with adventurism, the non-violent leadership of the black civil rights movement was temporarily displaced by Black Power separatism and the Black Panthers' strategy of armed self-defense.

Twenty years later, the dust has long settled from the explosion of the Weatherman townhouse bomb factory, and the Black Panthers are largely recognized as a tragic and suicidal expression of ghetto rage, but the New Left and the Movement have never reconstituted themselves as an effective political force in America. Since the takeover and destruction of SDS by Marxist-Leninists, there has been no broad forum for the expression and debate of that special brand of libertarian and decentralist democratic radicalism which Dwight Macdonald called "the American radical tradition." As has so frequently been the case in American history, the disruption of radical movements has left a series of discontinuities.

In the political vacuum created by the premature demise of the New Left, the new conservatism of the Reagan-Bush counterrevolution has energetically filled the void with avarice. Bolstered by the New (fundamentalist) Right, the reaction against the student movement and the New Left has virtually destroyed that watered-down American version of social democracy once called "the New Deal." Welfare state capitalism in the U.S. has been replaced by a politics of greed and corruption so insensitive to basic human needs that several million citizens of the wealthiest society in the history of the human race live homeless on the streets of this country and eat refuse from garbage cans. All this has been accomplished in the name of a supposed restoration of Judeo-Christian "morality," "family values," and "law and order." It is quite simply the triumph of selfishness and lies.

This social and political counterrevolution would not have been possible had the New Left not missed its chance to organize the new working class as a political force and to ally with blue-collar workers and the poor. Without this alliance, the old working class of industrial laborers has been decimated both by the flight of capital and jobs to cheap labor markets abroad and by the systematic destruction of its unions at home. Before long, there will be little for university-trained workers to ally with. The army of the poor grows apace. Young workers without college training enter a job market dominated by low-pay work as robots in hamburger stands, if they are able to enter it at all.

The exceedingly vigorous ecological and environmental movements have entered the political arena with a broad spectrum of organizations that raise considerable sums through mass mailings but seem to have missed out on the notion of democratic participation. Their members make few actual organizational or policy decisions apart from the exact amount of the contribution needed to salve their consciences. Additionally, the environmentalists (largely representative of "middle-class" constituencies) seem oblivious to the plight of racial minorities, industrial workers and the poor. Their ecological and aesthetic sensibilities are too often immune to social issues and they have generally missed opportunities to ally with workers against corporate interests, leaving the powerful to divide and conquer.

The liberal-labor alliance that was the social base of the New Deal and the force behind the construction of the welfare state is almost totally shattered. The New Left, which could have advanced the political agenda of the U.S., failed to fulfill its historic role, and a revitalized version of cutthroat corporate capitalism has easily replaced political progress with its own atavistic agenda.

As the planetary ecological crisis unfolds, one searches for strategies that will unite environmental and social issues with a democratic political agenda for the human community.

✦ Democratic Idealism and the Green Movement

The principles of democratic idealism that inspired the best of the New Left in the 1960s in the United States have spread in the succeeding two decades to every corner of the globe. Whether it is the West German Greens or the workers and students of Beijing, the notion that grassroots democracy and spiritual values can create a common political vision for a planetary politics has gained adherents in societies from the First World to the Fourth. A commitment to the realization of these ideals through nonviolence is a common theme as are the principles of feminism, gay liberation, and ecological sanity.

The Green movement has evolved a set of seven principles as the basis of the new politics: ecology, social responsibility, grassroots democracy, nonviolence, decentralization, post-patriarchal perspectives, and spirituality.[1] These principles represent the merger in theory of a spiritual-ecological and participatory-democratic politics that embody the best of SDS's democratic idealism in the *Port Huron Statement*, the nonviolence of the radical pacifists, and the spiritual-ecological vales of the counter culture as exemplified in Gary Snyder's manifesto "Buddhism and the Coming Revolution." This union, which was implicit in the Movement of the 1960s, would have continued to develop more easily if the New Left had not been torn apart by the separatist "politics of identity" and adventuristic violence. In my view, this coalescing, grounded in spiritual awareness, could have completed the new gestalt or political paradigm that emerged in the 1960s.

The power of this new politics, its ability to capture the imaginations of people worldwide, and its vision of a planetary grassroots-democratic and ecologically sane future on a decentralized basis appeared in a startling document, the *Green Buddhist Declaration*, prepared by members of the international Buddhist community on the occasion of the 14th General Conference of the World Fellowship of Buddhists in 1984 at Colombo, Sri Lanka. It reflects the far-flung influence of the language and vision of SDS's *Port Huron Statement* around the world.

This document states:

> In order to build an alternative to the current state and economic system, we believe it necessary to start change from the grassroots up and from the level of international cooperation down. We must "think globally, act locally." . . . Buddhism's priority is not the creation of a particular kind of state, but a culture based on non-violence and participatory democracy, putting the full development of human potential in community before the pursuit of national product.[2]

Furthermore, it reminds students of Eastern spiritual traditions that many of the structures which have accrued to the Buddhist tradition are "far from the voluntary simplicity and democratic decentralization of the early Sangha [community]."

Whether or not the emergence of Green politics implies the abolition of the traditional distinction between "left" and "right" as some have argued is debatable on several counts. (Two of its American supporters argue that "It is an ecological, holistic, and feminist movement that transcends the old political framework of left versus right."[3]) It is, in any case, undeniable that ecological politics has rendered obsolete the traditional opposition of the terms "radical" and "conservative". Grassroots democracy is certainly a "radical" position in the sense of being opposed to both corporate capitalist and state-socialist economic and social organization. When joined with ecological issues, however, the new politics is certainly more "conservative" in the true sense of that word than anything proposed by the traditional right. The idea of a democratic, ecological and spiritually motivated politics that is in the *forefront* of movements to preserve life on this planet is indeed exhilarating and seems to offer a sense of fresh political, psychological, and spiritual space which differs markedly from the traditional "left," overburdened with the antagonisms of the past. In a profound sense, this new outlook represents a fulfillment of the broken promise of a New Left that failed in its striving to be truly *new.* It remains to be seen whether ecological politics in America can grow beyond the sectarianism which it inherited from the break-up of the New Left and whether eco-philosophy can contribute to the world of political philosophy.

In the 1990s, we live in a world transformed by the message of participatory democracy and active nonviolence based on spiritual values which was the greatest gift of the American New Left of the 1960s to our brothers and sisters around the planet. And yet, our project of building in America a decentralist democracy of "communities human in scale" in which the full moral and spiritual development of each citizen would be the measure of the goodness of the whole polity remains sadly unfinished--even in disarray.

The revolutions in Eastern Europe and the Soviet Union force a rethinking of democratic strategies around the globe, and it is still too early to know what new decentralist spring may follow the thawing of the Cold War and the end of totalitarian state socialism. Surely the message of the New Left is more relevant than ever and its critique of corporate liberalism more integral to the achievement of real political and economic democracy in the 21st century.

One thing seems certain. The instinct of the young radicals of SDS who framed political debate in the 1960s in terms of *value-centered democratic political theory* laid the basis for the new political discourse that will guide radical democratic experimentation in the next generation. The discourse of democracy has won over all others and it now remains for us to deepen its meaning and fulfill its promises just as the framers of the *Port Huron Statement* insisted almost three decades ago.

✦ *The Inspiration of the Fourth World*

Although the gospel of participatory democracy was first promulgated by students from the First World, the vision of democratic idealism is nurtured by the survivors of humanity's long history of democratic, decentralist, and spiritually grounded cultures--the native peoples of the Americas and elsewhere on the planet who are a living link with the 50,000 years of our so-called "pre-history." These peoples, whom *we* have named the "Fourth World" are the guardians of what remains of the *real First World*--the world of paleolithic and early neolithic peoples who lived in decentralized democratic tribes and villages before the rise of what we dare to call "civilization"--as though that word implied a humane, uplifted culture instead of the brutal organization of humanity through "totalitarian technics" into what Lewis Mumford called the three great "human machines"--the war machine, the work machine, and bureaucracy[4]--all three present in what we now know as the modern militarized, industrialized nation state. Those native peoples represent the long history of a human world without standing armies, without slave brigades or factories, and without giant bureaucracies in the service of ruling classes or monarchs. They are the memory and the hope that humankind can live together in peace and in harmony with nature when it lives in tune with its natural spiritual promptings, its natural maternal instinct--the instinct for Mother Nature--and its natural egalitarian impulses.

Both capitalisms and socialisms pale before the awesome truth that human beings once knew who they were--one of the many species of sentient beings; that they revered the life of all beings--plant and animal; that they developed democratic technologies of appropriate scale; and that they experienced the "first post-scarcity society" in what we have contemptuously called "the Stone Age."[5] It is humbling to recognize that the explicit belief of Marxists and liberals that material abundance will bring us peace and prosperity is the idle dream of those who have equated empirical science, its technology, and the production of "things" (i.e., industrial goods) with human progress. The primary myth of the modern world is "matter" and 20th century science has been scrambling to save its dignity every since it split atoms into sub-atomic "particles" which could sometimes be seen as "waves" and since its greatest technological achievement, the thermonuclear bomb, exploded the fiction that the modern militarized state could protect anyone from anyone.

In the disarray following upon the loss of faith in the authority of science, technology, industrialism, and the nation state, democratic idealism has offered the only guidelines that seem to provide the necessary authority for radical political action--those that proceed from the heart. People of conscience turn for guidance to the spiritual and moral truths which American democratic radicals of the 18th century believed were self-evident in the inner hearts of all human beings.

Together with the collapse of modern materialist, centralized authority has come a revolution in the concept of appropriate size--the scaling down of patriarchal ego. The much vaunted "economies of scale" which were called upon to validate the proposition that "bigger is better" have given way to the notions of "small is beautiful," "human scale," and ecological balance.[6]

It is, I believe, an error (and the weakness of certain kinds of anarchist utopianism) to assume that humanity can somehow return to the "organic" or "natural" societies of the neolithic world, or that there is an end to politics. Human beings have left forever their neolithic past and life in the human realm can never be a simple return to nature. We have indeed lost our innocence, but with that loss we have gained in the dimension of ethical choice and a part of the growth of human moral life is the world of political choice. It remains our specifically human burden and blessing that we are no longer given a model of community by nature but must choose what kind of human communities we will build *in harmony with nature.* There is no god or goddess who will come as a savior to tell us the way. Attunement with nature--a fundamental necessity if we are to grow and survive--does not mean that a deified Nature can make choices for us. Only we can choose. The healing of human brokenness is a human task.

And yet, in the achievement of that task, peoples of the Fourth World--Native Americans of the Western Hemisphere in particular--provide a special inspiration to contemporary activists.

◆ Maximo and the Guatemalan Guerrilla Story

If it took almost twenty years for me to integrate my experiences of the New Left of the 1960s, it has taken even longer to allow an image to emerge from deep in my own mind during meditation: the image of a young boy standing in the sun on the hillside of a farm owned by his Finnish IWW grandparents, a boy bathed in the light of ancient sources of unconditional love that his peasant-worker grandmother bestowed on him while he stood on the earth of whose grace she was the channel and the true priestess, digging potatoes from the harsh soil with hands which had once ached from the toil of New England factories, and who sent money home to Wimpila in Central Finland to rebuild the roof of a round church, the symbol of earth itself and of community in that faraway Finnish village. When I uncovered the memory, I received a blessing, and the struggle to make history and mystery, his story and my story, coincide in a comprehensible whole finally merged in a poetic moment where the child of faith and the man of political acts met in a deep embrace. Another step on the journey of rebirth.

My story is never mine alone and there is another boy who has entered this tale now, a boy we met *as if by accident* on the shores of Lake Atitlan in Guatemala. He was ten years old when my companion and I met him selling shirts to gringo tourists from a bundle on his back. In full view of the four volcanoes which stand guard over that enchanted place we entered the Fourth World with this Cakchiquel-Mayan boy as our guide. ("When the student is ready, the teacher will appear.") I felt as though the spirit of my Finnish grandmother had led us there. Now the Guatemalan guerrilla story I had told as a metaphor of resistance and democratic organizing in the 1960s would come back to haunt me.

The peoples of the Western Highlands of Guatemala wage a resistance movement more than 450 years old. First against the Spanish, then against a series of domestic tyrants always allied with landed oligarchs and the army, now against the brutal attempt (with the help of our CIA and military) to quell the insurgent guerrillas by killing the Indians and uprooting their culture. Products of the First World and plastic containers threaten to turn this fragile economy into a garbage dump. Petty capitalism lurks on the fringes of village economies tenuously balanced between subsistence farming on tiny plots bolstered by communal institutions and the need to sell textiles to the tourists. Maximo worked in a small sweat shop for five quetzales (two dollars) a day at age eight. Work shifts: ten hours. "It was so boring," he complained. He doesn't speak a lot of Spanish. He doesn't read or write his own language. He's never been to school.

The bridge I want to build now is no longer only between the 1960s and the 1990s but between the boy on that Finnish farm in the Pacific Northwest and the son of the Cakchiquels in the Western Highlands of Guatemala, between the First and Fourth Worlds. Perhaps even more: between the world of my Finnish peasant ancestors and the world of Maximo's village, two parts of the planetary community before Western capitalism burst in upon their ancient communitarian traditions. I don't want Maximo to be forced to leave his lovely homeland to work for proletarian wages, to die far from the graves of his forebearers.

It is tempting here in the Fourth World to believe I can find fulfillment on the shores of a lake high among the Guatemalan volcanoes. There is even this ten-year-old Indian boy onto whom I project the archetypal child, and I weep for him because he works so hard. When I speak to him of my grandmother he falls into reverent silence because here in the Fourth World people know the meaning and importance of ancestors.

I am with my companion of fourteen years, Ken Carpenter, who went to prison for heeding the call of the draft resistance movement I helped organize. Our relationship has always been a symbol of resistance and hope as well as the fulfillment of a dream. I wonder what the Guatemalan Indian boys think when I tell them about the resistance movement. Their country has been torn for more than thirty years by a conflict our nation is largely responsible for sustaining.

In the face of an old Indian woman trying to sell firewood for a few pennies, I see the ancient weathered grace of my Finnish grandmother. Confusing tears of anger and love come to my eyes. I ask myself whether the brokenness I feel is the memory of the Movement, my own past, or the history of humanity itself and whether the world of these Indian villages in the Guatemalan highlands is the screen for my projections or whether the spirit of my Finnish Grandmother has led me home to a place and people who have resisted the destruction and encroachments of the Modern World. Was the identification with poor people that drew many of us into the early New Left a projection of our own pain and sense of inner poverty or did it also embody a longing for a simpler humanity that once lived in villages like these without armies, or factories, or bureaucracies or the state? Without modern science and technology or industrialization. Without many of the "goods" of technological society. But with spirit.

I stop and ask what freedom I have in the face of the encroaching plastic industrial war-mongering Modern World. Is resistance all that I can effectively do? An inner voice reminds me that resistance was never a simple saying "no," but the chance to live by a different set of spiritual values called the Movement and build the new world in the shell of the old.

NOTES

Preface

1. H. B. Acton, "Idealism," *The Encyclopedia of Philosophy* (New York: Macmillan, 1967), Vol. 4, p. 110.

2. Ernest Barker, *Greek Political Theory* (London: Methuen & Co, 1918; rpt., 1961), p. 150.

3. Abraham Maslow, *New Knowledge in Human Values* (New York: Harper, 1959).

4. Abraham Maslow, *Religions, Values, and Peak-Experiences* (New York: Viking, 1970), pp. viii and 18.

5. Gregory Bateson, *Mind and Nature: A Necessary Unity* (New York: E. P. Dutton, 1979).

6. Claudio Naranjo, *The One Quest* (New York: Ballantine Books, Inc., 1973).

7. Vaclav Havel, Speech before the U.S. Congress, February 21, 1990, *New York Times*, February 22, 1990, p. 8.

Introduction

1. Paul Potter, presentation to SDS reunion in Hell, Michigan, August 1977.

2. *Port Huron Statement* (1962; rpt. Chicago: Students for a Democratic Society, 1966); complete text available as "Appendix" in James Miller, *"Democracy Is in the Streets": From Port Huron to the Seige of Chicago* (New York: Simon and Schuster, 1987); reprinted in part in Mitchell Cohen and Dennis Hale, eds., *The New Student Left* (Boston: Beacon, 1966, rev. 1967), pp. 292 ff.; Paul Jacobs and Saul Landau, *The New Radicals* (New York: Random House, 1966), pp. 150 ff.; and Massimo Teodori, ed., *The New Left: A Documentary History* (Indianapolis: Bobbs-Merrill, 1969), pp. 163 ff.

3. Lauren Kessler, *After All These Years: A New Look At the Sixties Generation* (New York: Thunder's Mouth Press, 1990); Jack Whalen and Richard Flacks, *Beyond the Barricades: The Sixties Generation Grows Up* (Philadelphia: Temple University Press, 1989).

4. The major interpretive works on the New Left in the United States are: Wini Breines, *The Great Refusal: Community and Organization in the New Left* (New York: Praeger, 1982); Stewart Burns, *Social Movements of the 1960s: Searching for Democracy* (Boston: Twayne, 1990); Greg Calvert and Carol Neiman, *A Disrupted History: The New Left and the New Capitalism* (New York: Random House, 1971); Todd Gitlin, *The Whole World Is Watching: Mass Media in the Making and Unmaking of the New Left* (Berkely: University of California Press, 1980), and, *The Sixties: Years of Hope, Days of Rage* (New York: Bantam, 1987); Tom Hayden, *Reunion: A Memoir* (New York: Random House, 1988); James Miller, *"Democracy Is in the Streets": From Port Huron to the Siege of Chicago* (New York: Simon and Schuster, 1987); Kirkpatrick Sale, *SDS* (New York: Random House, Vintage edition, 1974); Irwin Unger, *The Movement: A History of the American New Left, 1959-1972* (New York: Harper

and Row, 1974); and Nigel Young, *An Infantile Disorder?: The Crisis and Decline of the New Left* (Boulder, Colo.: Westview Press, 1977).

5. Young, *An Infantile Disorder?*, pp. 11-13.

6. Sale, *SDS*, pp. 283-84.

7. See Chapter 2 following. The development of the nonviolent movement in the United States is chronicled in Robert Cooney and Helen Michalowski, *The Power of the People: Active Nonviolence in the United States* (Culver City, Calif.: Peace Press, 1977); and Staughton Lynd, ed., *Nonviolence in America: A Documentary History* (Indianapolis: Bobbs-Merrill, 1966).

8. On 17th century radicalism see Christopher Hill, *The World Turned Upside Down: Radical Ideas During the English Revolution* (New York: Viking Press, 1972). Useful surveys of decentralist thought and organization are found in the following works: Daniel Guérin, *Anarchism* (New York: Monthly Review Press, 1970); James Joll, *The Anarchists* (Boston: Harvard University Press, 1964); Kirkpatrick Sale, *Human Scale* (New York: G. P. Putnam Sons, 1980); and George Woodcock, *Anarchism: A History of Libertarian Ideas and Movements* (Cleveland: World Publishing, 1962).

9. I am indebted to Martin Verlet of the *Parti Communiste Français* for this formulation advanced in a discussion in 1967.

10. James Miller, *"Democracy Is in the Streets"*, p. 16. Miller's insistence that the New Left was indebted to "the tradition of civic republicanism that links Aristotle to John Dewey" seems to me essentially sound. He fails to recognize that this debt to the Western political tradition in no way obviates the New Left's equally great debt to the civil rights movement whose essential contribution he underrates. (See Chapter 4 below.)

11. Ernest Barker, *Greek Political Theory* (London: Methuen and Co., 1918), reprinted (New York: Barnes and Noble, 1960).

12. John H. Schaar, "Legitimacy in the Modern State," in *Legitimacy in the Modern State* (New Brunswick, N.J.: Transaction Books, 1981), pp. 15 ff.

13. Jürgen Habermas, *Legitimation Crisis*, trans. by Thomas McCarthy (Boston: Beacon Press, 1975).

14. Seymour Martin Lipset, *Political Man* (Baltimore: Johns Hopkins Press, 1981), p. 67.

15. Howard Zinn, *SNCC: The New Abolitionists* (Boston: Beacon, 1965), pp. 190 ff.; and Clayborne Carson, *In Struggle: SNCC and the Black Awakening of the 1960s* (Cambridge: Harvard University Press, 1981), pp. 111 ff.

Chapter 1

1. Letter from Allen Ginsberg to John Hollander, Fall 1958, quoted in Jane Kramer, *Allen Ginsberg in America* (New York: Random House, 1969), p. 174.

2. Gary Snyder, *Earth House Hold* (New York: New Directions Books, 1969), cover notes.

3. Jacques Ellul, *La Technique ou, l'enjeu du siècle* (Paris: Librairie Armand Colin, 1954), trans. by John Wilkinson, *Technological Society* (New York: Alfred A. Knopf, 1964).

4. Morris Dickstein, *Gates of Eden: American Culture in the Sixties* (New York: Basic Books, 1977), p. 85.

5. Walpola Rahula, *What the Buddha Taught* (London: G.Fraser, 1978), p. 21.

6. Alan Watts, *Beyond Theology* (New York: Vintage, 1973), p. 7.

7. *Ibid.*, pp. 82-83.

8. *Ibid.*, pp. 83-84.

9. *Ibid.*

10. Major secondary sources on the Beat Generation are: Morris Dickstein, *Gates of Eden*; Jane Kramer, *Allen Ginsberg in America*; Fred W. McDarrah, *Kerouac and Friends: A Beat Generation Album* (New York: William Morrow, 1985); Dennis McNally, *Desolate Angel: Jack Kerouac, the Beat Generation and America* (Random House: New York, 1979); and Gerald Nicosia, *Memory Babe: A Critical Biography of Jack Kerouac* (New York: Grove Press, 1983).

11. Jack Kerouac, *The Dharma Bums* (New York: New American Library, Signet edition, 1959), p. 10.

12. Unless otherwise indicated the following quotes are from Gary Snyder, "Buddhist Anarchism," *Journal for the Protection of All Beings*, Summer 1961.

13. Gary Snyder, "Buddhism and the Coming Revolution," in *Earth House Hold*.

14. Bruce Kokopeli and George Lakey, "More Power Than We Want: Masculine Sexuality and Violence," *WIN* magazine, July 29, 1976.

15. McNally, *Desolate Angel*, p. 202; see also Kramer, *Allen Ginsberg in America*.

16. William Carlos Williams, "Introduction," to *Howl! and Other Poems* by Allen Ginsberg (San Francisco: City Lights Books, 1959), pp. 7-8.

17. Thomas Merrill, *Allen Ginsberg* (Boston: Twayne, 1988), p. 12.

18. Snyder, *Earth House Hold*, p. 120.

19. Jean-Jacques Rousseau, *The Social Contract and Discourse on the Origin of Inequality*, edited by Lester G. Crocker (New York: Simon and Schuster Pocket edition, 1967).

20. Thomas Hobbes, *Leviathan*, edited by C. B. MacPherson (New York: Penguin Books, 1968).

21. *Ibid.*

22. Snyder, *Earth House Hold*, cover notes.

23. Snyder, "Politics and the Primitive," in *Earth House Hold*, pp. 121-122.

24. Snyder, "Why Tribe?" in *Earth House Hold*, pp. 113-114.

25. *Ibid.*, p. 114.

26. *Ibid.*, p. 115.

27. *Ibid.*

28. *Ibid.*, p. 116.

29. Biographical information on Kerouac taken from McNally, *Desolate Angel*, and Nicosia, *Memory Babe*.

30. Kerouac, *The Dharma Bums*.

31. McNally, *Desolate Angel*, p. 331.

Chapter 2

1. Eknath Easwaran, *Gandhi the Man* (Petaluma, CA: Nilgiri Press, 1978), p. 60.

2. See *Against the Tide: Pacifist Resistance in the Second World War* (New York: War Resisters League, 1983), a collection of oral histories of World War II draft resisters.

3. Biographical material on A. J. Muste is from Joann Ooiman Robinson, *Abraham Went Out: A Biography of A.J. Muste* (Philadelphia: Temple University Press, 1981). See also Nat Hentoff, *Peace Agitator: The Story Of A. J. Muste* (New York: McMillan, 1963).

4. Robinson, *Abraham Went Out*, pp. 42-43.

5. See Dave Dellinger's introduction to *Against The Tide*; also Cooney and Michalowski, *Power of the People*, pp. 88 ff.

6. Cooney and Michalowski, *Power of the People*, pp. 94-95. It should be noted that many of those imprisoned were Jehovah's Witnesses who were forbidden by church doctrine from cooperating in any way with "secular wars."

7. *Ibid.*, pp. 97, 112, 153, 189.

8. Robinson, *Abraham Went Out*, p. 79.

9. Cooney and Michalowski, *Power of the People*, p. 93.

10. *Ibid.*, p. 93.

11. *Ibid.*, p. 94.

12. *Ibid.*, p. 94.

13. Robinson, *Abraham Went Out*, p. XIV.

14. *Ibid.*, p. 137.

15. William D. Miller, *A Harsh and Dreadful Love: Dorothy Day and the Catholic Worker Movement* (Garden City, N.Y.: Doubleday Image Books, 1974), p. 21.

16. *Ibid.*, p. 89.

17. *Ibid.*, p. 93.

18. *Ibid.*, p. 93.

19. *Ibid.*, p. 95.

20. Cooney and Michalowski, *Power of the People*, p. 127.

21. *Ibid.*, p. 127.

22. "Tract for the Times," *Liberation*, March 1956, pp. 3-6. Reprinted in Paul Goodman, ed., *Seeds of Liberation* (New York: George Braziller, 1964), pp. 3-11. Except where otherwise indicated, the following quotations are all from this article.

23. *Liberation*, April 1956, p. 16.

24. Dwight Macdonald, "Introduction," *Politics Past: Essays in Political Criticism* (New York: Viking Press, 1957), pp. 17-22, and 25.

25. *Ibid.*, p. 29.

26. *Ibid.*, p. 28.

27. Dwight Macdonald, "The Question of God," *Partisan Review*, May-June, 1950; reprinted in *Politics Past*, pp. 369-373.

28. *Ibid.*, p. 371.

29. Macdonald, "Introduction," *Politics Past*, p. 30.

30. *Ibid.*, pp. 29-30.

31. *Ibid.*, p. 23.

32. *Ibid.*, p. 29.

33. McNally, *Desolate Angel*, p. 201.

34. Cooney and Michalowski, *Power of the People*, p. 187.

35. McNally, *Desolate Angel*, p. 203.
36. Snyder, "Buddhism and the Coming Revolution," p. 92.
37. Allen Ginsberg, *Howl! and Other Poems* (San Francisco: City Lights Books, 1956), p. 17.
38. Kramer, *Allen Ginsberg*, p. 174.

Chapter 3

1. Krishnalal Shridharani, *War Without Violence* (New York: Garland Publishing, 1972), p. 169.
2. *Ibid.*, p. 206.
3. Chris Orsinger, "Gandhi's Spiritual Rationale for Satyagraha (Nonviolent Direct Action)", unpublished paper, November 8, 1982.
4. M. K. Gandhi, *Non-Violent Resistance*, ed. by B. Kumarappa (New York: Schocken Books, 1961), p. iii.
5. Biographical material on King is drawn from Stephen B. Oates, *Let the Trumpet Sound: The Life of Martin Luther King, Jr.* (New York: New American Library, 1982).
6. *Ibid.*, p. 32.
7. Quoted in *Ibid.*, pp.39, 40.
8. *Ibid.*, p. 28.
9. *Ibid.*, p. 40.
10. *Ibid.*, pp. 102-3.
11. *Ibid.*, p. 106.
12. *Ibid.*, p. 108.
13. Cooney and Michalowski, *The Power of the People*, p. 157.
14. Aldon D. Morris, *The Origins of the Civil Rights Movement: Black Communities Organizing for Change* (New York: Macmillan, The Free Press, 1984), pp. 88-89.
15. *Ibid.*, p. 303 note 36.
16. *Ibid.* p. 91.
17. *Ibid.*
18. Richard Barnet, "The National Security Bureaucracy and Military Intervention," in Priscilla Long, ed., *The New Left: A Collection of Essays* (Boston: Porter Sargent, 1969) p. 87.
19. Michael Harrington, "The Mystical Militants," in *Beyond the New Left*, ed., Irving Howe (New York: Horizon Press, 1964).
20. Miller, *"Democracy Is in the Streets"*, p. 103.
21. *Ibid.*, p. 94.
22. Clayborne Carson, *In Struggle: SNCC and the Black Awakening of the 1960s* (Cambridge, Mass.: Harvard Univ. Press), pp. 9-10.
23. *Ibid.*, p. 23.
24. *Ibid.*, p. 22.
25. *Ibid.*, pp. 23-24.
26. See Leo Tolstoy, *On Civil Disobedience and Non-Violence* (New York: Signet Books, 1968.)
27. Mohandas K. Gandhi, *Gandhi: Selected Writings*, ed. by Ronald Duncan (New York: Harper & Row, 1972), p. 41.

28. Morris, *Origins of the Civil Rights Movement*, Chapter 3.

29. *Ibid.*, pp. 197 ff.

30. Clayborne Carson, *In Struggle*, p. 11. Carson's internal quote is from an article by Frederick Solomon and Jacob R. Fishman, "The Psychosocial Meaning of Nonviolence in Student Civil Rights Activities," *Psychiatry*, 27 (May 1964): 94-95. See Carson, p. 308 note 4.

31. Carson, *In Struggle*, pp. 11-12.

32. *Ibid.*, p. 2.

33. *Ibid.*, p. 19.

34. *Ibid.*, p. 2.

35. *Ibid.*, p. 3.

36. *Ibid.*

37. *Ibid.*, p. 21.

38. *Ibid.*, p. 16.

39. I am indebted for most of these insights to a seminar on ethnography given by Professor David Wellman of the Community Studies Board at the University of California at Santa Cruz in the winter of 1984. The seminar was entitled "From the Bottom Up: Ordinary People in Everyday Life."

40. Morris, *Origins of the Civil Rights Movement*, pp. 102-3.

41. Taped interview with Ella Baker, December 1970, in Gerda Lerner, ed., *Black Women in White America: A Documentary History* (New York: Random House, 1972), p. 351.

42. Morris, *Origins of the Civil Rights Movement*, p. 103.

43. *Ibid.*

44. *Ibid.*, p. 104.

45. Lerner, *Black Women in White America*, p. 352.

46. *Ibid.*, p. 351.

47. Morris, *Origins of the Civil Rights Movement*, pp. 215-18.

48. Carson, *In Struggle*, pp. 20, 24, and 30.

49. *Ibid.*, p. 66.

50. *Ibid.*

51. *Ibid.*

52. Staughton Lynd to Greg Calvert, 6-4-90 and 7-18-90.

Chapter 4

1. This interpretation is disputed in its essentials by James Miller in his book, *"Democracy Is in the Streets"*. In particular, Miller regards the notion "that [the New Left] owed its key ideas, including 'participatory democracy' to the example of black civil rights activists in the South" as one of the major "misleading assertions about the origins of the New Left." See p. 16. I regard his narrow focus on intellectual history and biography as responsible for his failure to recognize the importance that the SNCC experience had for the development of the political ideas of the New Left. Otherwise, his book is an invaluable source of information.

2. Sale, *SDS*, p. 23. Quoted in Morris, *Origins of the Civil Rights Movement*, p. 222.

3. *Ibid.*, p. 222.

4. *Ibid.*, based on an article by Richard Flacks, "Who Protests: The Social Bases of the Student Movement," in Julian Foster and Durward Long, eds., *Protest! Student Activism in America* (New York: William Morrow, 1970), pp. 134-57.

5. *Ibid.*

6. *Ibid.*, p. 223, from an interview with Robert Alan Haber, April 24, 1982, Berkeley, Calif.

7. *Ibid.*

8. Miller, *"Democracy Is in the Streets",* p. 23.

9. *Ibid.*, Chapter 2, "On the Road," pp. 41 ff.

10. *Ibid.*, Chapter 4, "The Prophet of the Powerless," pp. 78 ff.

11. *Ibid.*, p. 16.

12. Sheldon Wolin, *Politics and Vision* (Boston: Little, Brown and Company, 1960), Chapter 9, "Liberalism and the Decline of Political Philosophy," pp. 286 ff.

13. Miller, *"Democracy Is in the Streets",* p. 48.

14. *Ibid.*, pp. 48-50. See also, Sara Evans, *Personal Politics: The Roots of Women's Liberation in the Civil Rights Movement and the New Left* (New York: Random House, Vintage Books edition, 1980), pp. 33-34.

15. Miller, *"Democracy Is in the Streets",* pp.50-51.

16. *Ibid.*, pp.51-52.

17. *Ibid.*, p. 54.

18. *Ibid.*, pp. 55-56.

19. *Ibid.*, p. 56. Morris, *The Origins of the Civil Rights Movement,* p. 223.

20. Miller, *"Democracy Is in the Streets",* pp. 60-61.

21. *Ibid.*, p. 104.

22. *Ibid.*, pp. 110, 119.

23. *Port Huron Statement* (Students for a Democratic Society, 1962; reprinted Chicago, 1966), p. 6. Subsequent references will appear in the text. The complete text of the Statement is also available as an "Appendix" in Miller, *"Democracy Is in the Streets",* pp. 329-74.

24. See Evans, *Personal Politics.*

Chapter 5

1. Wini Breines, *The Great Refusal: Community and Organization in the New Left* (New York: Praeger, 1982), especially Chapter 7, "The Economic Research and Action Project." See also Todd Gitlin and Nanci Hollander, *Uptown: Poor Whites in Chicago* (New York: Harper and Row, 1970).

2. Carl Wittman and Thomas Hayden, "An Interracial Movement of the Poor," in Mitchell Cohen and Dennis Hale, eds., *The New Student Left: An Anthology* (Boston: Beacon Press, 1966), pp. 180-219.

3. See Todd Gitlin, *The Sixties: Years of Hope, Days of Rage* (New York: Bantam Books, 1987).

4. Carl Wittman, "A Gay Manifesto," *Liberation,* February, 1970, pp. 18-24.

5. Carl Wittman, *Students and Economic Action* (New York and Ann Arbor: Distributed by Students for a Democratic Society and its Economic Research and Action Project, [196-]), SDS microfilm Series 4B, No. 431; Carl

Wittman and Tom Hayden, *An Interracial Movement of the Poor* (New York and Ann Arbor: SDS and ERAP, [196-]), SDS microfilm Series 4B, No. 151; and, Carl Wittman and Tom Hayden, *Newark Community Union: Summer Project* (New York and Ann Arbor: SDS and ERAP, 1964), SDS microfilm Series 4B, No. 154.

6. Sale, *SDS,* pp. 136-150.

7. Carson, *In Struggle,* p. 96.

8. Staughton Lynd, "The New Radicals and Participatory Democracy," *Dissent* (Summer, 1965).

9. Carson, *In Struggle,* pp. 98-99.

10. *Ibid.,* pp. 114-115.

11. Clark Kerr, *The Uses of the University* (Cambridge: Harvard University Press, reprinted with "Postscript," 1972. Originally published 1963). Subsequent references will appear in the text.

12. Breines, *The Great Refusal,* pp. 115-122.

13. Jerry Farber, "The Student as Nigger," in his *The Student as Nigger* (New York: Pocket Books, 1970).

14. Paul Goodman, *Compulsory Mis-education and The Community of Scholars* (New York: Random House, Vintage Books, 1964).

15. P. A. Kropotkin, "The State: Its Historic Role," in Martin A. Miller, ed., *Selected Writings on Anarchism and Revolution* (Cambridge: The M.I.T. Press, 1970), pp. 210-264.

16. See Chapter 2 above.

17. Cooney and Michalowski, eds., *The Power of the People,* p. 190.

18. Paul Goodman, *Growing Up Absurd* (New York: Random House, 1960).

19. Paul Goodman, *Making Do* (New York: Macmillan, 1963).

20. Paul Goodman, *Compulsory Mis-education and the Community of Scholars,* p. 179.

21. Michael Ferber and Staughton Lynd, *The Resistance* (Boston: Beacon Press, 1971), pp. 121 ff.

22. Paul Goodman, "Memoirs of An Ancient Activist," *WIN,* November 15, 1969, pp.4-7.

23. Todd Gitlin, "Homage to Paul Goodman," *Busy Being Born* (San Francisco: Straight Arrow Books, 1974), p. 14.

24. Paul Goodman, Ralph F. Hefferline, and Fritz Perls, *Gestalt Therapy: Excitement and Growth in the Human Personality* (New York: Delta Press, 1951).

25. A. S. Neill, *Summerhill: A Radical Approach to Child Rearing* (New York: Hart Pub. Co., 1960).

26. Kropotkin, *Selected Writings,* p. 262.

27. Nigel Young, *An Infantile Disorder? The Crisis and Decline of the New Left* (Boulder: Westview Press, 1977), p. 40.

28. Goodman, *Compulsory Mis-education and The Community of Scholars,* pp. 273-274.

29. *Ibid.,* p. 240.

30. *Ibid.,* p. 238.

31. *Ibid.,* pp. 296-297.

32. *Ibid.*, pp. 316-318.

33. *Ibid.*, p. 332.

34. Carl Davidson, "Toward a Student Syndicalist Movement, or University Reform Revisited," *New Left Notes*, September 9, 1966. Reprinted in *Our Generation*, Vol. 5, No. 1, May 1967, and in Immanuel Wallerstein and Paul Starr, eds., *The University Crisis Reader*, Vol.II (New York: Vintage, 1971), p. 98.

35. Carl Davidson, Personal letter to the author, 9-26-88.

36. *Ibid.*

37. For a discussion of the use of the term "corporate liberal" and "corporate liberalism," see below, Chapter 6.

38. Davidson, "Toward a Student Syndicalist Movement," Wallerstein and Starr, eds., *The University Crisis Reader*, Vol. II, p. 99.

39. *Ibid.*, pp. 99-100.

40. Breines, *The Great Refusal*, pp. 102-110.

41. Carl Davidson, "The Multiversity: Crucible of the New Working Class," reprinted in Immanuel Wallerstein and Paul Starr, eds., *The University Crisis Reader*, Vol. II, (New York: Vintage, 1971.)

42. Davidson, "Toward a Student Syndicalist Movement," p. 100.

Chapter 6

1. Quoted in Ferber and Lynd, *The Resistance*, p. 114.

2. Sale, *SDS*, pp. 154-156.

3. The word "syndicalism" carries a certain ambivalence in Anglo-Saxon political discourse. In this work it is always equivalent to anarcho-syndicalism. The French word *syndicalisme* literally means "trade-unionism" but has a special meaning when attached to the theories of Georges Sorel--a French political thinker who defended the use of violence and has been regarded as proto-fascist by many critics.

4. Miller, *"Democracy Is in the Streets"*, pp. 369-370.

5. Sale, *SDS*, pp. 170-171.

6. Nancy Zaroulis and Gerald Sullivan, *Who Spoke Up?: American Protest Against the War in Vietnam 1963-1975* (New York: Holt, Rinehart and Winston, 1984), p. 27.

7. Paul Potter, "The Incredible War," in Massimo Teodori, ed., *The New Left: A Documentary History* (Bobbs-Merrill: In- dianapolis, 1969), pp. 246-248. Quoted in Sale, *SDS*, pp. 187-189.

8. Paul Potter, *A Name for Ourselves* (New York: Little, Brown, 1971).

9. Sale, *SDS*, pp. 198.

10. Carl Oglesby, "Trapped in a System," in Teodori, ed., *The New Left: A Documentary History*, pp. 182-188. The speech is mis-dated "October 27, 1965." See Sale, *SDS*, pp. 240-242.

11. Sale, *SDS*, p. 245 note.

12. R. Jeffrey Lustig, *Corporate Liberalism: The Origins of Modern American Political Theory, 1890-1920* (Berkeley: University of California Press), p. 14.

13. Martin Sklar, "Woodrow Wilson and the Political Economy of Modern

United States Liberalism," *Studies on the Left*, Vol. 1, No. 3, 1960. Cited in Lustig, *Corporate Liberalism*, note 84, p. 274.

14. Sklar, "Woodrow Wilson and the Political Economy of Modern United States Liberalism," p. 43.

15. *Ibid.*, pp. 40-41.

16. These discussions were an important source of my political education. Ella and John Laffey who, like Michael Harrington, were former associates of Max Schachtman, brought to these informal debates experience and knowledge without which my first graduate career would have lacked the political vitality that led me to activism. Others in these discussions who were later active in the New Left included Paul Breines, Wini Breines, and Mendy Samstein.

17. Sklar, "Woodrow Wilson and the Political Economy of Modern United States Liberalism," pp. 44-45.

18. See Chapter 7 below.

19. Breines, *The Great Refusal*.

20. Ferber and Lynd, *The Resistance*, pp. 50-51.

21. *Ibid.*, pp. 17-21 and 35.

22. *Ibid.*, pp. 29-33 and 126-127.

23. *Ibid.*, p.34.

24. Quoted in Sale, *SDS*, p. 206.

25. Ferber and Lynd, *The Resistance*, p. 52.

26. Sara Evans, *Personal Politics: The Roots of Women's Liberation in the Civil Rights Movement and the New Left* (New York: Vintage, 1980).

27. Ferber and Lynd, *The Resistance*, pp. 54-55

28. *Ibid.*, pp. 60-61; Sale, *SDS*, pp. 313-315.

29. Greg Calvert, "From Protest to Resistance," *New Left Notes*, January 13, 1967.

Chapter 7

1. Roger Weaver, *The Orange and Other Poems* (Portland, Or.: Press-22, 1978); *Standing on Earth, Throwing These Sequins at the Stars: A Handbook for Poets* (Salem, Or.: Joyce Publishers, 1989); and, *Twenty-One Waking Dreams* (Parkdale, Or.: Trout Creek Press, 1985).

2. Yu-t'ang Lin, ed., *The Wisdom of China and India* (New York: Random House), 1942.

3. Louis Fischer, *The Life of Mahatma Gandhi* (New York: Harper, 1950).

4. E. A. Burtt, ed., *The Teachings of the Compassionate Buddha* (New York: New American Library, 1955).

5. "Towards a Quaker View of Sex: An Essay by a Group of Friends," (Excerpts), *Liberation*, Summer, 1963, pp. 23-33.

6. Cooney and Michalowski, eds., *Power of the People*, p. 184.

7. Arthur Hirsh, *The French New Left: An Intellectual History from Sartre to Gorz* (Boston: South End Press, 1981), pp. 144-146.

8. See above Chapter 5.

9. Cathy Wilkerson, Interview with Ron Grele, transcript pp. 1-10 and 1-14, February 17, 1985, Columbia Oral History Project. Wilkerson copy of transcript. Hereafter referred to as Wilkerson-Grele Interview.

10. *Ibid.*, p. 1-35.

11. Quoted in Peter Henig, "Manpower Channeling," *New Left Notes*, January 20, 1967. Also quoted in Michael Ferber and Staughton Lynd, *The Resistance*, pp. 32-33.

12. André Gorz, *Strategy for Labor* (Boston: Beacon Press, 1967).

13. Serge Mallet, *Essays on the New Working Class*, edited and translated by Dick Howard (St. Louis: Telos Press, 1976).

14. Daniel Cohn-Bendit, *Le grand bazar* (Paris: Pierre Belfond, 1975).

15. Bob Gottlieb, Gerry Tenney, and Dave Gilbert, "Praxis and the New Left," *New Left Notes*, February 13, 1967.

16. Greg Calvert, "The Moderation of Cooptation--Doublethink and Student Dissent," *New Left Notes*, February 13, 1967.

17. Greg Calvert, "Democratic Decentralism," *New Left Notes*, February 20, 1967.

18. Carson, *In Struggle*, pp. 194-96.

19. Sale, *SDS*, p. 64.

20. This is a paraphrase of Gordon's performance based on my rather vivid memory of his presentation from the floor. For a description of the conference, see Jack Smith, *National Guardian*, March 4, 1967, p. 6.

21. Teodori, ed., *The New Left: A Documentary History*, p. 412.

22. Breines, *The Great Refusal*, pp. 88-89 and 98.

23. Herbert Marcuse, *Reason and Revolution: Hegel and the Rise of Social Theory* (New York: Oxford University Press, 1941).

24. Material in this section was developed in a paper this author prepared for the History of Consciousness program at the University of California at Santa Cruz in the Fall of 1982: Gregory A. Calvert, "Conversion to the Marxist Paradigm: From the Activist Sixties to the Academic Eighties," unpublished paper.

25. Robert S. and Helen Merrell Lynd, *Middletown: A Study in Contemporary American Culture* (New York: Harcourt, Brace & Company, 1929).

26. Staughton, Lynd, "The Right of Revolution," *New Left Notes*, February 13, 1967, pp. 6-8.

27. Staughton Lynd, *The Intellectual Origins of American Radicalism* (New York: Vintage, 1969).

28. Staughton Lynd to Greg Calvert, 2-22-89 and 2-23-89.

29. Lynd, *Intellectual Origins*, p. vii.

30. *Ibid.*, Chapter 1, "Truths Self-Evident," pp. 17-42.

31. Eugene Genovese, "Review of *Class Conflict, Slavery, and the United States Constitution* and *Intellectual Origins of American Radicalism*," *New York Review of Books*, September 26, 1968, Vol. XI, No. 5, pp. 69-74.

32. Staughton Lynd to Greg Calvert, 2-22-89 and 2-23-89.

33. *V. I. Lenin, Materialism and Empiro-Criticism* (Peking: Foreign Languages Press, 1972).

34. Simone Weil, "Fragments, 1933-1938," in *Oppression and Liberty*, trans. by Arthur Wills and John Petrie (Amherst: University of Massachusetts Press, 1958), p. 133.

Chapter 8

1. Carson, *In Struggle*, pp. 200-204.

2. *Ibid.*, pp. 208-209.

3. The most influential work on this subject is Theodore Roszak, *The Making of a Counter Culture: Reflections on the Technocratic Society and Its Youthful Opposition* (Garden City, N.Y.: Doubleday, 1969).

4. Robert Gottlieb, Gerry Tenney, and David Gilbert, "Towards a Theory of Social Change in America," *New Left Notes*, May 22, 1967, pp. 3-6.

5. David Albert of New Society Publishers has suggested to this author that the phrase was used by eco-anarchists in New York in the mid 1960s.

6. Paul Goodman, *Growing Up Absurd: Problems of Youth in the Organized System* (New York: Random House, 1960).

7. I am indebted to Professor John J. Schaar of the University of California at Santa Cruz for his helpful criticisms on this important point.

8. See Chapter 1 above.

9. Snyder, *Earth House Hold*, pp. 90-93.

10. Two excellent discussions of mind-active drugs and the problems of abuse and addiction are by a former director of the Haight-Ashbury Clinic, Andrew Weil, *The Natural Mind: A New Way of Looking at Drugs and the Higher Consciousness* (Boston: Houghton Mifflin, 1972), and *Chocolate to Morphine: Understanding Mind-active Drugs* (Boston: Houghton Mifflin, 1983).

11. Sale, *SDS*, pp. 282 and 285. The comment by Lee Webb, the unsuccessful candidate of the Old Guard for SDS President at Clear Lake, that "Nobody has heard from him since," is a long way from the truth. *Ibid.*, p. 282 n.

12. Sale, *SDS*, p. 287.

13. *Ibid.*, p. 347.

14. Paul Hofmann, "The New Left Turns to Mood of Violence in Place of Protest," *New York Times*, May 7, 1967. Quoted in Todd Gitlin, *The Whole World Is Watching: Mass Media in the Making and Unmaking of the New Left* (Berkeley: University of California Press, 1980), pp. 183-85. See also, Sale *SDS*, pp. 359-60.

15. Greg Calvert, "Response to the Sensational Press: Divide and Rule," *New Left Notes*, May 22, 1967, p. 2.

16. *Ibid.*

17. Régis Debray, *Revolution in the Revolution?*, trans. by Bobbye Ortiz (New York: Monthly Review Press, 1967).

18. At the final National Convention of SDS, the organization split into two factions both calling themselves the "Revolutionary Youth Movement." RYM I became the Guevaraist (or some would say "Debrayist") Weathermen and eventually the Weather Underground, while RYM II became an overtly Stalinist grouping with a "workerist" line.

19. Robinson, *Abraham Went Out*, pp. 220-21; Cooney and Michalowski, *Power of the People*, p. 189.

20. Staughton Lynd, "Coalition Politics or Nonviolent Revolution," *Liberation*, June-July 1965, pp. 18-21.

21. Young, *An Infantile Disorder?*, p. 31. Also see: Cooney and Michalowski, eds., *Power of the People*, p. 185; Zaroulis and Sullivan, *Who*

Spoke Up?, pp. 51-53.

22. Ferber and Lynd, *The Resistance*, p. 79; the following material is drawn largely from Chapter Six of that book, "David Harris and the Palo Alto Commune," pp. 78-91.

23. Ferber and Lynd, *The Resistance*, p. 52.

24. *Ibid.*, p. 78.

25. Carson, *In Struggle*, p. 278.

26. Eldridge Cleaver, *Soul on Ice* (New York: McGraw-Hill, 1968).

27. Sale, *SDS*, pp. 369-75.

28. Karen Wald, "The Promise of Oakland," *New Left Notes*, November 6, 1967, pp. 1-2. Quoted in part in Sale, *SDS*, p. 376.

29. Ferber and Lynd, *The Resistance*, pp. 141-42; Sale, SDS, p. 375 n.

30. John Veneziale, "Students," *New Left Notes*, September 25, 1967, pp. 1, 8.

31. The basic outline of this political vision is traced in David Dellinger, *Revolutionary Nonviolence* (Indianapolis: Bobbs-Merrill Company, 1970).

32. Barbara Deming, "On Revolution and Equilibrium," *Liberation*, February 1968, pp. 10-21.

33. Arthur Kinoy, *Rights on Trial: The Odyssey of a People's Lawyer* (Cambridge, Mass.: Harvard University Press, 1983).

34. Jean-Paul Sartre, Interview, *Nouvelle Observateur*, June 1975.

35. Marilyn Buck, "On the Right Side: To Resistance," *New Left Notes*, November 6, 1967, p. 3.

36. *New York Times*, August 3, 1988, Sec. 2, p. 3.

37. Sale, *SDS*, pp. 1-5.

38. See my speech at the Last Resistance Conference, Greg Calvert, "A Left-Wing Alternative," *Liberation*, May 1969, pp. 21-26. Also, Greg Calvert and Carol Neiman, *A Disrupted History: The New Left and the New Capitalism* (1971).

Notes Conclusion

1. Fritjof Capra and Charlene Spretnak, *Green Politics* (New York: E. P. Dutton, 1984), Chapter 2, pp. 29-56. See also the excellent overview of Green politics by Brian Tokar, *The Green Alternative: Creating an Ecological Future* (San Pedro, Ca.: R. & E. Miles, 1987), pp. 55 ff.

2. James Hughes, ed., *Green Buddhist Declaration* (Moratuwa, Sri Lanka: Sarvodaya Press, 1984).

3. Capra and Spretnak, *Green Politics*, p. xix.

4. Lewis Mumford, "Authoritarian and Democratic Technics," in *Technology and Culture*, Vol. 5, No. 1, pp. 1-8.

5. Marshall Sahlins, *Stone Age Economics* (Chicago: Aldine, 1972).

6. E. F. Schumacher, *Small Is Beautiful* (New York: Harper, 1973), and Kirkpatrick Sale, *Human Scale* (New York: G. P. Putnam's Sons, 1980).

BIBLIOGRAPHY

Barker, Ernest. *Greek Political Thought.* London: Methuen & Co., 1961.

Barnet, Richard. "The National Security Bureaucracy and Military Intervention." *The New Left: A Collection of Essays.* Edited by Priscilla Long.
Boston: Porter Sargent, 1969.

Bateson, Gregory. *Mind and Nature: A Necessary Unity.* New York: Dutton,
1979.

Breines, Paul, ed. *Critical Interruptions: New Left Perspectives on Herbert
Marcuse.* New York: Herder and Herder, 1970.

Breines, Wini. *The Great Refusal: Community and Organization in the New
Left.* New York: Praeger, 1982.

Burns, James MacGregor. *The Deadlock of Democracy: Four Party Politics in
America.* Englewood Cliffs, N.J.: Prentice Hall, 1963.

Burns, Stewart. *Social Movements of the 1960s: Searching for Democracy.*
Boston: Twayne Publishers, 1990.

Burtt, E. A., ed. *The Teachings of the Compassionate Buddha.* New York: New
American Library, 1955.

Calvert, Greg. "A Left-Wing Alternative." *Liberation,* May 1969.

-----. "Response to the Sensational Press: Divide and Rule." *New Left Notes,*
May 22, 1967.

-----. "Participatory Democracy, Collective Leadership and Political Responsibility." *New Left Notes,* December 18, 1967.

-----. "Review" of *The Great Refusal: Community and Organization in the New
Left* by Wini Breines. *Telos,* Winter 1982-83.

Calvert, Greg, and Neiman, Carol. *A Disrupted History: The New Left and the
New Capitalism.* New York: Random House, 1971.

Capra, Fritjof, and Spretnak, Charlene. *Green Politics.* New York: E. P. Dutton,
1984.

Carson, Clayborne. *In Struggle: SNCC and the Black Awakening of the 1960s.*
Cambridge: Harvard University Press, 1981.

Cleaver, Eldridge. *Soul on Ice.* New York: McGraw-Hill, 1968.

Cohen, Mitchell, and Hale, Dennis, eds. *The New Student Left.* Boston: Beacon
Press, 1966; rev. 1967.

Cohn-Bendit, Daniel. *Le grand bazar.* Paris: Pierre Belfond, 1975.

Cooney, Robert and Helen Michalowski. *The Power of the People: Active
Nonviolence in the United States.* Culver City, Ca.: Peace Press, 1977.

Davidson, Carl. "Toward a Student Syndicalist Movement, or University Reform
Revisited." *New Left Notes,* September 9, 1966. Reprinted in *Our
Generation,* May 1967, pp. 102-111.

-----. "The Multiversity: Crucible of the New Working Class." *The University
Crisis Reader,* Vol. 2. Edited by Immanuel Wallerstein and Paul Starr. New
York: Vintage, 1971.

Debray, Regis. *Revolution in the Revolution?* Translated by Bobbye Ortiz. New
York: Monthly Review Press, 1967.

Dellinger, David. *Revolutionary Nonviolence.* Indianapolis: Bobbs-Merrill Company, 1970.

Deming, Barbara. "On Revolution and Equilibrium." *Liberation*, February 1968.

Dickstein, Morris. *Gates of Eden: American Culture in the Sixties*. New York: Basic Books, 1977.

Dolgoff, Sam, ed. *Bakunin on Anarchism*. Montreal: Black Rose Press, 1980.

Ellul, Jacques. *Autopsy of Revolution*. New York: Alfred Knopf, 1971.

-----*La Technique ou, l'enjeu du siècle*. Librairie Armand Colin, 1954. Trans. by John Wilkinson. *The Technological Society*. New York: Alfred A. Knopf, 1964.

Evans, Sara. *Personal Politics: The Roots of Women's Liberation in the Civil Rights Movement and the New Left*. New York: Random House, Vintage Books, 1980.

Fanon, Frantz. *Black Skin, White Masks*. Translated by Charles Lam Markmann. New York: Grove Press, 1968.

-----. *The Wretched of the Earth*. Translated by Constance Farrington. New York: Grove Press, 1968.

Farber, Jerry. *The Student as Nigger*. New York: Pocket Books, 1970.

Ferber, Michael, and Staughton Lynd. *The Resistance*. Boston: Beacon Press, 1971.

Fischer, Louis. *The Life of Mahatma Gandhi*. New York: Harper, 1950.

Forman, James. *Liberation Will Come from a Black Thing*. Chicago: Students for a Democratic Society, 1967? SDS Microfilm, Series 4B, No. 94.

-----. *The Making of Black Revolutionaries*. New York: Macmillan, 1972.

Gandhi, M. K. *Non-Violent Resistance*. Edited by B. Kumarappa. New York: 1967.

-----. *Selected Writings*. Edited by Ronald Duncan. New York: Harper and Row, 1972.

Genovese, Eugene. Review of *Class Conflict, Slavery, and the United States Constitution* and *Intellectual Origins of American Radicalism*, by Staughton Lynd. *New York Review of Books*, September 26, 1968.

Ginsberg, Allen. *The Fall of America: Poems of These States, 1965-71*. San Francisco: City Lights Books, 1972.

-----. *Howl! and Other Poems*. San Francisco: City Lights Books, 1956.

Gish, Arthur. *The New Left and Christian Radicalism*. Grand Rapids, Mich.: William B. Eerdmans Publishing, 1970.

Gitlin, Todd. *The Sixties: Years of Hope, Days of Rage*. New York: Bantam, 1987.

-----. *The Whole World Is Watching: Mass Media in the Making and Unmaking of the New Left*. Berkeley: University of California Press, 1980.

-----, and Nanci Hollander. *Uptown: Poor Whites in Chicago*. New York: Harper and Row, 1970.

Goodman, Paul. *Compulsory Mis-education and The Community of Scholars*. New York: Random House, Vintage Books, 1964.

-----. *Growing Up Absurd*. New York: Random House, 1960.

-----. *Making Do*. New York: Random House, 1960.

-----. "Memoirs of an Ancient Activist." *Win* Magazine, November 15, 1969.

-----, Ralph Hefferline and Fritz Perls. *Gestalt Therapy: Excitement and Growth in the Human Personality*. New York: Delta Press, 1951.

Goodwyn, Lawrence. *Democratic Promise: The Populist Moment in America.* New York: Oxford University Press, 1976.

-----. *The Populist Moment: A Short History of the Agrarian Revolt in America.* New York: Oxford University Press, 1978.

Gorz, André. *Strategy for Labor.* Boston: Beacon Press, 1967.

Gottlieb, Bob, Gerry Tenney, and Dave Gilbert. "Praxis and the New Left." *New Left Notes,* February 13, 1967.

-----. "Towards a Theory of Social Change in America." *New Left Notes,* May 22, 1967.

Grof, Stanislav. *Realms of the Human Unconscious: Obversations from LSD Research.* New York: E. P. Dutton, 1976.

Guérin, Daniel. *Anarchism.* New York: Monthly Review Press, 1970.

Habermas, Jürgen. *Legitimation Crisis.* Translated by Thomas McCarthy. Boston: Beacon Press, 1975.

Harrington, Michael. "The Mystical Militants." *Beyond the New Left.* Edited by Irving Howe. New York: Horizon Press, 1964.

Hayden, Casey, and King, Mary. "Sex and Caste." *Liberation,* April 1966.

Hayden, Tom. *Reunion: A Memoir.* New York: Random House, 1988.

Henig, Peter. "Manpower Channeling." *New Left Notes,* January 20, 1967.

Hentoff, Nat, ed. *The Essays of A. J. Muste.* New York: Simon and Schuster, Clarion edition, 1970.

-----. *Peace Agitator: The Story of A. J. Muste.* New York: MacMillan, 1963.

Hill, Christopher. *The World Turned Upside Down: Radical Ideas During the English Revolution.* New York: Viking Press, 1972.

Hirsch, Arthur. *The French New Left: An Intellectual History from Sartre to Gorz.* Boston: South End Press, 1981.

Hobbes, Thomas. *Leviathan.* Edited by C. B. Macpherson. New York: Penguin Books, 1968.

Horowitz, David, ed. *The Moral Foundations of the American Republic,* 2nd edition. Charlottesville: University Press of Virginia, 1979.

Hughes, James, ed. *Green Buddhist Declaration.* Moratuwa, Sri Lanka: Sarvodaya Press, 1984.

Isserman, Maurice. *If I Had a Hammer--: The Death of the Old Left and the Birth of the New Left.* New York: Basic Books, 1987.

Jacobs, Paul and Saul Landau. *The New Radicals.* New York: Random House, 1966.

Joll, James. *The Anarchists.* Boston: Harvard University Press, 1964.

Katz, Nathan. *Buddhist and Western Philosophy.* Atlantic Highlands: Humanities Press, 1981.

Kerr, Clark. *The Uses of the University.* Cambridge: Harvard University Press, reprinted with "Postscript," 1972. Originally published 1963.

Kerouac, Jack. *The Dharma Bums.* New York: New American Library, Signet edition, 1959.

Kessler, Lauren. *After All These Years: A New Look At the Sixties Generation.* New York: Thunder's Mouth Press, 1990.

Kinoy, Arthur. *Rights on Trial: The Odyssey of a People's Lawyer.* Cambridge, Mass.: Harvard University Press, 1983.

Kokopeli, Bruce and George Lakey. "More Power Than We Want: Masculine

Sexuality and Violence." *Win* Magazine, July 19, 1976.

Kramer, Jane. *Allen Ginsberg in America*. New York: Random House, 1969.

Kropotkin, P. A. *Selected Writings on Anarchism and Revolution*. Cambridge: M.I.T. Press, 1970.

Lenin, V. I. *Materialism and Empiro-Criticism*. Peking: Foreign Languages Press, 1972.

Lerner, Gerda, ed. *Black Women in America: A Documentary History*. New York: Random House, 1972.

Lin, Yu-t'ang, ed. *The Wisdom of China and India*. New York: Random House, 1942.

Lipset, Seymour Martin. *Political Man*. Baltimore: Johns Hopkins University Press, 1981.

Lustig, R. Jeffrey. *Corporate Liberalism: The Origins of Modern American Political Theory, 1890-1920*. Berkeley: University of California Press.

Lynd, Staughton. "Coalition Politics or Nonviolent Revolution." *Liberation*, June-July 1965.

-----. "The Movement: A New Beginning." *Liberation*, May 1969.

-----. "The New Radicals and Participatory Democracy." *Dissent*, Summer 1965.

-----. "Radical Politics and Nonviolent Revolution." *Liberation*, April 1966.

----. "A Radical Speaks in Defense of SNCC." *New Left Notes*, September 25, 1967.

-----. "The Right of Revolution." *New Left Notes*, February 13, 1967.

-----. *The Intellectual Origins of American Radicalism*. New York: Vintage, 1969.

-----, ed. *Nonviolence in America: A Documentary History*. Indianapolis: Bobbs Merrill, 1966.

-----, and Thomas Hayden, *The Other Side*. New York: New American Library, 1966.

MacDonald, Dwight. *Politics Past: Essays in Political Criticism*. New York: Viking Press, 1970.

Macpherson, C. B. *Democratic Theory: Essays in Retrieval*. Oxford: Oxford University Press, 1973.

McDarrah, Fred W. *Kerouac and Friends: A Beat Generation Album*. New York: William Morrow, 1985.

McLuhan, Marshall and Quentin Fiore, *The Medium Is the Massage*. New York: Random House, 1967.

McNally, Dennis. *Desolate Angel: Jack Kerouac, the Beat Generation, and America*. New York: McGraw Hill, 1979.

Mallet, Serge. *Essays on the New Working Class*. Edited and translated by Dick Howard. St. Louis: Telos Press, 1976.

Marcuse, Herbert. *Eros and Civilization*. Boston: Beacon Press, 1955.

-----. *Reason and Revolution: Hegel and the Rise of Social Theory*. New York: Oxford University Press, 1941.

Martin, Robert K. *The Homosexual Tradition in American Poetry*. Austin: University of Texas Press, 1979.

Maslow, Abraham H., ed. *New Knowledge in Human Values*. New York: Harper, 1959.

-----. *The Farther Reaches of Human Nature*. New York: Viking Press, 1971.

-----. *Religions, Values, and Peak Experiences.* New York: Viking Press, 1970.

Merrill, Thomas F. *Allen Ginsberg.* Boston: Twayne, 1988.

Michels, Robert. *Political Parties.* Glencoe: Free Press, 1962.

Miller, James. *"Democracy Is in the Streets": From Port Huron to the Siege of Chicago.* New York: Simon and Schuster, 1987.

Miller, William D. *A Harsh and Dreadful Love: Dorothy Day and the Catholic Worker Movement.* Garden City, N.Y.: Doubleday, Image edition, 1974.

Millet, Kate. "Sexual Politics: A Manifesto for Revolution." *Notes from the Second Year.* New York: Radical Feminism, 1970.

-----. *Sexual Politics.* Garden City, N.Y.: Doubleday, 1970.

Montagu, Ashley. *Man's Most Dangerous Myth: The Fallacy of Race.* New York: Harper, 1952.

Morris, Aldon D. *The Origins of the Civil Rights Movement: Black Communities Organizing for Change.* New York: Macmillan, The Free Press, 1984.

Mumford, Lewis. "Authoritarian and Democratic Technics." *Technology and Culture.* Vol. 5, No. 1.

Naranjo, Claudio. *The Healing Journey: New Approaches to Consciousness.* New York: Pantheon, 1974.

-----. *The One Quest.* New York: Ballantine Books, 1973.

Neill, A. S. Summerhill: *A Radical Approach to Child Rearing.* New York: Hart Pub. Co., 1960.

Nicosia, Gerald. *Memory Babe: A Critical Biography of Jack Kerouac.* New York: Grove Press, 1983.

Oates, Stephen B. *Let the Trumpet Sound: The Life of Martin Luther King, Jr.* New York: New American Library, 1982.

Oglesby, Carl. "Trapped in a System." *The New Left: A Documentary History.* Edited by Massimo Teodori. Indianapolis: Bobbs-Merrill Co., 1969

Potter, Paul. "The Incredible War." *The New Left: A Documentary History.* Edited by Massimo Teodori. Indianapolis: Bobbs-Merrill Co., 1969.

-----. *A Name for Ourselves.* New York: Little, Brown & Company, 1971.

Port Huron Statement. Students for a Democratic Society, 1962.

Rahula, Walpola. *What the Buddha Taught.* London: G. Fraser, 1978.

Robinson, Jo Ann Ooiman. *Abraham Went Out: A Biography of A. J. Muste.* Philadelphia: Temple University Press, 1981.

Roszak, Theodore. *The Making of a Counter Culture: Reflections on the Technocratic Society and its Youthful Opposition.* Garden City, N.Y.: Doubleday, 1969.

Rousseau, Jean-Jacques. *The Social Contract and Discourse on the Origins of Inequality.* Edited by Lester G. Crocker. New York: Simon and Schuster, Pocket Books edition, 1967.

Sahlins, Marshall. *Stone Age Economics.* Chicago: Aldine, 1972.

Sale, Kirkpatrick. *Human Scale.* New York: Putnam, 1980.

-----. *SDS.* New York: Random House, Vintage edition, 1974.

Schaar, John. *Legitimacy in the Modern State.* New Brunswick, N.J.: Transaction Books, 1981.

Schridharani, Krishnalal. *War Without Violence.* New York: Garland, 1972

Schumacher, E. F. *Small Is Beautiful.* New York: Harper, 1973.

Sklar, Martin. "Woodrow Wilson and the Political Economy of Modern United

States Liberalism." *Studies on the Left,* Vol. 1, No. 3, 1960.

Snyder, Gary. "Buddhist Anarchism," *Journal for the Protection of All Beings.* San Francisco: City Lights Books, 1961.

-----. *Earth House Hold.* New York: New Directions, 1969.

Teodori, Massimo, ed. *The New Left: A Documentary History.* Indianapolis: Bobbs Merrill, 1969.

Tokar, Brian. *The Green Alternative: Creating an Ecological Future.* San Pedro, Ca.: R. & E. Miles, 1987.

"Towards a Quaker View of Sex: An Essay by a Group of Friends." *Liberation,* Summer 1963.

Unger, Irwin. *The Movement: A History of the American New Left.* New York: Harper and Row, 1974.

Wallerstein, Immanual and Paul Starr, eds. *The University Crisis Reader,* 2 vols. New York: Vintage, 1971.

War Resisters League. *Against the Tide: Pacifist Resistance in the Second World War.* New York: War Resisters League, 1983.

Watts, Alan. *Beyond Theology: The Art of Godmanship.* New York: Vintage, 1973.

-----. *Psychotherapy, East and West.* New York: Pantheon Books, 1961.

-----. *Nature, Man, and Woman.* New York: Pantheon Books, 1958.

Weil, Andrew. *The Natural Mind: A New Way of Looking at Drugs and the Higher Consciousness.* Boston: Houghton Mifflin, 1972.

-----. *Chocolate to Morphine: Understanding Mind-active Drugs.* Boston: Houghton Mifflin, 1983.

Weil, Simone. "Fragments, 1933-1938." In *Oppression and Liberty.* Translated by Arthur Wills and John Petrie. Amherst: University of Massachusetts Press, 1958.

Weinstein, James. *Ambiguous Legacy: The Left in American Politics.* New York: New Viewpoints, 1975.

Whalen, Jack and Richard Flacks. *Beyond the Barricades: The Sixties Generation Grows Up.* Philadelphia: Temple University Press, 1989.

Wittman, Carl. "A Gay Manifesto." *Liberation,* February 1970.

-----. "Waves of the Resistance." *Liberation,* November 1968.

Wittman, Carl, and Thomas Hayden. "An Interracial Movement of the Poor." *The New Student Left.* Edited by Mitchell Cohen and Dennis Hale. Boston: Beacon Press, 1966.

Wolin, Sheldon. *Politics and Vision.* Boston: Little, Brown and Company, 1960.

Woodcock, George. *Anarchism: A History of Libertarian Ideas.* Cleveland: World Publishing, 1962.

-----, ed. *The Anarchist Reader.* Hassocks, Sussex: Harvester Press, 1977.

Young, Allen. *Gays Under the Cuban Revolution.* San Francisco: Grey Fox Press, 1981.

Young, Nigel. *An Infantile Disorder?: The Crisis and Decline of the New Left.* Boulder: Westview Press, 1977.

Zaroulis, Nancy, and Sullivan, Gerald. *Who Spoke Up?: American Protest Against the War in Vietnam, 1963-1975.* New York: Holt, Rinehart and Winston, 1984.

Zinn, Howard. *SNCC: The New Abolitionists.* Boston: Beacon, 1965.

INDEX